D1596214

Memory and Architecture

Memory and ARCHITECTURE

Edited by Eleni Bastéa

UNIVERSITY OF NEW MEXICO PRESS   ℭ   ALBUQUERQUE

08   07   06   05   04   1   2   3   4   5

LIBRARY OF CONGRESS CATALOGING-IN-PUBLICATION DATA

Memory and architecture / edited by Eleni Bastéa.— 1st ed.
      p. cm.
   Includes bibliographical references and index.
   ISBN 0-8263-3269-2 (cloth : alk. paper)
  1. Space (Architecture)—Psychological aspects.
2. Memory—Social aspects.
3. Architecture and literature.
4. Architectural design—Philosophy.
I. Bastéa, Eleni.

   NA2765.M46 2004
   720'.1'03—dc22

                                   2004015743

℘

Cover photos: Susan Hicks Bryant, 1996
Coleman Gallery, Albuquerque, New Mexico

Book design and type composition: Kathleen Sparkes

This book is set in Sabon 10/14
The Display type is Cezanne and Helvetica Neue

To our children,
may they live in peaceful times

Contents

Acknowledgments

$\mathcal{S}$everal of the chapters in this volume were first presented at a conference on Memory and Architecture in the fall of 1998.* I am grateful to all the conference participants, speakers, and moderators, who helped engender a most stimulating debate on the role of memory in architecture. In the process of preparing this anthology, however, the conference became a distant memory, and the book acquired a life of its own—as it should be. As the scope of the book expanded, we added contributions from Eric Sandweiss, Mark Jarzombek, Eleni Bastéa, and V. B. Price. I would like to thank all the authors for their engagement, patience, and support.

Of course, you wouldn't be holding this book in your hands were it not for the careful work of everyone at the University of New Mexico Press, who embraced the project enthusiastically and guided it through the last but crucial publication steps. I am indebted to University of New Mexico Press director, Luther Wilson, for his continual support; to Evelyn Schlatter, David Holtby, Mary Rodarte, and Adam Kane for their editorial care and attention; to the members of the design team for their magic; and to Lynne Bluestein for her quiet friendship and advice on ceramics.

As the manuscript began taking shape, several colleagues were instrumental in shaping and refining the whole and the parts, as they provided valuable editorial and publishing advice. I am indebted to Tom Fisher, Mark Forte, Laurie Kain Hart, Mark Jarzombek, Wendy Lochner, Andy Pressman, and Eric Sandweiss. This is not to say, however, that the final work responds to all the comments and questions that are invariably raised when one introduces the subjects of memory and architecture. The authors studied the intersections of memory and architecture in a kaleidoscopic fashion and brought in only those sources that were integral to these particular chapters and points of view. Taken together, this collection offers a cross section of the current research, without attempting to be comprehensive or encyclopedic. We hope that the strong personal voices of the authors will inspire and engender further dialogue and research among our readers, now and later.

Personal, national, and international events have indelibly marked our lives during the last five years. Most notably, the tragic terrorist attack on the World Trade Center in New York on September 11, 2001, gave rise to an unprecedented outpour of public and private reflection on the intersections of buildings and memory. We have left those discussions outside of this volume, as the book manuscript was conceived and mostly written before the attacks. And sadly, the more recent destruction of both ancient and modern sites in Iraq echoes some of the themes already explored in our papers, even though their focus may lie on different cities and different times.

During the book's gestation period, several of the contributors became new parents.

We dedicate this book to our children, wishing them a peaceful world.

—*Eleni Bastéa, Albuquerque, New Mexico*

*The conference took place at Washington University in St. Louis, Missouri, under the auspices of the West Central Region of the Association of Collegiate Schools of Architecture. Despite the "regional" appellation, the open call for papers brought several international submissions, some of which are included in this volume. Eleni Bastéa (then faculty at Washington University) and Gia Daskalakis co-organized the conference, with Bastéa overseeing the paper sessions, and Daskalakis overseeing the design sessions.

Notes on Contributors

ELENI BASTÉA is associate professor at the School of Architecture and Planning at the University of New Mexico. She is the author of *The Creation of Modern Athens: Planning the Myth* (Cambridge, UK: Cambridge University Press, 2000), which won the John D. Criticos Prize. Her current project focuses on the memory of place in contemporary Greece and Turkey.

CAREL BERTRAM is assistant professor in the Department of Humanities at San Francisco State University. Her work is on architecture as allegory, with a concentration on the late Ottoman and post-Ottoman urban environment, especially in Anatolia and the Balkans. Her dissertation is titled "The Turkish House: An Effort of Memory" (UCLA, 1998).

THOMAS FISHER is professor and dean of the College of Architecture and Landscape Architecture at the University of Minnesota. He has served as the editorial director of *Progressive Architecture* and *Building Renovation* magazines and is the author of *In the Scheme of Things: Alternative Thinking on the Practice of Architecture* (Minneapolis: University of Minnesota Press, 2000) and *Salmela, Architect* (Minneapolis: University of Minnesota Press, 2005, forthcoming).

CHRISTINE GORBY is an architect and associate professor in the Department of Architecture at Pennsylvania State University. She teaches upper-level thesis design studio and lectures on the history and theory of urban form. Her research considers spiritual experience and place making in the city. Gorby received a master of architecture from Harvard University in 1988.

CATHERINE HAMEL is assistant professor in the Faculty of Environmental Design at the University of Calgary, Canada. Her research projects focus on groups that have been subjected to the pressures of transformation, particularly immigrants and refugees. In 2003, she held a solo exhibit of drawings at the Nickel Arts Museum, University of Calgary, entitled *displace/graft/retrace.*

RACHEL HURST and JANE LAWRENCE are senior lecturers in the Louis Laybourne Smith School of Architecture and Design at the University of South Australia. They have developed, refined, and implemented an innovative collaborative-architecture and interior-design studio teaching practice; they also share research interests in alliances between architecture and gastronomy.

MARK JARZOMBEK is associate professor in the History, Theory, and Criticism section of the Department of Architecture at MIT. He is the author of *On Leon Baptista Alberti: His Literary and Aesthetic Theories* (Cambridge, Mass.: The MIT Press, 1989) and *The Psychologizing of Modernity: Art, Architecture, and History* (Cambridge, UK: Cambridge University Press, 2000).

SABIR KHAN is associate professor and associate dean of undergraduate studies at the College of Architecture at the Georgia Institute of Technology, USA. His primary research interests are in studio-based design pedagogy and in exploring what a cross-cultural framework may offer to the production, consumption, and reception of architecture and design. A new research project, Hyphen-nation, looks at the way race and ethnicity play out in contemporary American spaces and culture.

FERNANDO LARA is a practicing architect and assistant professor of architecture in the Taubman College of Architecture and Urban Planning at the University of Michigan. His dissertation is titled "Popular Modernism: An Analysis of the Acceptance of Modern Architecture in 1950s Brazil" (University of Michigan, 2001).

MARIA DE LOURDES LUZ is trained in architecture and the visual arts. She is dean of the School of Design and Visual Arts of the Veiga de Almeida University in Rio de Janeiro. She also holds a Ph.D. from the Beaux Arts School of the UFRJ—Universidade Federal do Rio de Janeiro.

BARBARA MANN is associate professor of Hebrew Literature at the Jewish Theological Seminary in New York. She is the author of the forthcoming book, *A Place in History: Modernism, Tel Aviv and the Creation of Jewish Urban Space* (Stanford, Calif.: Stanford University Press, 2005).

V. B. PRICE, journalist and poet, teaches in the University Honors Program at the University of New Mexico. He is the author of *A City at the End of the World* (Albuquerque: University of New Mexico Press, 1992, revised 2003) and coeditor (with Baker H. Morrow) of *Anasazi Architecture and American Design* (UNM Press, 1997). He is also the author of several poetry collections and of a novel, *The Oddity* (UNM Press, 2004).

ERIC SANDWEISS is Carmony Associate Professor of History at Indiana University, Bloomington. He is also the editor of *Indiana Magazine of History*. He is the author of *St. Louis: The Evolution of an American Urban Landscape* (Philadelphia: Temple University Press, 2001) and the editor of *St. Louis in the Century of Henry Shaw: A View beyond the Garden Wall* (Columbia: University of Missouri Press, 2003).

ANA LUCIA VIEIRA DOS SANTOS is trained in architecture and historic preservation. She is professor at the School of Design and Visual Arts at the Veiga de Almeida University in Rio de Janeiro. She is also a doctorate student at the History Faculty of the Universidade Federal Fluminense (Rio de Janeiro).

SHEONA THOMSON teaches in the architecture program at the Queensland University of Technology, Brisbane, Australia. She also writes regularly about architecture and interiors for the Australian design magazines *Artichoke* and *Houses*.

Introduction

ELENI BASTÉA

The great majority [of a city's inhabitants] may
well be more sensitive to a certain street being torn
up, or a certain building or home being razed, than
to the gravest national, political, or religious events.
That is why great upheavals may severely shake
society without altering the appearance of the city.
Their effects are blunted as they filter down to
those people who are closer to the stones than to
men—the shoemaker in his shop; the artisan at his
bench; the merchant in his store; the people in the
market; the walker strolling about the streets, idling
at the wharf, or visiting the garden terraces; the
children playing on the corner; the old man
enjoying the sunny wall or sitting on a stone
bench; the beggar squatting by a city landmark.
  —Maurice Halbwachs, "Space and the
          Collective Memory," 1939

*A*rchitecture can transform words, needs, and desires into space. It can capture fleeting or insistent memories into tangible, buildable, or unbuildable forms. Architecture provides the stage on which we can enact our lives. Memory, however, creates a special relationship with space, holding on to the essence of it, the best and the worst, letting the rest of the details fade into gray. Reflecting on their individual backgrounds and perspectives, the authors in this volume examine the relationship between memory and architecture as it is experienced in design, teaching, and writing.

"[T]he manipulation of images in memory must always to some extent involve the psyche as a whole," wrote Frances A. Yates in *The Art of Memory*.[1] If one of our roles as teachers is to nurture the memories that each one of our students cherishes, openly or secretly, is it also our role to challenge those memories, as they become juxtaposed to the greater and ever-richer mosaic of our students' collective experiences? As writers, scholars, and architects we are constantly in an open dialogue between form and culture, space and memory, images and the psyche. As we open up our private treasure chests of Mnemosyne and articulate our memories of place, we bequeath to the world reflections of our soul. In the process, we engage both ourselves and our audiences in the search for a common ground, the foundation for all future dialogue.

Memory and Architecture is oriented toward a general theory of memory and the built environment. Drawing from the methods of architecture, comparative literature, and cultural studies, the authors examine the politics of memory and space, at both the personal and the national levels. Engaged but not dogmatic, they draw from the existing literature, questioning some of the accepted paradigms and describing their own research questions and methods. We trust that our work will serve as a catalyst for further dialogue, debate, and research on the intersections of memory and the built environment. It is a very timely and critically exciting area that is at the center of current research in the sciences and the humanities. Our aim is to make a scholarly *and* personally engaged contribution to the theory of memory and place.

Personal Reflections

One of the first projects I was asked to design when I entered architecture school was a single-family, detached house. That was in 1979 at Berkeley, but I imagine that my experience was common. Most of us had just discovered Gaston Bachelard's *The Poetics of Space,* and we read it eagerly searching for inspiration for our designs. Having grown up in an apartment in Greece, I could not retreat into Bachelard's idealized childhood house, hiding in my own room, daydreaming in the attic, or withdrawing in the basement. "When we recall the old house in its longitudinal detail," he wrote, "everything that ascends and descends comes to life again dynamically."

And quoting Joë Bousquet, Bachelard added: "He was a man with only one story: he had his cellar in his attic."[2] I realized then and there that I was a woman with only one story.

It seemed impossible to design a typical, middle-class, American house, without being able to conjure one in my memory. Fortunately, I had spent a summer in Philadelphia, living in an old stone house near Germantown. Though I did not tell anybody at the time, it was this Philadelphia house that I kept trying to re-create in my first designs—its comfortable window sill, generous stair, and wild, tiny garden. It became my emblematic house in this country. At twenty-one, I was not ready to admit the decisive role of memory in design and education. But today, almost twenty-five years later, I see memory squarely at the root of our learning experience. Why do we visit significant buildings whenever we can, wherever we are, if not to imprint them in our memory, to learn their spaces by passing our body through them, to make them part of us in some ways, and maybe to draw from them in our own designs? How do we communicate the experience of being in a particular building, be it an icon of architecture, like Frank Lloyd Wright's Falling Water, or a common, roadside building, when most of our students may have never visited it? How do we talk about buildings that *we* have never visited? Where is the common ground, if there is one?

I often ask my students to take a few minutes in class and write a poem about their home. They write of "neighborhoods neatly woven together, and reinforced with Oak Alleys."[3] And about "the blackness of the basement. . . . The blackness [that] became jungles and river beds, faraway cities and places only dreamed. I remember the freedom of the dark."[4] "I remember standing at the window, watching the Christmas trees go up block by block, corner after corner."[5] Yet once, a few years back, one of my students concluded a powerful photographic essay on the home as follows: "But I had to go away from home to find the comfort that home should've provided; and it's unsettling for me to realize, now, as I write this, that the most fucked-up place I've ever been [in] is home."[6] Perhaps others had similar memories that they buried deeper inside, reluctant to bring them out into the broad daylight of the classroom. How do we deal with these memories? "And perhaps architecture has always wanted to be a theater of memory," wrote Umberto Eco.[7] But whose memory? While some memories nourish us, others may kill the spirit, leading us to the dark labyrinths of a disabling past. What, then, comes in their stead?

Let me quote from Italo Calvino's *Invisible Cities,* which describes an imaginary exchange between Marco Polo and Kublai Khan:

> "Sire [said Marco Polo to Kublai Khan], now I have told you about all the cities I know."
> "There is still one of which you never speak."
> Marco Polo bowed his head.
> "Venice," the Khan said.
> Marco smiled. "What else do you believe I have been talking to you about?"
> The emperor did not turn a hair. "And yet I have never heard you mention that name."
> And Polo said: "Every time I describe a city I am saying something about Venice."
> "When I ask you about other cities, I want to hear about them. And about Venice, when I ask you about Venice. . . . "
> "Memory's images, once they are fixed in words, are erased," Polo said. "Perhaps I am afraid of losing Venice all at once, if I speak of it. Or perhaps, speaking of other cities, I have already lost it, little by little."[8]

Are the cities we believe we know and understand simply a reinterpretation of our own Venice, encountered again and again under different guises? Is our own hometown in Minnesota, Brazil, or Australia the yardstick with which we measure all other cities? Does our own home, for better or worse, become the standard of comparison?

The writer André Aciman reflected on the power of certain places to evoke other, familiar, beloved places in his essay "Shadow Cities." Beginning with Straus Park in New York, he found himself remembering other cities he had lived in, loved, and longed for: Paris, Rome, London. And, at the end, all of those cities, New York included, were but shadow cities of the city of his own youth—Alexandria: "I come to Straus Park to remember Alexandria, be it an unreal Alexandria, an Alexandria that does not exist, that I've invented, or learned to cultivate in Rome as in Paris, so that in the end the Paris and the Rome I retrieve here are really the shadow of the shadow of Alexandria."[9]

I often come back to a line from Carole Maso's novel *Ava*: "So primary is homesickness as a motive for writing fiction, so powerful the yearning to memorialize what we've lived, inhabited, been hurt by and loved."[10] I believe that in some deeper way all creation is born out of our incurable homesickness and "the yearning to memorialize what we've lived [and] inhabited." Yet most of us in academia would never admit nostalgia's creative agency. Maybe it is not considered professional, relevant, or academic enough to allow one's dreams and experiences to explain, in part, the inception of a building, a scholarly paper, or a book. We have perpetuated the myths that architectural design and research are rational processes, based on past history and factual considerations. Silencing the role of memory in the creative process effectively silences the personal voices of all new architecture students. As we sever the connection between memory and architecture, we rob our students of their most significant reservoir of ideas, references, and strength. We dismiss the significance of their own past, culture, and knowledge. Ultimately, we curtail their creative potential. It is time to revisit the role of memory in architecture.

It is easier for writers to articulate their debts to memory. The narrative form lends itself to self-reflection in a way that no work of architecture ever will. Nevertheless, it is constructive to review how writers have drawn from their personal past because, fundamentally, both writers and architects strive to express their inner, ancient, lingering visions in contemporary, legible forms. "The true paradises are the paradises we have lost," wrote Marcel Proust in *Swann's Way*, part of his complex and monumental *À la recherché du temps perdu*.[11] Proust's novel has since served as a reference point and a road map to many other writers battling with the demons of their pasts. "I think I began writing a long novel," reflected the British writer A. S. Byatt, "because, having read Proust, I saw it as a solution to the problem of being haunted by 'glittering' memories which appeared to solicit a place, a hearing."[12] Memory's voices, once recognized, command us to create, and to memorialize, what we remember. Both writers and architects endow their "glittering" memories with form and prepare places for them to rest.[13]

A. S. Byatt describes two types of memory within a text: "There is memory of its own contents and coherence, and there is memory of the outside events—the madeleine, and beyond the madeleine the walled garden of

Combray, and beyond the walled garden of Combray the walled garden of Paradise Lost—which are or will be part of this particular text."[14] Let us focus now on the first type: the memory within a text's contents and coherence. Byatt likens writing to remembering: "If you are writing a long novel there is a sense in which you do, precisely, *remember* all of it, including in some sense the part which is not written, which feels like a projected memory-image or mnemonic. . . . [A] rhythm begins to sing, a grammatical structure begins to hold, and the 'right' precise words take their places in the structure. . . . "[15]

Design is also about recognition. The recognition of the memory within a text, of what feels right in a text that the writer is composing, is akin, I believe, to what design teachers frequently point out to their students. At a certain point, a design acquires its own structure and personality. An experienced teacher can recognize that structure within the mess of sketches and images that clutter the desk and can facilitate its delivery. Designing presupposes an open and vulnerable self, an ear that stays close to the ground, listening to the sounds of our imagination, trusting that eventually, we will begin to recognize the hidden coherence of the project. Teaching design brings us closer to our students' private memories of place, memories that we urge them to consider also within the wider context of our culture.

Memory inspires us to create or re-create a fleeting vision from a dream or from our waking moments. As that yearning and nostalgia for the visible and invisible past flare up, they inform and enrich our present. At some deeper level we may view all writing and design as works of autobiography, since we bring ourselves into our work, imprinting our identity into our creations. Acknowledging the self as the primary source of all work, however, can bring us down the slippery slopes of solipsism. Is our private vision obscuring a view of the rest of the world? Reflecting on autobiographical writing, Patricia Hampl remarked: "True memoir is written, like all literature, in an attempt to find not only a self but a world."[16] That is precisely the confirmation of the role of private memory in design and in all creative work. By reaching into ourselves we trust that we can come closer to the world around us, to the world of the past, and of the future.

More and more, I have come to see teaching also as a ritual for remembering and commemorating our own teachers, our past, and ourselves. We teach because we do not want to be forgotten. Like the ancient troubadours, we sing the stories of our lives with chalk and slides, notes and sketches;

we praise the wisdom of our own teachers and share the insights we have attained from our travels—travels out in the world or deep into our soul—slowly initiating our students into the inner chambers of architecture's universe, the language and lore of our tribe. Good teachers can describe places they visited in such a way that they become part of our own vocabulary, part of our own experience. They will their stories to their students, handing them down as part of their students' own patrimony, to be remembered and transmitted. Travel stories about Salonica, Siena, or St. Louis, special lectures and readings that we share with our students, become reference points for everyone in the class, laying the foundations for a common ground. And as we return to our favorite sites and citations again and again, we continue revisiting and cultivating the same ground with each new group of students, constructing with them a common language of space that incorporates their memories and ours. Slowly we come to understand the world around us a little better, layering the memories of our teachers and their teachers over our own memories. Gradually, all personal memories are endowed to the world. This is not unlike the way family stories are handed down to the younger generations, keeping alive the life and works of relatives who have long passed on. We read in Tracy Kidder's novel, *Old Friends*: "Heard only twice, Lou's memories could seem monotonous. Heard many times, they were like old friends. They were comforting. . . . Lou's memories contained such a density of life that in their presence death seemed impossible."[17]

Adrienne Rich has called one of her poetry collections *The Dream of a Common Language*.[18] The dream of a common language is also our aspiration as writers, architects, and teachers. Built space can become the basis for a larger narrative that not only respects the unique characteristics of the local and national stories, but also acknowledges their common myths and begins to compare them. Our histories are bound in space, just as they are bound in time. While grounded in the precepts of the discipline of architecture and cultural history, this language of space is alive. It is ours to learn, nurture, expand, and transmit. This common language of space is our legacy to the next generations.

We try to understand the past by reading its traces on the landscape, entering into a dialogue with it, like the fortune-teller studying the coffee grounds in the demitasse cup. "In fortune-telling, the reading is generally a conversation, and that's what I want to do, create work that encourages a dialogue," writes the artist Canan Tolon.[19] I find that teaching is also akin to fortune-telling, an ongoing dialogue in the classroom and the studio, as we try to decipher what the future holds by studying the patterns of our shared memories, words, and visions.

Perspectives from History and Psychology

In his pioneering studies on collective memory, *Les cadres sociaux de la mémoire* (1925) and *La mémoire collective* (1950), Maurice Halbwachs argued that every recollection, even the most personal and private thought and sentiment, exists in relationship to a social group. Our memories are localized within a social group, situated in the mental and material spaces provided by that group. The apparent stability of these material spaces surrounding us allows us to conserve our recollections.[20] In 1958 the philosopher Gaston Bachelard wrote *The Poetics of Space,* an eloquent and evocative work that continues to engage students in architecture and literature with the questions of space and the self. Yet Bachelard describes a very stable experience of space, assuming that we all grew up in the prototypical, middle-class, single-family house, to which we can still go back at will.

On one level, no one of us can go home again. Without trivializing the trauma of immigration and forced dislocation, we have to acknowledge that, seen in a global perspective, the loss of home may have now become the norm. Many of us grew up in someone else's house of memory. We are all carrying our memories around, looking for a new home for them to rest.

More recently, the historian John R. Gillis points out in his introduction to *Commemorations: The Politics of National Identity* that "both identity and memory are political and social constructs, and should be treated as such. . . . Identities and memories are not things we think *about,* but things we think *with.*"[21] The philosopher Ian Hacking posits that in the late nineteenth century, "memory, already regarded as a criterion of personal identity, became a scientific key to the soul, so that by investigating memory (to find out its facts) one would conquer the spiritual domain of the soul and replace it by a surrogate, knowledge about memory."[22] In reviewing the recent Anglophone literature on memory I have also found that references to personal memory are often described with the gravity and resonance that would have been reserved for references to one's soul a century earlier.

Recent work among historians and anthropologists has also begun to establish connections among memory, history, and space. One of the most prominent and ambitious efforts is the multivolume study on French history *Les lieux de mémoire (1984–1992),* by Pierre Nora and his colleagues. In Nora's words, their work underscores the "importance of memory and the search for the *lieux* that embody it, the return to our collective heritage and focus on the country's shattered identities."[23] Maurice Halbwachs had left historical developments mostly outside his analysis of collective memory.[24] Nora and his colleagues, on the other hand, concentrated on the collective memory of the French republic in their effort "to write a history in multiple voices. . . . [A] history . . . less interested in 'what actually happened' than in its perpetual reuse and misuse, its influence on successive presents. . . . [A] history that is interested in memory not as remembrance but as the overall structure of the past within the present."[25] By focusing on the idea of the French nation, the work has downplayed the existence of opposing political communities and their own collective memories.[26] As other historians have pointed out, there has been a consistent local opposition to the concept of the French nation both from among the conservatives and from the peasantry.[27] Nevertheless, Nora's work, with its emphasis on the multiple voices and its search for common cultural agents, offers a viable model for the study of national memories, as shown in some of the chapters in this volume.

We have learned from psychology that we perceive and remember visual designs and spatial locations by employing the right side of the brain. We remember verbal information with the left side of our brain.[28] The right side of the brain "sees" space and images, while the left "narrates." Put in that way, the memory of "our own home" is encoded through the right side of the brain. It is based on personal, *lived* experience. The memory of "our own nation" is encoded through the left side of our brain. It is a *learned* concept that has been transmitted and reinforced through our education, socialization, media, state rhetoric, and so forth. I believe that we perceive the two entities fairly independently and are able to negotiate between them and draw connections between them without, however, considering the home to be a subset of the nation.

Expanding on the earlier distinction between *lived* and *learned* memory of space, we can now examine Body Memory and Mind Memory.

Body Memory refers to memories of space derived from personal, lived experience, like the layout of our bedroom, the old childhood home, or the streets of our hometown. They appear to be directly imprinted or encoded in our bodies. Motor memory, a component of body memory, involves remembering how to ride a bicycle, swim, or dial familiar phone numbers without thinking or rehearsing.[29] In *Searching for Memory*, the psychologist Daniel L. Schacter describes the case of a patient who, although she "could not recollect even a sliver of her personal past," was able to dial her mother's telephone number when she was handed a telephone.[30]

Mind Memory refers to indirect memories of space, narrated experiences that have been passed down to us through our family, community, schooling, and so forth. They could be a relative's home we have never seen, architectural landmarks we studied but have not visited, or the national borders of our country. Stories we heard about places also become part of our autobiographical memory.

How does autobiographical memory work? First comes the encoding process. "We remember only what we have encoded, and what we encode depends on who we are," points out Schacter.[31] Not all encoding happens consciously, however. A significant aspect of our memory comes from *implicit memory*, events and experiences that happened in the past without our having the awareness that we are remembering them.[32] Current research suggests that "the brain structures that support implicit memory are in place before the systems needed for explicit memory."[33] Once children develop language skills, they are able to impose their own narrative structure on their experiences.[34] Studies on literary autobiography focus on the significance of narrative. Our memories would remain an amorphous mass were we not able to give them form, to shape them into a coherent narrative.

Remembering involves the process of *retrieval*, the unearthing of a past experience from the treasure chests of Mnemosyne. This is a complicated process, as retrieval presupposes the active, conscious altering and adjustment of the old experiences to fit the present circumstances. Autobiographies are not documentaries,[35] as the brain actively engages in the "construction" of a memory during the retrieval process.[36] "When we remember, we complete a pattern with the best match available in memory; we do not shine a spotlight on a stored picture."[37] Images and events stored in our memory are not etched in stone, as was previously believed, but are rather subject to a selective, continuous recasting that reflects our current experiences and preoccupations.

Memory of place seems to work in a similar fashion. We revisit our earlier experiences, adjust them, edit them, alter them, or erase them. We might experience architecture through our body but we remember it in our mind and heart. "The unfolding drama of life is revealed more by the telling than by the actual events told. Stories are not merely 'chronicles,' like a secretary's minutes of a meeting. . . . Stories are less about facts and more about meanings. In the subjective and embellished telling of the past, the past is constructed—history is made," writes psychologist Dan McAdams.[38]

Interestingly, all of the research on autobiographical memory concurs that "few vivid memories are reported after early adulthood."[39] As psychologists John A. Robinson and Leslie R. Taylor point out, "[t]his difference is consistent with a developmental account of self-narratives and memory if we assume that few new formative experiences occur after early childhood."[40] And not only are most memories related to our childhood, but "memory seems to improve, not decay, over time."[41] Encoded memory appears to become more resistant to forgetting as time passes. This is consistent with the general tendency I have observed both among students and academic colleagues to zoom into the house or garden of their childhood when asked to describe their memories of place.

The architectural theorist Frances Downing has examined extensively the personal spatial references of architecture students in her remarkable book *Remembrance and the Design of Place*.[42] In describing her method and findings, Downing reflected on the impossibility of recording scientifically the experience of the memory of place:

> I began to realize that the design of my research would force an analytic tracing of general relationships among the interviewees' memorable places. Although this was, in fact, my aim and the things that I discovered were extremely useful, I couldn't "record" the holistic content of memorable experience as it *presented* itself to the consciousness of each participant. Slowly it dawned on me that somehow I was missing the power of the act of remembrance as I pursued more analytical concerns about memory. I realized, too, that capturing this elusive quality and translating it into words that conveyed the content of in-sight would be a complex undertaking indeed. It is only indirectly, then, that I can refer to the acts of remembrance I witnessed.[43]

Equally important is her observation that "what is significant about a memorable place experience is not the actual feeling, but the *ideas* of feeling which *present* meaning to designers."[44] We could connect this insight with our earlier discussion of right- and left-brain activity and the significance of the narrative in recalling memories. Perhaps a physical (right-brain) memory of place remains dormant in our mind until we can put its significance in words, until we can narrate the ideas that make it meaningful and memorable by employing also the left brain.

I would venture that going back to a *place* of the past may be the best way we have to take ourselves back in *time*. While I am writing this chapter from our home in New Mexico, I can remember sitting at the balcony of my good friend and teacher Tina Godhi, in Thessaloniki, Greece. As I picture us sitting and talking there, I can relive my visits to her house from many years ago.

The assertion that we recast and reinterpret our memories every time we bring them out is reflected also in the work of anthropologist Keith Basso, who observes a similar process of reinterpretation not only among individuals, but among societies, as well. In his book *Wisdom Sits in Places,* he concurs:

> Building and sharing place-worlds . . . is not only a means
> of reviving former times but also of *revising* them, a means of
> exploring not merely how things might have been but also how,
> just possibly, they might have been different from what others
> supposed. . . . [F]or what people make of their places is closely
> connected to what they make of themselves as members of society
> and inhabitants of the earth, and while the two activities may
> be separable in principle, they are deeply joined in practice.
> If place-making is a way of constructing the past, a venerable
> means of *doing* human history, it is also a way of constructing
> social traditions and, in the process, personal and social identities.
> We *are,* in a sense, the place-worlds we imagine.[45]

Individual Contributions

The book is divided into four sections: I. Designing National Memories; II. Literary Memory Spaces; III. Personal Cartographies; and IV. Voices from the Studio.

Part I, "Designing National Memories," addresses the broad issues of national memories and the individuals and institutions that construct those memories. As each author or team of authors concentrates on a particular question, site, and historical period, it becomes apparent that many of the current assumptions on the social and historical memory of place may need reconsideration or revision. With regard to the categories discussed earlier, the creation of national memories reflects primarily a left-brain activity. As citizens, we are taught, through literature, education, and other processes of socialization, to picture the past in certain terms. The authors examine some of these historical reconstructions of the built environment and question their basis. Furthermore, they caution us against generalizations and the easy application of one historical model of explanation to a variety of situations.

In reviewing research from psychology and literature earlier, we examined the role of the personal narrative in giving form and shape to our memories and making them coherent, both to ourselves and to others. In the first chapter, "Framing Urban Memory: The Changing Role of History Museums in the American City," Eric Sandweiss examines the museums' role in writing the historical narratives, as a necessary part of making the museum experience legible and instructive. Sandweiss proposes that American urban history museums are the paramount repositories of urban memory and examines the lasting, inherent problems they encounter as they seek to fulfill their mission. The main question here has to do with the "intrinsic, organic quality of the urban memory," which, Sandweiss claims, Americans "have never comfortably accepted." Can the memory of a city ever sit still to be portrayed in an urban history museum? Does the impossibility of unchanging urban memory, of "the city [as] a posed subject" make the "urban history museum" an oxymoron? And does the effort toward selective preservation in fact accelerate "the loss of a deeper sense of memory"?

In the next chapter, "Disguised Visibilities: Dresden/'Dresden,'" Mark Jarzombek examines several of the city's new reconstruction projects. These, he criticizes, aim to create an imaginary "historical Dresden" that willfully ignores the city's complex and competing actual pasts. He denounces the current trend in Dresden and other cities, where the "construction of urban history [tends to] parallel state-supported discourses." Dresden's past, he posits, is represented not by a single, linear history, but by a multiple layer of conflicting histories, still reflected on its built fabric. It is these histories that need to be acknowledged, challenged, or preserved, before the current feverish reconstruction activity creates a homogeneous, "historical Dresden." Does the selective physical reconstruction of the city make it difficult to narrate the city's actual history? And finally, is there a place for Maurice Halbwachs's "collective memory" in a city with overlapping layers of a Jewish, Nazi, Socialist, and now postunification history?

In "Designed Memories: The Roots of Brazilian Modernism," Fernando Lara demonstrates that Brazilian modern architecture followed a radically different route from the earlier European modernist movements. Instead of posing the national against the international and the modern against the traditional, Brazilian architecture opted for the blending of these apparent opposites. From the beginning, Brazilian modernism respected local cultural memories and turned repeatedly to local building traditions. While acknowledging that this was a constructed past, and, by extension, a constructed memory, Lara's analysis presents the development of Brazilian architecture as an autonomous response to the local, Brazilian conditions and not as an anemic imitation of western European formulas.

In "Patrimony and Cultural Identity: The Coffee Plantation System— Paraíba Valley, Rio de Janeiro, Brazil," Maria de Lourdes Luz and Ana Lúcia Vieira Dos Santos examine the history of nineteenth- and twentieth-century Brazil through the prism of the coffee plantation system. Radically shifting the perspective from Lara's earlier essay on Brazilian modernism allows us to revisit some of the issues on modernism addressed by Lara, while highlighting the significance of the culture of the African slaves, a culture that, until now, has remained "forgotten," absent from the various constructions of Brazil's national past. Through their detailed exposition, Luz and Santos outline how they have used the study of coffee production and the architecture of the coffee plantations to introduce their students to the concepts of memory, patrimony, and cultural identity. By focusing on the architecture of the slave quarters, the authors aim "to provide a link between the different stages of the transformation of free people into slaves" and connect the patterns of habitation with "the memory of African cultural patterns."

Part II, "Literary Memory Spaces," delves into the literary depictions of memory spaces and examines the impact of literature onto architecture and of architecture onto literature. Whereas part one depicted the construction of national memories from the top down, this part examines the power of the personal voice, the poet and fiction writer, who is inevitably part of the larger nation-building myth, but who is also able to resist, question, and transcend this myth. These studies join a growing literature on the impact of political upheavals and border partitions on works of fiction.[46]

In "Memory Work: The Reciprocal Framing of Self and Place in Émigré Autobiographies," Sabir Khan focuses on the work of two South Asian émigré women writers: Attia Hosain's autobiographical novel, *Sunlight on a Broken Column,* and Sara Suleri's memoir, *Meatless Days.* Khan begins with the insight that remembering is predicated on disjunction. He examines how space is remembered in moments of crisis or loss and how literary depictions of early memories of space are used to reflect the characters' souls and states of minds. Perhaps the image of the childhood home becomes a symbol for Paradise Lost, as it is continuously re-created in the writer's mind and memory, and shared, as a pact of trust, with the reader.

In "Memory and Diaspora in Tel Aviv's Old Cemetery," Barbara Mann addresses the question of memory versus history. She examines a particular site of memory, the Old Cemetery in Tel Aviv, through the lenses of poetry, history, and physical form. Unlike other Jewish cemeteries in Europe and Israel, Tel Aviv's Old Cemetery appears ignored by the local guidebooks and neglected by the inhabitants themselves. Mann suggests that the cemetery's state reflects precisely the two opposing sensibilities that were present at the city's birth: "nostalgia for the founding vision of Tel Aviv as an intimate 'Garden City' by the sea . . . [and] a feeling of outsiderness in a place where much of the city's history, most of its inhabitants were born elsewhere." Can a "site of memory," to use Pierre Nora's term, also be about forgetting?

In her chapter "Housing the Symbolic Universe in Early Republican Turkey: Architecture, Memory, and 'the Felt Real'," Carel Bertram employs the concept of "emotional memory" to describe feelings and emotions that people in Turkey have about the traditional Turkish house. Whereas the literary domestic spaces described in Khan's article stemmed from personal, lived childhood experience, Bertram describes an equally powerful literary topos that is rather imagined. In fact, she suggests that the image of the Turkish house in Turkish novels resonated with the readers not because they had lived in these houses, but because the image of the Turkish house embodied all that was old, spiritual, national, and, ultimately, threatened with destruction. Her analysis of the imagined but "felt real" past echoes current approaches of psychoanalysis. As Hacking points out, "even traditional psychoanalysis tends not to question the underlying definiteness of the past. The analyst will be indifferent as to whether a recollected event really occurred. The present emotional meaning of the recollection is what counts."[47]

In "Storied Cities: Literary Memories of Thessaloniki and Istanbul," I examine representative literary works about the two cities, questioning the writers' emphasis on the ethnic homogeneity of the present. I propose that one of the reasons for this evident historical amnesia can be attributed to the writers' personal childhood memories and to the successful nation-building project of each country that was constructed on the premise of ethnic and cultural homogeneity. As an architectural historian, I was trained to assume that buildings speak to us of their past. These forays into comparative literature began to cast doubt on my earlier suppositions.

In Part III, "Personal Cartographies," the authors describe their own experiences with familiar and foreign cities and the reverberations of dislocation and exile. "You won't find a new country, won't find another shore. / This city will always pursue you," reflected the poet C. P. Cavafy.[48] Or, perhaps, the city pursues us, as we, simultaneously, pursue it. For natives of a city, like Catherine Hamel and V. B. Price, political and economic changes may bring changes to their cities, without, however, rendering them unrecognizable. For an outsider, like Christine Gorby, trying to decipher a complex city that hides its secrets may remain an unattainable, lifelong pursuit.

Can cities bury their pasts in order to heal the wounds inflicted on their people? The following two chapters examine two cities that have been divided by war: Beirut and West Belfast. Catherine Hamel reflects on memory and forgetting in her chapter, "Beirut, Exile, and the Scars of Reconstruction," written in the form of a letter addressed to the city of Beirut. The looser form of the letter, enhanced by her original drawings, allows Hamel to weave together her own recollections and memories with others' writings and haunting reminiscences about their beloved city—a personal meditation on the stages and experiences of exile. She writes: "'Do you go back often?' I am repeatedly asked. A faint smile lingers in my silent gaze. I never left."

In "Diffused Spaces: A Sacred Study of West Belfast, North Ireland," Christine Gorby ventures to territories where even angels fear to tread today: spaces marking religion, life, and death. West Belfast, however, refuses to be mapped, as mapping facilitates access, and access spells danger. "According to one visitor," she remarks, "the best guide to the city is the invisible map that 'all locals carry around in their heads.'" In fact, the walls that divide the city are not depicted on the maps of the city. Her challenge is to map both the physical and the invisible city of West Belfast in a way that makes sense to an outsider, while remaining true to the citizens' own image of their city.

In "Profaning Sacred Space: Los Angeles in New Mexico," V. B. Price examines his own memory culture as a longtime resident, writer, and urban critic of New Mexico and as a willing exile of Los Angeles. On the surface of it, this chapter criticizes the unchecked growth of New Mexico and the generic urban development of the Rio Grande Valley. But underneath the public voice of the architectural and environmental critic, there is also the private voice of the Los Angeles exile, whose deep love for New Mexico never challenged his attachment to the city of his youth. While he continues to criticize the Californication of New Mexico, he is also reflecting on his own "antipathy to Los Angeles, which has oddly dissipated as I have grown older."

Finally, in Part IV, "Voices from the Studio," we examine how some of these questions regarding personal and historical memory of place may apply to the teachings and design going on in the studio and the architect's drawing board. The authors here describe their own approaches to design teaching and criticism, incorporating those theoretical works that are directly related to their projects.

In "What Memory? Whose Memory?" Thomas Fisher confronts directly the state of architectural education and practice today, arguing for a reconsideration of the role of personal and cultural memory in design. He examines architectural education and practice, drawing from his experience as a student, educator, and former editor of *Progressive Architecture*. While considering the unique strengths of our discipline's "peculiarly Socratic way," he also alerts us to a weakness of this method, as Socrates himself distrusted memory. A distrust, or even disregard for memory has become a badge of honor for many architects, who fear that acknowledging influences from the past might relegate them to the dreaded status of preservationists. Fisher exhorts architects to value the collective memory of the people and the places for which they build, and to make spaces that accommodate the memory and imaginations of others.

The following two chapters examine closely the role of memory in the classroom: Rachel Hurst and Jane Lawrence coauthored "(Re)Placing, Remembering, Revealing: Understanding through Memory and Making," which describes the first-year architecture studio that they teach jointly at the University of South Australia. Hurst and Lawrence draw upon their students' collective and individual cultural experiences and focus on the design qualities of familiar, everyday places: the beach and the bush, the street and the shed. Many of the studio projects take place off campus, in order "to let the unadulterated and sometimes humble spaces . . . reveal solutions and prime the students for lessons that become ingrained not just metaphorically, but literally."

In "Places within and without: Memory, the Literary Imagination, and the Project in the Design Studio," Sheona Thomson examines the relationship between the spaces of architecture and the spaces of literature, as she outlines her approach to teaching first-year design studio. "Why couldn't we be drawn more often into learning about architecture by studying how it has been painted by Giotto, or described by Virginia Woolf, or, for that matter, by being asked to reflect on our own recollections of place?" she asks. Working with evocative literary descriptions of places, Thomson seeks to engage and heighten her students' imagination and guide them as they begin to discover the power of their own personal memories and experiences of place. Gradually, the thread that connects the known, the imagined, and the remembered space becomes apparent.

⌒

From a number of different perspectives, all of the contributors in this volume have examined the powerful and ever-present memory of our built environment. Their testimonies counter Pierre Nora's assertion, frequently repeated by other historians, that "we speak so much of memory because there is so little left."[49]

Notes

The epigraph is from Maurice Halbwachs, "Space and the Collective Memory," in *The Collective Memory,* by Maurice Halbwachs, trans. Francis J. Ditter Jr. and Vida Yazdi Ditter (New York: Harper Colophon Books, 1980), 131–32.

1. Frances A. Yates, *The Art of Memory* (Chicago: University of Chicago Press, 1966), xi.

2. Gaston Bachelard, *The Poetics of Space,* trans. Maria Jolas (Boston: Beacon Press, 1964), 26. First published in French in 1958. Joë Bousquet, *La neige d'un autre âge,* 100, cited in Bachelard, 26.

3. Ragini Gupta. This and the quotations immediately following were written by students in the course "Memory and Architecture," offered by the Comparative Literature Program at Washington University in St. Louis, in the fall 1998 semester. I developed and taught the course in collaboration with Randolph Pope, professor of Spanish and Comparative Literature, and now a member of the University of Virginia faculty.

4. Matt Teichner.

5. Kathryn Friedman.

6. G. G., student in the course "Visualizing Experience: Body and Space," co-taught by Eleni Bastéa and Libby Reuter, Washington University, 1995.

7. Umberto Eco, "Architecture and Memory," trans. William Weaver, in *VIA,* Journal of the Graduate School of Fine Arts, University of Pennsylvania, vol. 8, "Architecture and Literature" (1986): 94.

8. Italo Calvino, *Invisible Cities,* trans. William Weaver (New York: Harcourt Brace Jovanovich, 1974), 86–87.

9. André Aciman, "Shadow Cities," *The New York Review of Books,* Dec. 18, 1997, p. 37. Also in *Letters of Transit: Reflections on Exile, Identity, Language, and Loss,* ed. André Aciman (New York: The New Press and The New York Public Library, 1999), 33–34. I would like to thank Engin Akarlı for bringing the essay to my attention.

10. Carole Maso, *Ava* (Normal, Ill.: Dalkey Archive Press, 1993), 176.

11. Cited in A. S. Byatt, "Memory and the Making of Fiction," in *Memory,* eds. Patricia Fara and Karalyn Patterson (Cambridge, UK: Cambridge University Press, 1998), 60.

12. Ibid., 61.

13. Ibid., 47.

14. Ibid., 65.

15. Ibid., 64–65.

16. Patricia Hampl, "Memory and Imagination," in *I Could Tell You Stories,* by Patricia Hampl (New York: Norton, 1999), 35. "Memory and Imagination" originally appeared in *The Dolphin Reader II,* comp. Douglas Hunt (Boston: Houghton Mifflin, 1986).

17. Tracy Kidder, *Old Friends* (New York: Houghton Mifflin, 1993), 184, cited in Daniel L. Schacter, *Searching for Memory: The Brain, the Mind, and the Past* (New York: Basic Books, 1996), 294.

18. Adrienne Rich, *The Dream of a Common Language: Poems, 1974–1977* (New York: W. W. Norton, 1978).

19. Canan Tolon, *Limbo* (Istanbul: Galeri Nev, 1998), 66.

20. Paul Connerton, *How Societies Remember* (Cambridge, UK: Cambridge University Press, 1989), 36–37; Halbwachs, *The Collective Memory,* 52–55.

21. John R. Gillis, "Introduction," in *Commemorations: The Politics of National Identity,* ed. John R. Gillis (Princeton, N.J.: Princeton University Press, 1994), 5.

22. Ian Hacking, *Rewriting the Soul: Multiple Personality and the Sciences of Memory* (Princeton, N.J.: Princeton University Press, 1995), 198.

23. Pierre Nora, "From *Lieux de mémoire* to Realms of Memory," in *Realms of Memory: Rethinking the French Past,* vol. 1, under the direction of Pierre Nora, trans. Arthur Goldhammer, English-language edition ed. Lawrence D. Kritzman (New York: Columbia University Press, 1996), xxiii–xxiv.

24. In his essay "Space, Time, and the Politics of Memory," Jonathan Boyarin pointed out that "Halbwachs failed to historicize memory; not surprisingly, virtually all of his examples are of the sort that could be found in France in the early twentieth century, and a rather stereotyped, native-born, middle-class France at that." Jonathan Boyarin, ed., *Remapping Memory: The Politics of TimeSpace* (Minneapolis: University of Minnesota Press, 1994), 24.

25. Nora, "From *Lieux de mémoire,*" xxiv.

26. Robert Gildea, *The Past in French History* (New Haven, Conn.: Yale University Press, 1994), 10–11. Gildea also remarked that "[i]f *Les Lieux de Mémoire* had a shortcoming in the earlier volumes it was to establish an archaeology of objects of memory rather than to show how collective memories were shaped and reshaped by given communities." Gildea, ibid., 11. Boyarin criticized the work's effort "to reinvent 'la France profonde' as a defense against the onslaught within France of Others making claims for their own collective rights and identities." Boyarin, *Remapping Memory,* 19.

27. Refusing, at first, to participate in the national anniversaries, the conservative aristocrats commemorated instead the life of the Bourbons, while the peasants remained attached to local history and memory until almost World War I. See Gillis, "Introduction," 8–9.

28. Schacter, *Searching for Memory,* 141.

29. Ibid., 231.

30. Ibid. On pp. 62 and 79, Schacter discusses personal experiences he has had with the recall of familiar spaces, but does not elaborate further on the available literature and research.

31. Ibid., 52.

32. Ibid., 161.

33. See D. L. Schacter and Morris Moscovitch, "Infants, Amnesiacs, and Dissociable Memory Systems," in *Infant Memory,* ed. M. Moscovitch (New York: Plenum, 1984), 173–216. Cited in Schacter, *Searching for Memory,* 174.

34. Schacter, *Searching for Memory,* 175.

35. John A. Robinson and Leslie R. Taylor, "Autobiographical Memory and Self-Narratives: A Tale of Two Stories," in *Autobiographical Memory: Theoretical and Applied Perspectives*, Charles P. Thompson et al., eds. (Mahwah, N.J.: Lawrence Erlbaum Associates, 1998), 126.
36. Schacter, *Searching for Memory*, 66.
37. Ibid., 71.
38. D. P. McAdams, *The Stories We Live By: Personal Myths and the Making of the Self* (New York: Morrow, 1993), 28, cited in Schacter, *Searching for Memory*, 93.
39. Robinson and Taylor, "Autobiographical Memory," 125.
40. Ibid., 125–26.
41. Schacter, *Searching for Memory*, 82.
42. Frances Downing, *Remembrance and the Design of Place* (College Station, Tex.: Texas A & M University Press, 2000). I would like to thank my UNM colleague Alf Simon for bringing Downing's work to my attention. Unfortunately, I was not able to engage Downing's findings in this anthology, as most of the text was already completed when I read her book.
43. Ibid., 9.
44. Ibid., 11.
45. Keith H. Basso, *Wisdom Sits in Places* (Albuquerque: University of New Mexico Press, 1996), 6–7. I would like to thank Juan Rojas Routon for bringing this book to my attention.
46. For representative examples, see Susan Slyomovics, *The Object of Memory: Arab and Jew Narrate the Palestinian Village* (Philadelphia: University of Pennsylvania Press, 1998); Mary N. Layoun, *Wedded to the Land? Gender, Boundaries, and Nationalism in Crisis* (Durham, N.C.: Duke University Press, 2001); Mehmet Yashin, ed., *Step-mothertongue: From Nationalism to Multiculturalism; Literatures of Cyprus, Greece and Turkey* (London: Middlesex University Press, 2000); Joe Cleary, *Literature, Partition and the Nation State: Culture and Conflict in Ireland, Israel and Palestine* (Cambridge, UK: Cambridge University Press, 2002); and Antoinette Burton, *Dwelling in the Archive: Women Writing House, Home, and History in Late Colonial India* (New York: Oxford University Press, 2003).
47. Hacking, *Rewriting the Soul*, 246.
48. C. P. Cavafy, "The City," 1910, in *C. P. Cavafy: Collected Poems*, trans. Edmund Keeley and Philip Sherrard (Princeton, N.J.: Princeton University Press, 1975), 27.
49. Pierre Nora, "Between Memory and History: *Les lieux de Mémoire*," *Representations* 26 (spring 1989), 7.

Part One

Designing National Memories

chapter one

Framing Urban Memory

The Changing Role of History
Museums in the American City

ERIC SANDWEISS

*H*uman memory is both heightened and endangered in the urban landscape. Etched into their hardened fabrics of brick and stone, records of
human interaction mark cities as sites of endurance as well as of change.
It is perhaps this fact that distinguishes cities as cultural creations, above the
more tangible economic and bureaucratic functions that social thinkers—
in the traditions of Marx and Weber—have ascribed to them. Lewis Mumford
proposed something of the sort when, after a career spent seeking to capture
the essential significance of "the city in history," he identified the task of
"enlarg[ing] the scope of all human activities, extending them backwards and
forwards in time."

Mumford knew well, of course, that this conveyer of memory has
proved a powerful tool of erasure, as well, and that it might as likely become
the seat of civilization's demise as of its salvation. Change is, almost by
definition, one of the few constants of city life. We come to the city to transform things: raw resources into finished products, services into money,
diminished expectations into new opportunities. How, then, do urban citizens and institutions nourish this vibrancy while still fulfilling Mumford's
vision of the city's equally essential function as a storehouse of memory, a
durable stratum of experience upon which to "lay a new foundation for
urban life" in times of change and crisis?[1]

As I want to demonstrate in this chapter, Americans in particular have never comfortably accepted the intrinsic, organic quality of the urban memory of which Mumford wrote. Onto his open-ended formulation of the city as a site of both endurance and transformation, as a palimpsest of meanings to be revealed or concealed from the shifting vantage points of a culture in constant transformation, we have continually felt compelled to project an additional layer of explicit, unchanging memory (consciously refashioned as "history")—to make of the city a posed subject, suitable for framing and protected from the presumably corrosive forces of time. This contrived historical memory, different by its nature from Mumford's formulation of the city as a living repository of human experience, has indeed preserved an image of the past. Yet, as others before me have shown and as I hope to expand upon here, the act of singling out for preservation elements of the historical urban landscape and urban experience has itself proved instrumental in accelerating the loss of a deeper sense of memory that might come through the experience of change and even loss.[2]

In order to add new perspective to the problem of posed memory, I would like first to examine generally the ways in which the American city has been imaged and packaged for interpretation and memory in the very process of its formation. Then, I will look more specifically at the institution most directly responsible for maintaining and enlarging that mnemonic function: the city history museum. While no other place should be better suited to the challenge of "extending the scope of human activities forward in time," the case of the history museum only highlights the basic paradox of any attempt to connect with an urban past by thwarting the dynamic flow of urban change. What we perceive as memory, in this process, depends for its success upon a deliberate act of forgetting.

$\mathcal{C}\!\mathit{o}$

The representations to which memory affixes itself are crafted not simply in the retrospective act of remembering cities, but also in the prospective act of constructing them. Henri Lefebvre's distinction between intertwined "spatial practice," "representations of space," and "representational space"—or, as he phrases it alternately, the "lived, conceived, and perceived realms" of space—provides us with one means for distinguishing the closely woven threads of production, abstraction, and imaginative depiction that together shape the city.³ Every city's landscape is both fact—the sum of an equation of cultural, social, economic decisions, played out in space—and the raw stuff (*"matériel,"* in Lefebvre's terms) of the further representations and images by which we make sense of that otherwise confusing jumble of intentions and results. Even before they are laid out in brick and stone, cities are ready for their close-ups: the maps, views, and memories that come to seem, to us, the place itself. Memory fixes upon such representations in a way that melds the urban image to the circumstances of its making.

For years, historians have obliged the posed subject, treating the represented city as though it were the sum and substance of the real. Drawing from a tradition dating back to Patrick Geddes's efforts to link planning with a more organic theory of urban history, historians of the urban environment have in large part drawn from studies of the history of self-conscious or professional urban planning—an act akin to studying cosmetology in order to learn anatomy.⁴ Yet to look critically at the historiographic tradition that represents urban growth through its most self-conscious expressions is not to say that the represented city need stand wholly apart from the real; it is very much a part *of* it. The problem facing the historian, as it faces anyone seeking to activate the latent memory residing within the urban landscape, is not to peel away the representation (any more than it should have been to be seduced by it in the first place) but to be aware of its role as a trigger of memory and cultural meaning.

While Lefebvre and others have argued that such meanings have developed within a broader Western context of modernization, there is nevertheless room for individual cultural or political distinctions in the overall framework. From as far back as John Winthrop's vision of a "City on a Hill," or the planning of ideal towns like New Haven, Connecticut, Americans have been working to merge practice with representation, to project onto the transient urban landscape a lasting image of their paired ideals of equality and liberty. While this is most famously true of such (rare) consciously symbolic city plans as that of Washington, D.C., it accounts as well for some measure of the popularity of more ordinary landscapes. Both moral and economic imperatives bolstered the visually apprehensible gridiron street plans, like William Penn's seventeenth-century Philadelphia and the New York Commissioners' 1811 Manhattan grid, marking themselves as the prototype for towns large and small across the continent. Although the "imageability" of those plans,

to borrow from Kevin Lynch, was no doubt aided by their geometric simplicity, it was further enhanced by their cultural import as egalitarian landscapes
that nevertheless allowed for unfettered individual initiative.[5]

Once built, our means for describing such landscapes have abetted the
conceit of the city as a series of intentional, memorable spaces. As their titles
indicated, early published histories, like James Mease's 1811 *Picture of
Philadelphia,* attempted to paint in words a finely detailed image of the place
at hand—usually down to the tonnage of cargo sitting on the levee—while
later city guides typically promised block-by-block tours through what they
called the "Lights and Shadows" of the urban landscape. Artistic techniques
for imaging cities, particularly through the commanding perspectives of the
bird's-eye view and the panoramic photograph, presented nineteenth-century Americans with visual evidence of the inexorable accommodation of the
American land to a regime of order, progress, and prosperity. The ideal of the
posed, exposed city served both God and Mammon: clarity and light were as
much the hallmarks of the New Jerusalem as they were of the exchange hall.
As such, they constituted versatile tools for Americans who were busy constructing for posterity spatial images of their drive for perfection and uplift.[6]

But if the books and printed images soon offered a wealth of tools for
remembering an imagined and unchanging moment in city life, the urban
landscape itself presented a more difficult case. Cityscapes, and American
ones in particular, have been notoriously bad at sitting still for their portraits. The city is a place not just of appearance but of concealment, not only
of protection but of danger, not only of permanence but of change. From
very early in the nation's history, a strong countermovement frustrated the
work of those planners and artists concerned with posing and framing the
urban landscape. American investors literally banked on the impermanence
of the urban landscape, calculating the moment at which the value of a given
structure would depreciate to a level beneath that of the land on which it
stood, at which point the time would come to tear it down and build anew.
As architect Cass Gilbert described, developers built buildings primarily as
"machines that make the land pay"—tools for maximizing return on investment (over a frankly limited period), rather than settings for humane social
intercourse. In shaping the geography of the city, profit has been a force far
greater than religious or civic virtue. It has not been easy to paint a lasting
portrait of such a fidgety subject, or to draw from the continual process of
destruction a fixed point on which memory can alight.[7]

The malleability of American urban space is only one aspect of the larger problem of the effect of change upon memory. When one adds to the impermanence of urban structures and property the shifting makeup of the population dwelling within them, one sees how even the hastiest sketch could never hope to present more than a moment's truth faithfully. From the pages of countless travelers' diaries to the crafted prose of a returned Henry James, gazing with wonder across the Common toward downtown Boston, or the sour rant of William Burroughs, debarking from the train station in his home town of St. Louis and wondering how the city fathers could have replaced a perfectly respectable neighborhood of tattoo parlors and brothels with an arid stretch of landscaped parkway, the tradition of the disoriented urban wanderer runs deep through American letters.[8] Edward Bellamy, aware of the deep familiarity of this convention, inverted it for polemical effect when he brought his time-traveling narrator, in *Looking Backward,* to a future Boston cleansed once and for all of the unplanned, the irregular, the unpleasant. Expectably, the city had changed, yes—but only to restore itself to a stable, futuristic version of the ever-elusive City on a Hill.

Like literature, history itself can be, and in fact has been, employed not to reveal the unsettling variability of the urban environment, but to manage it: to spread varnish across it, stick a frame around it, place a label under it—in short, to project a "representational" city over the more obscure "lived" city. Nowhere has that tendency been clearer than in the case of city history museums and historical societies. Their origin was an almost desperate effort to gain bearings amidst the changes of the early republic, of the Progressive Era, and ultimately of the contemporary period, when institutions seek to memorialize their cities in the face of urban decline. Historical societies and their associated museums have sought to resolve—but in the end deepened—the paradox of fostering memory within a site that, if fully remembered, would actually reveal itself as having been the nexus of constant change, disorientation, and forgetting. A review of historical societies' and their museums' own history will help to bring this role into clearer focus.

As museums go, the idea of a building devoted to the display of artifacts related strictly to the historical past—as opposed to artifacts of art or natural history—is not particularly old. It postdates, at any rate, the long tradition of curiosity cabinets, royal galleries, and expositions that constitutes the more general lineage of the modern-day museum. The notion of focusing the history museum's mission strictly upon a city, rather than on a broader political or geographic terrain, is more recent still. Although American historical societies were established within the cities of the new republic as early as the 1790s, a century would pass before they developed what we would recognize as the city-history museum, alongside their more established function as libraries adorned by galleries of portraits and miscellaneous curios. By the 1970s, however, American city-history museums had acquired an aura of antiquity in their own right. Seemingly filled with the belongings of an elite few, little concerned with capturing either changing audiences or the changing spirit of their times, many languished at the brink of bankruptcy, even as nearby art museums drew broader and more diverse crowds than ever before.[9] Amidst a great deal of public attention, museum boards, directors, and staff have subsequently gone great distances in seeking to overturn that unfortunate legacy. Although their efforts have paid off in a number of ways, the question of how well museums function to enhance the city's potential as a conveyance of memory is dogged by two facts: one, the continual difficulty, already outlined above, of reconciling the represented city—and representation is the museum's stock in trade—with the city of spatial practice; and two, the peculiarly troubled history of the institutions themselves as places of consensus over public memory.

Those troubles appeared in the United States as soon as did history museums. In 1790, after only a scant few years of independence, New Yorker John Pintard established his American Museum in an effort to preserve the heritage of the city and the new nation. Fifteen years later, with Pintard's original vision already foundering beneath the weight of public neglect, he led a group of prominent New Yorkers seeking to supplant the museum with something more solid. The group, constituting themselves the New-York Historical Society, called on their fellow citizens to join in a broad-based, public search for records that might recover the details of a past already imperiled, they thought, by "ingenious conjectures and amusing fables." Here, again, the cause of providing a formal venue for the preservation of urban memory proved tenuous in its appeal. The most significant reply to the New-York Historical Society's initial public notice came from the writer Washington Irving, whose *History of New York, from the Beginning of the World to the*

End of the Dutch Dynasty, narrated by a fictional curmudgeon named Diedrich Knickerbocker, offered a volume full of amusing fables in response. Irving, granting that "cities, of themselves, are nothing without an historian," had supplied his own city with a perfect parody of the historian's craft (taking as his model, in fact, an 1811 publication called *A Picture of New York*); he granted historically insecure New Yorkers a legitimacy on a cosmic scale. The novelist was, no doubt, gratified to hear DeWitt Clinton, mayor of the city and one of the founders of the new historical society, denounce this "unnatural combination of fiction and history" as being "disgusting to good taste." His satiric point was taken, and it still merits taking today: life produces no end of memories—most of them readily dismissible, should we choose to do so, as "ingenious conjectures and amusing fables." History, to the extent that it excludes memory, leaves itself no less susceptible to error of another sort, though it makes itself more questionable by virtue of its pretense of a higher truth.[10]

Still, the elderly Knickerbocker, stuffing his pockets full of the useless minutiae of his city's past, proved an apt caricature of Clinton and others who followed in his footsteps. The effort "to collect and preserve," as the organization's charter put it, "whatever may relate to the natural, civil, or ecclesiastical History of the United States in general and of this state in particular" represented as focused a mission as early historical societies cared to articulate. In their sweeping goals they reflected a familiar, Enlightenment-derived confidence that all could ultimately be known. They also reflected something newer: an anxiety that to seek less would be to miss some vital answer to the problem of how to anchor memory within an increasingly fluid society.[11]

That anxiety was soon translated into similar action in other cities across the country. In one case after another, the early historical societies' notion of just who should partake of such research was as narrow as its scope was wide. William Barry, elected the first secretary of the Chicago Historical Society in 1857, had described his colleagues as "fit, though few," comprising a selection of "our oldest, most respected citizens"; Barry warned soon thereafter that only a "compact and harmonious" organization would resist the "popular excitement" that seemed to an old-line Whig such as himself as dangerous to good history as it was to good governance. In St. Louis, a self-described group of "old residents . . . who have spent the flower of their lives in advancing [the city's] interest" met in the county courthouse in 1866 "for the purpose of saving from oblivion the early history of our city and our state"—a meeting that resulted in the establishment of the Missouri Historical Society. As such "old residents" diminished in number, the stakes of their success seemed to grow higher. In the same year, New-York Historical Society director Frederic de Peyster warned that his city's growing ranks of immigrants "exposed [New York] to the vices of the great cities abroad." De Peyster set a high bar for a historical society, contending that "to counteract the evils, which irreligion, folly and wickedness have thus transplanted, it becomes our duty to control their effects, and then eradicate them, by . . . stem[ming] this flood and mak[ing] it subservient to . . . social progress." Across America, then, these Knickerbockers set a tone for historical societies—particularly big-city societies—that has persisted, in some cases, to our own time. They represented their own interests, their own memories, as those of the city, and left no room for anyone to argue otherwise. In the name of "social progress," they gathered up every bit of evidence that might reflect (or justify) their ascendance to power.[12]

Material progress, on the other hand—reflected more readily in the landscape itself than in the halls of the museum—coexisted uneasily with the founders' original goals. History museums owed their existence to the profits earned on things scraped from the earth, melted in furnaces, heaped on trains, slashed under blades. Economic progress underlay, as well, the basic plot of the stories crafted by the early historical societies—but it was also the cause of that effacement of landscape and of memory that made those societies seem necessary in the first place. The very function of the museum, as we think of it—displaying and interpreting material artifacts—was hardly a given motivation to historical-society organizers. Instead, the early groups typically stressed their moral rise above the commercial realm they celebrated and memorialized. "It would be unworthy of the spirit of historical Chicago," wrote the Chicago Historical Society's president in 1882 in campaigning for a new building, "that it should have nothing to show for the future but piles of boxes and bales. . . . There should be some fitting memorial, in no way connected with trade . . . which shall not be touched by the spirit of profit or dividend." The president of the Missouri Historical Society, George Leighton, wrote the following year of his desire for a "philosophical history" of St. Louis, one that went beyond "the mere compilation of commercial and manufacturing statistics."[13]

And yet, the spirit of accumulation underlay the impulse to preserving memory, just as it had the impulse to wealth. Already, in urban literature,

James Mease's *Picture of Philadelphia* had set the tone with its avowal that the "chief objective" of city history "ought to be the multiplication of facts"; a half-century later, an observer of the young Chicago Historical Society justified that institution's mission with the observation that "our generalizations, our theories, are right in proportion to the comprehensiveness of the mass of facts from which they are deduced."[14] The relentless thoroughness that Irving had mocked in his *History* continued to provide civic leaders with intellectual armor against the untrustworthy and fragmented experience that limited the truth of individual memories.

It was through amassment of the printed word, then—not of "boxes and bales"—that the early societies sought to anchor and to regulate memory in the changing city. (Significantly, the area in which they did evince a consistent interest in museum collecting and exhibition was in the area of "aboriginal"—that is, preliterate—culture, for which no accompanying narrative existed. This "cabinet" of prehistoric relics, as the museum arm was usually known, was solely an adjunct to the larger archiving function that seemed to the founders so urgent; in fact, as of the late 1700s, the term "museum" referred as much to magazines as it did to buildings).[15] Although historical societies' collections soon grew to include more historical urban artifacts, their buildings remained, in essence, decorated reading rooms, and their role as keepers of public memory was fulfilled through the amassing of textual material. Symptomatic of this textual bias was the director's position at the New-York Historical Society, which continued to be listed as "librarian" until the 1930s. For these groups, collection and care of the documentary record was the key to holding onto a coherent vision of a more orderly past. The memory of the city was in this way safely protected from the vicissitudes of the city itself.

The move to separate memory from change and appearance—and therefore to protect and sanctify it as "history"—reflected scholarly attitudes toward the museum generally. By the 1860s, museums had acquired something of a tarnished reputation—in part because they were already a fixture of the shifting urban landscape that historical societies sought to rise above. It was in 1865 that P. T. Barnum's American Museum, in downtown Manhattan, was destroyed by fire—an act that has been taken as a kind of coda for the hurly-burly of Jacksonian America. But the distinction between museum-as-entertainment and museum-as-education had never been firm in the antebellum years. In terms of practical collecting

FIG. 1.1. *Like many of the early city museums, MHS was first housed in a building erected for other purposes; the museum, or "cabinet," was itself a secondary element of the institution's missions. Missouri Historical Society, ca. 1909. Courtesy of the Missouri Historical Society.*

strategies, relatively little distance separated Barnum, searching the country for "albinoes, fat boys, giants, [and] dwarfs," from Philadelphia's Charles Willson Peale, keeper of the nation's best-known early museum, and his desire to present "rational amusements" in the service of revealing "divine wisdom." In fact, Peale's collection itself was partially absorbed by Barnum in his continuing quest for more objects. So, too, was John Pintard's original museum, which, not coincidentally, had borne the same name as Barnum's (carried through several changes of ownership, Pintard's brainchild actually formed the basis of Barnum's collection). In Cincinnati and in St. Louis, wherever urbanization led in the antebellum decades, new "museums" promised the curious public mastodon bones beside three-dimensional re-creations of Hell, mermaids next to arrowheads. Sensation—exposure to "the world in miniature," as Peale sought—never stood far from sensationalism, Barnum's "superfluity of novelties." What they shared was precisely what the early societies sought to avoid: a reliance on *things* to trigger a more immediate form of understanding—revelation not cerebration, emotion not distance. In place of the mannerist pose, they offered the impressionist glimpse. In place of "reliable," documented memory, they presented unmediated experience.[16]

A superfluity of novelties, of course, was what the city itself offered. Barnum, in a manner that Mumford himself might have appreciated, saw his own operation as exemplary of "the novelties of the town": an experience of the kind that country people couldn't see elsewhere. Indeed, there was a decided resemblance between mounting criticisms of the opacity and disorder of the urban landscape and the ways in which civic and intellectual leaders saw the contents of the museums themselves. The Smithsonian Institution's pioneering curator, George Brown Goode, criticized the typical history museum as a "chance assemblage of curiosities," while various observers sniped that the belongings of the New-York Historical Society were "distributed about in dark corridors," or that the Chicago Historical Society's collections were "cheap and cheerless" and "full of queer old things." The Missouri Historical Society, after only seven years of existence, was judged to be "nearly as much of a fossil as the specimens which crowd its cabinets." Such language matched the concern of late-nineteenth-century urban observers like Jacob Riis, Frederick Law Olmsted, and Charles Mulford Robinson for the ostensibly chaotic city that they sought to reform and re-form, outside of the museum's walls.[17]

Historical societies responded by expanding and systematizing their artifactual collections in a way that might make objects the agents of instruction rather than mere sensation. From the 1880s on, the once-incidental cabinets, or museums, were reconceived as transparent interior landscapes, readable and reliable contrasts to the difficult world of the street. The museum of the future, in Goode's words, would comprise "a collection of instructive labels each illustrated by a well-selected specimen." If objects were indeed a part of the historical society's purview, they would at least be put to the service of ideas; the museum would become a classroom, not a laboratory. This controlling urge was complemented by the decision of a number of organizations to push toward their long-held goals of erecting buildings that might, themselves, serve as instructive objects. It was at the end of the nineteenth and beginning of the twentieth century that history museums joined the trend of other urban institutions seeking to realize Edward Bellamy's 1887 vision of a future city adorned by "public buildings of a colossal size and an architectural grandeur, unparalleled" in the period that Mumford would later dub aptly, the "brown decades." The lure of a "city beautiful," a place in which representation at last controlled practice, clearly appealed to the keepers of the still largely marginal historical societies, who had sought unsuccessfully to fashion such a unity in words, from within the dim chambers of their downtown libraries.[18]

But even as the colonnades were rising on their new park-front sites, historical societies continued to suffer from public protests of the futility of seeking to capture a meaningful memory of something as dynamic as the modern city, whether in their libraries (often parodied as sleeping lounges for aging capitalists), their tedious lecture series ("gaseous secretions of vanity and dilettantism," to the New York diarist George Templeton Strong), or their long rows of glass cases. Again, the city had outpaced its chroniclers' ability to make sense of what they saw. Across the disciplines of American intellectual culture in the 1890s, while city-history museums invested heavily in the taxonomic model of explanation, others had begun to conceive of the city as a more strictly social phenomenon, to make of its protean quality a positive thing, not a danger. The economist Adna Weber, one of the first of the master theorists of urban culture, had tried to sum up the importance of nineteenth-century cities in terms of their role as the incubators of "a broader and freer judgment and a great inclination to and appreciation of new thoughts, manners, and ideals." Others, including George Herbert Mead

FIG. 1.2. *In 1915, MHS joined the trend of history museums moving
to purpose-built structures in parklike settings set apart from
the surrounding urban fabric. Missouri Historical Society,
ca. 1933. Courtesy of the Missouri Historical Society.*

and John Dewey, were framing their new concepts of selfhood in social terms,
and finding in the city the ultimate laboratory for human interchange at its
most complex. The intellectual conception of the early-twentieth-century city
was better captured by the social dynamism of Louis Wirth's "Urbanism as
a Way of Life" than it was by the concreteness of the old "Picture of one
place or another" variety. Such ideas only cast harsher light on the problem
of how to memorialize this dynamism, this fluidity, within the museum,
which, by its nature, honored the concrete over the abstract, the constant
over the changing.[19]

The suggestions for integrating memory-as-representation with a more
active program of social engagement appeared in fits and starts. "Why
confine the aim of the society," wrote a *New York Times* editorialist of that

city's historical society in the 1890s, "to the comparatively narrow object
of historical research?" In place of the society's plans for a new showcase
on Central Park West, the author suggested a "museum for artisans"—a
building open in a site, and at times, convenient to working-class New
Yorkers, a place where they might investigate the beauty and importance of
their own lives, rather than be reminded of their own relative insignificance.
In 1903, the influential librarian John Cotton Dana proposed that the "chief
concern" of urban cultural institutions like libraries was "the process, not
the product, of education," and that they ought to be seen as sites primarily "for diffusing sound principles of social and political action."[20]

The populist turn affected even the stuffiest of the historical organizations—not just such predictably progressive stalwarts as Wisconsin's state historical society. Chicago, the society that had once bragged of its "fit, though
few" members, dedicated its new building in 1896 not to "any sect or clique,"
but "to [the] benefit of the whole community." A generation later, the Chicago
Historical Society moved yet again, this time to its current Georgian quarters
at the southern edge of Lincoln Park. With the move, the institution sought
to reform at one stroke its architectural image, the content of its collections,
and the manner of their display. In turning from the previously popular stylistic language of the classical revival to the more domesticated Georgian, or
colonial revival, they identified themselves as one of a growing breed of museums, like the Museum of the City of New York, established across Central
Park from the more exclusive New-York Historical Society, aspiring to a more
accessible image within the city. The Chicago Historical Society bought the
vast estate of a local confectioner named Charles Gunther, who had operated his own museum of curiosities above his State Street candy store—including the mummy of Moses's mother and the original serpent of the Garden of
Eden—and who had once taken down, brick by brick, the Confederate Libby
Prison from its site in Richmond, Virginia, and reconstructed it as a tourist
attraction on Chicago's South Side. Just prior to the move, the Chicago
Historical Society announced its desire to appeal to a wide popular audience,
as well as its willingness to foreground artifacts, rather than archives, as its
primary medium for conveying knowledge. And finally, in installing its new
collections in dioramas and re-created period rooms, the museum joined a
growing number of similar institutions seeking to replace entirely the now
ill-favored method of taxonomic display with a more emotive, more all-
encompassing form of display, one which made of the viewer an ostensible

participant in, rather than critic of, the past. "An antidote for the prevalent movie habit," gushed a local arts critic of the new museum, while another journalist praised the Chicago Historical Society for "breathing new life into its collections" by removing its "relics" from their "dreary glass cases." Not long after, in Detroit, a Streets of Detroit exhibition, carefully separated from the real streets of Detroit by a new, windowless modernist museum structure on Woodward Avenue, provided a similar thrill to citizens whose only previous local history-museum experiences had taken place in a suite of rooms, crowded with shelves and cases, tucked away on a high floor in a downtown skyscraper.[21]

But the suggestion of "breathing new life" and the comparisons to movie-going pointed to the continuing problem of conceiving of the historical society as the repository of urban memory, even more than they suggested some new level of success. If verisimilitude was what museums now sought, they could never possibly keep up with movies and radio—let alone with reality. In cities across the country, local groups had already begun the practice of erecting plaques on historic buildings—framing the street itself as a museum-like experience. In Williamsburg, Virginia, and in Dearborn, Michigan, the era's great capitalists, Rockefeller and Ford, were busy investing their millions in the full-scale renovation or re-creation of entire buildings. Meanwhile, in Charleston, South Carolina; Santa Fe, New Mexico; and New Orleans, Louisiana, the new legal tool of historic district zoning made outdoor museums of entire urban districts. The urban landscape itself was increasingly framed within historical reference points.[22]

A long period of relative quietude commenced that culminated, in the 1970s, in new calls for a more proper practice of history to inform the work of the nation's aging history museums. Under the rubric of inclusivity and critical social history, museums returned to Goode's century-old preference for "instructive labels illustrated by well-selected specimens"—in the eyes of its critics, a "book-on-the-wall" approach to exhibition. Beneath a guise of intellectual rigor and democratic concern, they ventured the same "evocation of a presumptive community," as historian Michael Frisch called it, that had characterized the work of their patrician forebears. Once again, they separated urban memory from its more fluid and contested grounding in the changing landscape. Asked in 1992 about his approach to exhibitions, Ellsworth Brown, then-director of the Chicago Historical Society, stated, with somewhat too much insistence, that "exhibitions should be about

FIGS. 1.3 AND 1.4.
Paul Revere House Gallery (n.d.), and Thorne Rooms (ca. 1938).
CHS's move to new quarters in the 1920s marked the continuation
of the society's effort to arrange materials—through dioramas and
reconstructed rooms—in a manner that surpassed the realism of earlier
display techniques. Courtesy of the Chicago Historical Society.

ideas." Rick Beard, then director of the Museum of the City of New York and later of the Atlanta History Center, explained that he began the process by "creating . . . a very long monograph with appropriate scholarly apparatus, bibliography, and some notes, and our interpretations come from that document for the various media we employ." Such thinking was encouraged, in material ways, by the criteria of one of the most important funding agencies for museum exhibitions, the National Endowment for the Humanities. NEH standards have indeed imparted a measure of intellectual discipline to many exhibitions. But in using such criteria, inadvertently, to shortchange the *medium* of their craft for its *message*, many museum professionals today have laid aside Peale's and Barnum's simple insights into the stimulating effect of a "superfluity of novelties." They have rejected "the novelties of the town"—the vivid if unreliable evidence of the past that, as Mumford saw it, permeates the urban landscape—in favor of their earliest predecessors' distrust of unmediated sensation. That the narratives of today's idea-driven exhibits focus more on the once-forgotten, or excluded, rather than on the more familiar denizens of corporate boardrooms or society blue books does not change the fact that they are usually developed by groups who, if forced to, would still have to describe themselves as "fit, though few."[23]

Figures within the very landscapes that they purport to represent, museums have come to seem time-bound, historical artifacts in their own right. In their initial efforts at amassing written records toward the end of reconstructing accurately and completely an imagined civic unity, in their subsequent drift toward attempting to re-create the dynamism of the landscape itself, they offered two models for "extending [human activity] . . . forward in time." Neither proved particularly successful, in terms of garnering public credibility and acceptance. The former tendency, echoed in the recent turn back toward a more intellectual approach to historical interpretation, suffers from the general disenchantment over monadic historical interpretation that has affected both the academy and the public in the period since the early era of museum building. The latter, meanwhile, can only suffer from comparison to what landscape historian Denis Cosgrove has termed "the ever more seamless elision of experience and landscape" that characterizes our own time.[24] The representational city is realized less effectively, today, within museum walls than it is through large-scale historic preservation projects, in consumption-oriented spaces, or in the verisimilitude of film and electronic media—all of which have more powerfully influenced our collective memory of the urban past.[25] Our highly developed state of capitalism has, instead of overtly rejecting the past, embraced it, placing a comfortable, commodified frame of memory around the whole world. Under the guise of expanded access to information, and with it of well-preserved memory, we inhabit a world managed by ever fewer producers, fewer interpreters, fewer true alternatives to the comfortable habits that we fashioned so successfully from the labors of our predecessors. Amidst this conflation of "lived," "perceived," and "conceived" space, life itself seems as though it were set within a museum or upon a stage—a seeming rush of color, noise, and experience that actually plays itself out in well-packaged, well-sponsored segments.

As American cities passed through a long period of extraordinary fluidity and change, museums struggled to provide a stable venue within which memory—albeit of a highly selective sort—might be protected from the destructive forces of capitalist society and thence converted to an authoritative historical record, all toward the end of maintaining a stable social order. Today, as the city reaches what geographer James Lemon calls "nature's limits"[26]—that is, as the basis for urban wealth shifts from the exploitation of a continually expanding quantity of natural resources to the management of finite resources and information—the need for such a preserve has diminished. "Memory," framed and matted for presentation, is all around us. And yet, as that memory has become its own sort of product, a modern-day equivalent of the "boxes and bales" that cultural leaders once sought to rise above, history museums are left high and dry. Perhaps for the future, their sanctified walls could shelter and nourish the more truly endangered aspects of the contemporary American city: change, unpredictability, and social fluidity. These forces, all of which once seemed to threaten our ability to connect urban past to urban future, now stand in danger of becoming memories in their own right.

Notes

1. Lewis Mumford, *The City in History: Its Origins, Its Transformations, and Its Prospects* (New York: Harcourt, Brace, & World, 1961), 569, 3.

2. The critical literature on preservation and its problematic relation to history and memory is large and continues to grow. Among the many works useful in the preparation of this study, see M. Christine Boyer, *The City of Collective Memory: Its Historical Imagery and Architectural Entertainments* (Cambridge, Mass.: The MIT Press, 1994); David Lowenthal, *Possessed by the Past: The Heritage Crusade and the Spoils of History* (New York: Free Press, 1996); Françoise Choay, *The Invention of the Historic Monument* (New York: Cambridge University Press, 2001); Larry Bennett, *Fragments of Cities: The New American Downtowns and Neighborhoods* (Columbus: Ohio State University Press, 1990); Dolores Hayden, *The Power of Place: Urban Landscapes as Public History* (Cambridge, Mass.: The MIT Press, 1995); Max Page, *The Creative Destruction of Manhattan, 1900–1940* (Chicago: University of Chicago Press, 1999). On the development of professional standards of historical objectivity see Peter Novick, *That Noble Dream: The Objectivity Question and the American Historical Profession* (Cambridge, UK: Cambridge University Press, 1988).
On commemoration and the construction of public memory within the United States, see Michael Kammen, *Mystic Chords of Memory: The Transformation of Tradition in American Culture* (New York: Knopf, 1991) and John Bodnar, *Remaking America: Public Memory, Commemoration, and Patriotism in the Twentieth Century* (Princeton, N.J.: Princeton University Press, 1992).

3. Henri Lefebvre, *The Production of Space*, trans. Donald Nicholson-Smith (Oxford: Blackwell Publishers, 1991), 38–40.

4. Patrick Geddes, *Cities in Evolution: An Introduction to the Town Planning Movement and to the Study of Civics* (London: Williams & Norgate, 1915). Among the influential histories of physical planning, see John Reps, *The Making of Urban America: A History of City Planning in the United States* (Princeton, N.J.: Princeton University Press, 1965); Mel Scott, *American City Planning since 1890: A History Commemorating the Fiftieth Anniversary of the American Institute of Planners* (Berkeley: University of California Press, 1961); and Spiro Kostof's simultaneously released *The City Assembled: The Elements of Urban Form through History* and *The City Shaped: Urban Patterns and Meanings through History* (Boston: Little, Brown, 1991).

5. Darrett Bruce Rutman, *Winthrop's Boston: Portrait of a Puritan Town, 1630–1649* (Chapel Hill: published for the Institute of Early American History and Culture at Williamsburg, Va., by the University of North

Carolina Press, 1965); John Archer, "Puritan Town Planning in New Haven," *Journal of the Society of Architectural Historians* 34, no. 2 (May 1975): 140–66; Dell Upton, "The City as Material Culture," chap. 3, in *The Art and Mystery of Historical Archaeology: Essays in Honor of James Deetz,* eds. Anne Elizabeth Yentsch and Mary C. Beaudry (Boca Raton: CRC Press, 1992); Kevin Lynch, *The Image of the City* (Cambridge, Mass.: The MIT Press, 1960).

6. James Mease, *The Picture of Philadelphia,* rev. ed. (1811; repr., New York: Arno Press, 1970); Helen Campbell, *Darkness and Daylight; or, Lights and Shadows of New York Life. A Woman's Story of Gospel, Temperance, Mission, and Rescue Work* (Hartford, Conn.: A. D. Worthington and Co., 1893); James D. McCabe, *Lights and Shadows of New York Life; or, the Sights and Sensations of the Great City,* rev. ed. (1872; repr., New York: Farrar, Straus, and Giroux, 1970). On the tradition of nineteenth-century lithographic bird's-eye views, see the many relevant works of John W. Reps, including *Views and Viewmakers of Urban America: Lithographs of Towns and Cities in the United States and Canada; Notes on the Artists and Publishers, and a Union Catalog of Their Work, 1825–1925* (Columbia: University of Missouri Press, 1984). On panoramic urban photography, see Peter B. Hales, *Silver Cities: The Photography of American Urbanization, 1839–1915* (Philadelphia: Temple University Press, 1984) and David Harris, with Eric Sandweiss, *Eadweard Muybridge and the Photographic Panorama of San Francisco, 1850–1880* (Montreal: Canadian Centre for Architecture, 1993).

7. On land depreciation and early real estate practices generally, see Richard M. Hurd, *Principles of City Land Values,* 2nd ed. (New York: Record and Guide, 1905); Cass Gilbert, "The Financial Importance of Rapid Building," *Engineering Record* 41 (1900): 624.

8. Henry James, *The American Scene* (1907; repr., Bloomington, Ind.: Indiana University Press, 1968), 231; William S. Burroughs, "St. Louis Return," in *Seeking St. Louis: Voices from a River City, 1670–2000,* ed. Lee Ann Sandweiss (St. Louis: Missouri Historical Society Press, 2000), 735.

9. On the early historical societies, see Walter Muir Whitehill, *Independent Historical Societies: An Enquiry into Their Research and Publication Functions and Their Financial Future* (Boston: The Atheneum, 1962) and Julian P. Boyd, "State and Local Historical Societies in the United States," *American Historical Review* 40, no. 1 (Oct. 1934): 10–37. On the evolution of museums in American culture, see Steven Conn, *Museums and American Intellectual Life, 1876–1926* (Chicago: University of Chicago Press, 1998). On the more recent troubles facing historical museums, see Kevin M. Guthrie, *The New-York Historical Society: Lessons from One Nonprofit's Struggle for Survival* (San Francisco: Jossey-Bass, 1996); Mike Wallace, *Mickey Mouse History and Other Essays on American Memory*

(Philadelphia: Temple University Press, 1996); Susan Porter Benson, Stephen Brier, and Roy Rosenzweig, eds., *Presenting the Past: Essays on History and the Public* (Philadelphia: Temple University Press, 1986).

10. On New-York Historical Society generally, see R. W. G. Vail, *Knickerbocker Birthday: A Sesquicentennial History of the New-York Historical Society, 1804–1954* (New York: New-York Historical Society Press, 1954) and Pamela Spence Richards, *Scholars and Gentlemen: The Library of the New-York Historical Society, 1804–1982* (Hamden, Conn.: Archon Books, 1984). See also Washington Irving, *A History of New York, from the Beginning of the World to the End of the Dutch Dynasty* (New York: A. L. Burt, 1848) and Samuel L. Mitchill, *The Picture of New-York, or the Traveler's Guide through the Commercial Metropolis of the United States* (New York: I. Riley, 1807). Clinton quoted in Mary Weatherspoon Bowden, "Knickerbocker's *History* and the 'Enlightened' Men of New York City," *American Literature* 47, no. 2 (1975): 159.

11. Vail, *Knickerbocker Birthday,* 23.

12. "Fit, though few": William Barry to L. A. Lapham, Apr. 29, 1856, folder 1, William Barry Papers, Chicago Historical Society Archives; "compact and harmonious," cited in Paul M. Angle, *The Chicago Historical Society, 1856–1956: An Unconventional Chronicle* (New York: Rand McNally, 1956), 23; "old residents": public notice, Aug. 1, 1866, included in *Missouri Historical Society Collections* 1, no. 1 (n.d.): 25; "saving from oblivion": "The Origin of the Missouri Historical Society," *The Invincible Magazine* 1, no. 1 (1913): 9; Frederic DePeyster, *The Moral and Intellectual Influence of Libraries upon Social Progress* (New York: New-York Historical Society, 1866), 48.

13. *Historical Chicago: Past, Present, and Future; Address of Emery A. Storrs for the Benefit of the Chicago Historical Society* (Chicago: 1882), 10; George Leighton, "Annual Address of the President, Jan. 16, 1883," *Missouri Historical Society Collections* 1, no. 7 (1883): 10–11.

14. Mease, *Picture of Philadelphia,* xi; *Chicago Tribune,* Feb. 9, 1865.

15. See, among many similar titles in the late 1700s, *The Massachusetts Magazine; or, Monthly Museum of Knowledge and Rational Entertainment* (1789–1796).

16. P. T. Barnum, *Struggles and Triumphs; or, Forty Years' Recollections,* rev. ed. (1889; repr., New York: Penguin, 1987), 103; Peale cited in Neil Harris, *Humbug: The Art of P. T. Barnum* (Boston: Little-Brown, 1973), 34 and David R. Brigham, *Public Culture in the Early Republic: Peale's Museum and Its Audience* (Washington, D.C.: Smithsonian Institution Press, 1995), 20–21. On the Peale-Pintard-Barnum connection, see Barnum, *Struggles and Triumphs,* 101–2 and John Rickards Betts, "P. T. Barnum and the Popularization of Natural History," *Journal of the History of Ideas* 20, no. 3 (June–Sept. 1959): 353–68; M. H. Dunlop, "Curiosities too Numerous

to Mention: Early Regionalism and Cincinnati's Western Museum,"
American Quarterly 36, no. 4 (fall 1984): 524–48; John F. McDermott,
"Museums in Early St. Louis," *Bulletin of the Missouri Historical Society* 4,
no. 3 (Apr. 1948): 30ff.

17. Barnum, *Struggles and Triumphs,* 136; Goode cited in Archie F. Key,
Beyond Four Walls: The Origin and Development of Canadian Museums
(Toronto: McClelland and Stewart, 1973), 91; New-York Historical Society:
New York Evening Post, Dec. 26, 1884, cited in Vail, *Knickerbocker
Birthday,* 157; Chicago Historical Society: *Chicago Herald,* June 20, 1886,
cited in Angle, *The Chicago Historical Society,* 118; Missouri Historical
Society: W. H. H. Russell, "The Missouri Historical Society," *The Central
Magazine* 3, no. 1 (July 1873): 417.

18. Goode cited in Kenneth Hudson, *A Social History of Museums: What the
Visitors Thought* (London: Macmillan, 1975), 68. Lewis Mumford, *Brown
Decades, 1865–1895: A Study of the Arts in America,* 2nd ed. (New
York: Dover Publications, 1955); William H. Wilson, *The City Beautiful
Movement* (Baltimore: Johns Hopkins University Press, 1989). Typical
of the monumental cultural institutions erected in the late 1800s and early
1900s were the structures of the museums examined in this study, including
the New-York Historical Society (1906), Museum of the City of New York
(1932), the Chicago Historical Society (1896, with another new building
in 1932), and the Missouri Historical Society (1915).

19. Strong cited in Vail, *Knickerbocker Birthday,* 114; Adna Ferrin Weber, *The
Growth of Cities in the Nineteenth Century: A Study in Statistics* (New
York: Macmillan, 1899), 432–34; George Herbert Mead, *Mind, Self, and
Society: From the Standpoint of a Behaviorist,* ed. and with an introduction
by Charles W. Morris (Chicago: University of Chicago Press, 1934); John
Dewey, *Democracy and Education: An Introduction to the Philosophy of
Education* (New York: Macmillan, 1926); Louis Wirth, "Urbanism as a
Way of Life," *American Journal of Sociology* 44 (1938): 1–26.

20. "A Museum for Artisans," *New York Times,* Apr. 24, 1892; John Cotton
Dana, *A Library Primer,* 3rd ed. (Chicago: Little-Brown, 1903), 13.

21. "Sect or clique" cited in Angle, *The Chicago Historical Society,* 137. On
the Lincoln Park building see ibid., 195ff.; on the Museum of the City of
New York see "'A Vanished City Is Restored': Inventing and Displaying the
Past at the Museum of the City of New York," chap. 5, in Page, *Creative
Destruction;* on Gunther's museum, see Clement Silvestro, "The Candy
Man's Mixed Bag," *Chicago History* 2, no. 2 (fall 1972): 86–99, as well
as Gunther Scrapbook, Chicago Historical Society Archives; "breathing
new life": *Dallas News,* Oct. 20, 1938, cited in Angle, *The Chicago
Historical Society,* 214; on Detroit, see Henry D. Brown, "Our New
Museum: A Building—A Program," *Bulletin of the Detroit Historical
Society* 9 (May 1949): 5–12.

22. On Williamsburg and Greenfield Village, see Michael Wallace, "History Museums in the United States," in Benson et al., *Presenting the Past*. On New Orleans, see "Invented Traditions and Cityscapes," chap. 6, in Boyer, *City of Collective Memory;* on Santa Fe, see Chris Wilson, *The Myth of Santa Fe: Creating a Modern Regional Tradition* (Albuquerque: University of New Mexico Press, 1997). (It is, interestingly, this same period that generated a great counter-current, in American literature, of regret for the landscape of an irretrievable past: the melancholic drama, memoir, and fiction of Thomas Wolfe, Alfred Kazin, Tennessee Williams, and so many others in the 1930s, '40s, and '50s).

23. Bruce M. Stave, "A Conversation with Rick Beard," *Journal of Urban History* 23, no. 5 (1997): 204; Bruce M. Stave, "A Conversation with Ellsworth Brown," *Journal of Urban History* 18, no. 4 (1992): 479; Michael Frisch, "The Presentation of Urban History in Big-City Museums," in *History Museums in the United States,* eds. Roy Rosenzweig and Warren Leon (Urbana: University of Illinois Press, 1989), 40.

24. Denis E. Cosgrove, *Social Formation and Symbolic Landscape* (Madison: University of Wisconsin Press, 1998), xxiv.

25. See Michael Sorkin, ed., *Variations on a Theme Park: The New American City and the End of Public Space* (New York: Hill and Wang, 1997).

26. James T. Lemon, *Liberal Dreams and Nature's Limits: Great Cities of North America since 1600* (New York: Oxford University Press, 1997).

chapter two

Disguised Visibilities

Dresden / "Dresden"

MARK JARZOMBEK

The New Dresden

When the *Boston Globe* recently proclaimed in a headline, "Dresden Builds a Future: German City Reconstructs Its Demolished Past," the words, inadvertently, raised some intriguing questions.[1] What does it mean "to build a future?" What is the nature of that "demolished past?" Even the first word, *Dresden,* is something of a conundrum. The city actually consists of two cities, one on each side of the Elbe. On the north side one finds Dresden-Neustadt, which was laid out in 1732 over the ruins of the old medieval township that had burned in a massive conflagration in 1685. A good portion of that "New City" is now, ironically, the oldest part, since sections of it were spared in the bombing raids of 1945. By contrast, the part of Dresden south of the Elbe that had been destroyed in the war had been rebuilt by the Socialists in a Marxist modernist manner. As the article proclaims, Dresden is presently again in the process of being worked over. This newest of the "new" Dresdens is divided into two zones. The area closer to the train station is becoming a postmodern-styled commercial center, while the area along the Elbe, containing the castle, ministry buildings, and museums, as well as that famed eighteenth-century baroque

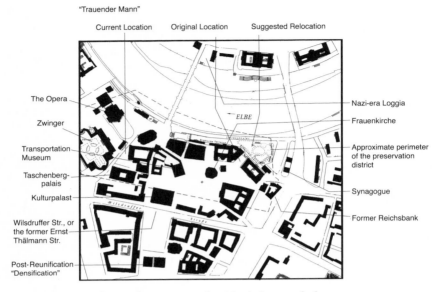

FIG. 2.1. *Plan of Dresden. Drawn by Mark Jarzombek.*

masterpiece, the Frauenkirche, is in the process of becoming Dresden's reconstituted historical quarter.

The restorers' hope, in particular, is to recapture the silhouette of Dresden's once-famous skyline as seen from Dresden-Neustadt.

Before one can attempt to critique these developments, the Nazi-era Dresden must also be taken into consideration. Part of the problem, however, is that the Nazis did not add any major buildings to the city's center but adapted old structures to their purposes. The Taschenbergpalais, located just behind the castle, was used, for example, as the Nazi army command headquarters. But when the multimillion-dollar restoration of the building was recently completed, the book that celebrated that event mentioned its wartime use only vaguely as something that the "old timers remember."[2] Not only does one wonder what those memories might consist of, but one may also ask, why is it mentioned as a "memory" and not as a fact?

As it turns out, the Nazis contributed more than just "memories" to the urban landscape of Dresden. Along the foundations of the Elbe Bridge that links Neustadt to Dresden, at the very point from which Dresden's famous

FIG. 2.2. *Nighttime illumination of Dresden's new skyline, from* Dresdener Neueste Nachrichten 9, *no. 16/80 (Jan. 20, 1999): 1.*

silhouette can best be seen, Hans Nadler designed a loggia in 1935 that houses a set of enameled panels depicting the building of Dresden-Neustadt.

The theme of the panels, showing a confident ruler looking down at broad-shouldered workers, is certainly innocuous, but one should not forget that the Nazis perceived Dresden as a perfect Germanic city, with the only disturbing element the nineteenth-century synagogue that had been designed by Gottfried Semper and located in a prominent spot close to the Elbe. And so, in 1939, after the building had already been firebombed on Kristallnacht, it was blasted into oblivion. Though a new synagogue has recently been built on the same site as the old, it is a low, modern building, not visible in the newly reconstructed skyline. In that sense, the contemporary Dresden skyline still carries the imprint of the Nazi-era vision of the city.[3]

The history of Dresden is thus not only a history of multiple "Dresdens," but also a history of the problematic interweaving of overlapping and

FIG. 2.3. *Loggia containing* History of Shipping on the Elbe, *Hans Nadler, 1935. Photo by Mark Jarzombek.*

competing narratives about its past and future. This comes very well into focus in the movie that is shown to today's tourists at the Transportation Museum located in the very heart of Dresden's newly created heritage district. The film, entitled *Das alte Dresden, in den 30-er Jahren* (The Old Dresden, in the 1930s), shows tourists being driven through the city on buses to view the sites.

With similar buses still being used for the same purpose, and parked not too far away, the film tries to evoke a sense of continuity with the 1930s. That some of the movie's clips derive from Nazi propaganda films is not revealed and might not be evident to the viewer. Nor have the current directors as of yet made any attempt to provide a more accurate picture of what everyday life was like in Dresden during the 1930s. Furthermore, even though the film was made by the Socialists with an accusatory agenda, the film is shown today to bracket out not only the city's destruction but also the equally problematic presence of the Socialist modernism that had left the church abandoned. In other words, when one exits

FIG. 2.4. *Detail of* History of Shipping on the Elbe.
Photo by Mark Jarzombek.

the Transportation Museum, after viewing the movie, and looks directly at the Frauenkirche across the street, one could easily get the impression that the movie had just recently been conceived as a promotional film for the rebuilding of the city.

My point is to draw forth awareness of the complex nature of the history of a city like Dresden, or of any city for that matter, when studied from the perspective of its representational elucidations, whether that be a film, a building, or a monument. Though these elucidations all exist within the public domain, and may appear relatively innocuous, they are all part of the history of multiple and overlapping claims to modernity. The historian must thus be on guard to transcend the false pairing of memory and modernity, where memory, by implication, is assigned a positive value and modernity a negative one. Dresden's "memory," like its history, is very much a modernist construction and can be discussed only in those terms. This does not mean that one has to diminish the horror of its destruction on February 13, 1945, only that

FIG. 2.5. *View of an advertisement for the film* Das alte Dresden. *Photo by Mark Jarzombek.*

Dresden's contemporary history should be defined by the complex accumulation of narratives that exist within the fabric of the city itself.

My concern is born of urgency, for the city—already being primed for its eight-hundredth birthday celebration in 2006—is being rebuilt and transformed at such a fast pace that it is increasingly difficult to differentiate the still-potent, bricolaged layers of Dresden's mnemonic structure. Soon the moment will be lost and indeed become irrelevant. The dust that hovers over the city's numerous construction sites will settle, and the layered, dynamic, and complex nature of Dresden's history will be lost.

Rebuilding and Forgetting

After the war it was more or less assumed that Dresden's Frauenkirche would be rebuilt, but this did not happen during the four decades of Socialist rule. Instead, the ruins were left abandoned and the heap of blackened stones were designated a memorial to Allied atrocity. And so, when, in the early 1990s, in the euphoria of German reunification, the decision was finally made to rebuild the church, the announcement opened a floodgate of pent-up remembrances not only about the circumstances of the church's destruction but also about the destruction of the city itself. Overnight, the Frauenkirche became the symbol of the city's past, its survival, and its rebirth.

The announcement, accompanied by the commensurate rhetoric, not only reawakened Dresden's civic spirit but also heralded the return of religion after decades of "god-less" Socialist rule. For political and economic reasons, speed was of the essence, especially since the West, in rebuilding the church, felt that it was atoning for the damage done by the Allies in the war. Framing the enterprise were speeches by politicians, visits by dignitaries, candlelit prayers, and somber memorial services. Queen Elisabeth, the Duke of Kent, and other English notables were invited to Dresden for various ceremonies of reconciliation. Even Henry Kissinger has weighed in on the matter: "The rebuilding of Dresden's Frauenkirche demonstrates an international commitment to overcome the cruelties of war and to build bridges among nations."[4]

But it would be a mistake to reduce the architectural history of this building to an official narrative of the building's destruction, subsequent "neglect," and, with the reunification of Germany, its reconstruction.[5] The task itself was undertaken with the help of an advanced French computer modeling system known as CATIA, which had been developed for the design of military aircraft. This technology was also used for the Guggenheim Museum in Bilbao, and indeed, there is something uncannily similar about these two buildings, as both are central to a narrative in which political symbolism, regional identity, and international tourism are conflated. Nor should the irony that the very aviational technology that once facilitated the bombing of the building was now helping to repair it, be lost on us.

One of the pressing problems of the Frauenkirche was what to do with the heap of old stones. Should one discard them and start over or accept and preserve their accusatory meaning, Socialist-inspired or not?

FIG. 2.6. *Frauenkirche, 2002. Photo by Mark Jarzombek.*

The controversy filled many pages in the German press, but it is largely an either-or debate.[6] Finally, the decision was made to treat the stones as elements of a vast, DNA-like research puzzle. They were separated, measured, analyzed, and then placed into the fabric of the new walls of the church, hopefully at the very spot where they once belonged. Preservationists call this a "critical restoration." Yet, despite all the technology and science that went into the church's rebuilding, the placement of most of the old stones was quite arbitrary. Some of the stones were parts of capitals and moldings, but many were generic blocks that could be put anywhere. They were thus sprinkled around to make it look as if the preservationists had indeed figured out where they had come from. As a result, what started as an honest attempt to make a building with "embedded memory" became an aesthetic governed by the positivistic conceits of the restorers. It could even be argued that the Socialist monument was, in essence, dispersed throughout the fabric of the building so that it was no longer possible to read its former presence back into existence.

FIG. 2.7. Trauender Mann, *Wieland Förster, 1985.*
Photo by Mark Jarzombek.

But where then, one may ask, can citizens mourn their dead or reflect on the painful events of the recent past on a human and secular level not tainted by the paradoxes of the reconstruction industry? Oddly enough, there are such places, although largely overlooked by "official" historians. On the busy Sophienstrasse next to the castle, for example, one encounters the figure of *Trauender Mann* (Mourning Man), created in 1985 by the Dresden-born Wieland Förster.[7]

The sculpture depicts a man with knees pulled up tightly to cover his face in a way that was intended by the artist to express not only grief but also shame. Like the Greek Niobe, who averts her face in silent grief, the *Trauender Mann* evokes the profound anguish of self-inflicted tragedy. Initially, during the height of the Socialist regime, the statue had been rejected, no doubt because it was seen as too ambiguous and self-indulgent. But in the 1980s, with the arrival of glasnost, permission was granted for its display.[8] Though many Socialist sculptures were removed after reunification, this one survived the "cleansing," as it was not considered overtly ideological.

The statue, in our current phraseology, qualifies as both a memorial and a counter-memorial. It is classical and profound, and yet, because it not only states the human tragedy of war but also, historically, evokes the memory of a Socialist optic, it might be perceived by some as deeply unsettling. The West likes to think that it has mastered the trauma of war more effectively than the Socialist regime it replaced. But Socialist modernity, especially in this particular case, should certainly not be denied its rightful place in the space of urban reflection. The statue's siting will be critical in this respect. Originally, the sculpture was placed in the Georg-Treu-Platz, only a few steps from the Frauenkirche. It was moved to the more remote Sophienstrasse, however, because of construction work in the area. Though it is likely that the statue will be returned to the Georg-Treu-Platz, I would argue that it be brought to a location somewhere between the Frauenkirche and the nearby synagogue to expand its message to include also the Jewish victims of the city. I would also argue that this equidistance be noted in a sign so that the statue is understood as a memorial to all human suffering that occurred in Dresden—the Jewish suffering not excluded—as a symbol of reconciliation in grief.

I make these claims mainly to critique the tendency of urban historians to parallel state-supported discourses. Heinz Quinger's art and architectural guide, *Dresden und Umgebung* (Dresden and Environs, 1993), for example, mentions in its very first sentence the wartime destruction of the city, but without any mention of the Nazi past or the complete destruction of Dresden's Jewish community. For sure, this is not out of any disrespect, but a forgetting nevertheless, because the image of the new postreunification "Dresden" is built almost entirely around the narrative of the church's destruction and rebuilding, with the intervening Socialist phase left a blank. The *Trauender Mann* is briefly mentioned but only on page 152.[9] The more recent book, *Dresden: A City Reborn,* a work that deals with the broad spectrum of Dresden's history, is not much better in this respect. It was authored by English scholars—with an introduction by the Duke of Kent—and is dutifully laudatory of the English contribution to the rebuilding of the Frauenkirche. The new golden orb, made by English craftsmen and personally handed over to the city by the duke himself, is featured in the only color plate of the book's first edition. The globe is now proudly displayed in front of the church, awaiting its final placement on the top of the dome. In contrast to such works of art, the Socialist contributions are described as "primitive," and their politics as a combination of "scandalous neglect" and "ideological desecration."[10] Clearly one ideological bias has superceded another.

The Question of the New Synagogue

The attempt to narrate the history of Dresden through the lens of its various representational modalities is made difficult by the overwhelming immensity and invasiveness of the current reconstruction. It is one of the largest urban preservation projects ever attempted in all of Europe. Buildings that had been restored to their original appearance under the Socialists, like the Zwinger and the Dresden Opera House, were reappropriated into an overarching scheme that includes the reconstruction of the Schloss, its stables, the Brühlsche Terrasse, as well as former government buildings, palaces, and museums. Everything in that preservation zone is designed to replicate the configuration prior to the bombing, down to the last finial. A notable exception is the rebuilding of the erstwhile synagogue.

Built in 1840, it had formed the eastern anchor of Dresden's great Elbe silhouette, the western one having been defined by Semper's other building, the famous Opera House. Though the synagogue may never have been as remarkable a piece of architecture as the opera house, it represented, in human and visual terms, the attempt to integrate Jews into German culture. In political terms, it came to represent the aspirations of the Jewish emancipation of 1848.

It was precisely the synagogue's historical and architectural significance in that respect that caused Nazis to vent their fury against it with such excessive venom. The building was not only burnt in Kristallnacht, in 1938, but consequently blasted away to make a military training film demonstrating how to "scientifically" demolish buildings.[11] To add insult to injury, the name Rathenau Platz, on which the synagogue had fronted, was replaced with the name Schlageterplatz, after Leo Schlageter, one of the earliest members of the Nazi party.[12] He was among the first "martyrs" for the Nazi cause, having been arrested and shot in 1923 by the French for dynamiting a bridge in protest of the French occupation of the Alsace. His deed resonated triumphantly over the ruins of the devastated synagogue.

Though the Socialists erected an elegant memorial on the site, it was decided with reunification to build a new synagogue despite the fact that

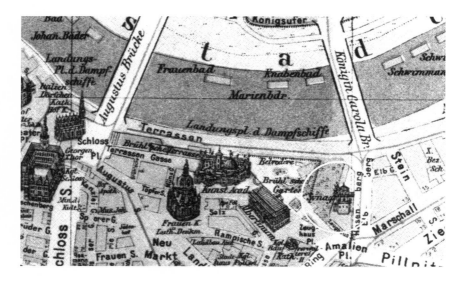

FIG. 2.8. *Plan showing the location of the former synagogue, from
"Mein Haus werde Genannt: ein Haus der Andach allen
Völkern," a pamphlet published by Förderverein Bau der
Synagoge Dresden, ca. 2002.*

there were barely sixty Jews, most of them secularized newcomers from
Russia, then living in Dresden. But the government pressed ahead, with
Saxony's Minister President Kurt Biedenkopf reminding Dresdeners that the
synagogue needed to be built not only as a symbol of justice and restitution,
but also because it had once been "an important element in the picture of
the city."[13] So what then is the nature of that "picture" today?

Sadly, Semper's building could not be reconstituted, since the conditions of the site had been significantly altered by the construction of a
Socialist-era bridge embankment.[14] The new building, completed in 2002,
was designed by the architectural firm Wandel, Hoefer, Lorch, from
Saarbrücken, and consists of two almost prismatic boxes facing each other
over an open courtyard.[15] One box is twisted as it rises, apparently so that
the orientation of its top faces Jerusalem. In the courtyard between the two
boxes, the architects, in an effort to introduce the site's "memory" into the
design, delineated the footprint of Semper's synagogue.

FIG. 2.9. *View of the Dresden Synagogue, designed by Wandel, Hoefer, Lorch, 2002. Photo by Mark Jarzombek.*

The building has been well received in the professional press, but as an uncompromising statement of formal purity, it sets in play a series of problems that, though perhaps inadvertent, are nonetheless troubling. For example, it is not mandated by Jewish law or custom that a synagogue face Jerusalem. It should, if possible, face east. It seems that the designers got Judaism confused with Islam, where mosques have to face Mecca. An even more complex problem stems from the fact that unlike the rebuilt churches and palaces of the city center, which will regain, at least visually, their "age-value," as Alois Riegl might have put it, this building, because of its bold modern design, will always point to the problematics of Jewish "otherness." Jews, invited to grow new roots in Dresden, are given a modern building in which to do so, whereas the rest of the Dresdeners can practice their religion in the re-created historical context of the city center. In other words, the synagogue does not belong—and will never belong—to the "picture" of the reconstructed city center.

FIG. 2.10. *View of the Dresden Synagogue, south along* Hasenberg Strasse. *Photo by Mark Jarzombek.*

The situation is not made any better by the fact that within the immediate urban context of the synagogue one finds several other examples of unwanted modernity. The cornice of the synagogue, for example, lines up with the imposing façade of the neighboring former Reichsbank, designed by Heinrich Wolf in 1928. Wolf was to become an important Nazi-era architect. The synagogue also blends in with the Socialist-era housing blocks on the other side of the street to the south. This set of three buildings constitutes a perhaps inadvertent but nevertheless telling ensemble all its own, one that uncomfortably puts the Jews, the Nazis, and the Socialists into an enforced visual and historiographic grouping that contrasts with the neohistoricist core of the beloved Dresden.

What we have with the Frauenkirche and the synagogue, and their associated silhouettes, is a situation where they are constructed as "witnesses" to two different events, the bombing of World War II and the Holocaust. Both silhouettes are thought to form a barrier against the past. Both, in that sense, do the honorable thing. And for this there most be some credit. But

FIG. 2.11. *View of the Dresden Synagogue, east.*
Photo by Mark Jarzombek.

in reality both are bound up with a catastrophe of another kind. One building is a manifestation of healing, the other of trauma, creating once again
the illusion that modernity and tradition are two separate entities. History
and memory are all placed in the premodern category along with the rein-
forcements of preservation and tourism. Modernity, rupture, Socialism, and
the Holocaust are put into another category. Out of that paradox comes a
particular type of victory, for the ambiguity of the Jewish space in Dresden
parallels the ambiguity of other spaces, the Socialist space, and the Nazi
space, all unified into the framework of the trauma of modernity. If conventional trauma theory emphasized the destructive repetition of the trauma
necessitating the intervention of science and healing, a more postmodern
reading of trauma suggests that healing is really a question of technology
and capital. Trauma is not the rupture of the flow of history, but a historiographic force that, when properly understood, can set the stage for an
awakening into consciousness of the temporally mutilated entanglements
of memory and history.

FIG. 2.12. *View, ca. 1967, of the former city center of Dresden. Courtesy of Sächsische Landesbibliothek.*

From Apocalyptic Picture to Socialist Civitas

The Socialist contributions to the city's structure and appearance are clearly foundational to this representational complexity. Some contemporary Dresdeners, like the historian Jürgen Paul, have claimed that if Dresden's first destruction came with the Allied bombing of 1945, the "second destruction" came with the failed Socialist attempt to rebuild the city.[16] The Socialists, he argued, transformed Dresden into little more than "a chaos of disconnected fragments." But that is, of course, a question of perspective, and could easily be applied to the current rebuilding efforts as well. Nevertheless, the photograph of the flattened landscape of Dresden's center from the 1960s showing the extent of the demolition takes one's breath away. But the claim that the socialists failed in their effort needs to be reassessed.

The most important feature of Socialist Dresden was the monumentally scaled, east-west Ernst Thälmann Strasse that ran parallel to the Elbe and that bisects what once was the old city.[17] A comparison of that project with a map of old Dresden helps visualize its dramatic scale. The street's name itself served a symbolic purpose, having to do with Thälmann himself. Born

FIG. 2.13. *Kulturpalast, designed by the firm Wolfgang Hänsch,
Herbert Löschau and Heinz Zimmermann, 1969.
Courtesy of Sächsische Landesbibliothek.*

in 1886, and rising to prominence after the death of Karl Liebknecht, he
became the first president of the German Communist Party. Steering a
course close to the policies of Stalin, he ran in the bitter 1933 national elec-
tion against Hitler. The success of Hitler sealed his fate. He was arrested by
the Gestapo, sent to prison, and eventually died in Buchenwald.[18] A
Socialist-era film, shown at schools throughout East Germany, *Ernst
Thälmann—Sohn seiner Klasse* (Ernst Thälmann—Son of the Working
Class), directed by Kurt Maetzig, gives us a glimpse of his role. The film,
taking place in 1918, shows the young Thälmann on the German western
front, sitting in a small hut, drawing up a manifesto that calls on the soldiers to turn their guns away from the alleged enemy on the front and point
them instead against the real enemy in their own land.

Not only did the Ernst Thälmann Strasse appear to carry out this puri-
fying logic, but so, too, did the Kulturpalast.[19] It was a simple and elegant
glass box, not unlike what one might have found in the West at that time,
except that the building's five bronze doors featured a vivid history lesson
of the city's past as seen through the lens of Socialist historiography. They

FIGS. 2.14 (above), 2.15 (below), AND 2.16 (facing).
Bronze panels of Kulturpalast, by Gerd Jaeger, 1969.
Photos by Mark Jarzombek.

show the people's oppression by the feudal and bourgeois overlords and how this led in the end to a—for the Communists—fortuitous destruction of the city, a destruction that cleared the field for the triumphant victory of the Socialist working class.

This arrival of the new age was demarcated quite literally on the sidewalk around the Kulturpalast by a red pavement that not only emphasized Dresden's allegiance to Moscow, but also pointed out the metaphysical ground on which a new Socialist city has to stand. This red "ground" was meant to triumph over the memories of the bourgeois world that lay in ruins below it. In 1974, the *Jahrbuch zur Geschichte Dresdens* continued the historical "readjustment" of Dresden's urban consciousness by listing events deemed of importance to the history of the working class in Dresden. A new *Museum für Geschichte der Dresdner Arbeiterbewegung* (Museum for the History of Dresden's Worker's Movement) was set up, and there were, of course, statues, rituals, parades, exhibitions, and street namings.[20]

Other aspects of the city were incorporated into this message. Unlike the Frauenkirche, which was left abandoned, the Renaissance-era palace known as the Johanneum, which lies between the Kulturpalast and the Frauenkirche,

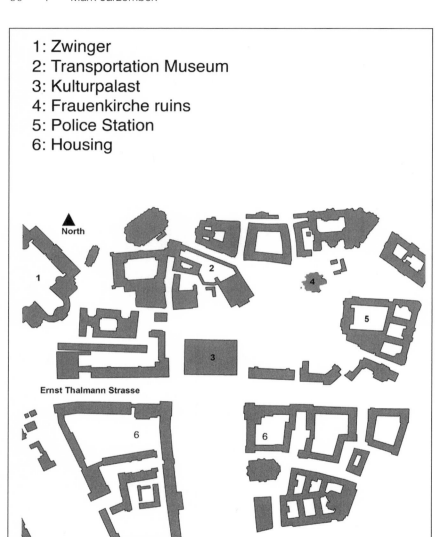

1: Zwinger
2: Transportation Museum
3: Kulturpalast
4: Frauenkirche ruins
5: Police Station
6: Housing

FIG. 2.17. *General plan of the Socialist city. Drawn by Mark Jarzombek.*
1. Zwinger; 2. Transportation Museum; 3. Kulturpalast;
4. Frauenkirche ruins; 5. Police station; 6. Housing

and which survived the bombardment with most of its walls standing, was rebuilt. Its antiquated "bourgeois" historical form was meant to stand in contrast to its new contents, a Museum of Transportation, which exhibited the latest in socialist tractors and railway engines.[21] The tactic, similar to one used after the French Revolution, put the usurpation of the building on display to demonstrate, in this case, the triumph of Communist industrialism. Dresden's cultural heritage was also not overlooked. In fact, it is remarkable how much was actually rebuilt. But even the restoration of the Zwinger, one of Germany's most famous baroque buildings, was not without a heavy-handed dose of ideology.[22] The considerable expense of reconstruction was partially justified by the claim that the building, designed by Daniel Poppelmann, a merchant's son, demonstrated the "emergence of the bourgeoisie" from the oppression of the feudal aristocracy, a necessary in-between step in the Marxist topos.[23] Semper's Opera House was also slowly rebuilt, as were parts of the famous Brühlsche Terrasse that overlooked the Elbe.

In summary, what emerged was a powerfully effective three-dimensional map of a Socialist *civitas*, all in all, no small accomplishment.[24]

The New "New Dresden"

Whether or not the Socialist city constituted Dresden's first rebuilding or Dresden's second destruction, there was no escaping the fact that what was done was a far cry from what was envisioned. The fault lay not only with the perpetually depleted coffers of the *Deutsche Demokratische Republik*, but also with the type of modernity into which the Socialist regime had entrapped itself. Nonetheless, after reunification in 1989, the city planners, most having been trained in West Germany, felt that they had to undo the "utopian" message of the Socialist planners. The principal strategy was to divide the city's core into two zones, one given over to preservation and tourism and the other to commerce. "Civic identity" was equated almost exclusively with the "premodern," the only exception being, of course, the synagogue. As for the commercial center, the planners used an approach called *Verdichtung,* or densification, in which buildings were inserted into the Socialist fabric to simulate a more compact, nineteenth-century urban grid.

A team of urban design professionals was assembled by the Saxon government to come up with studies and make suggestions to the local planning

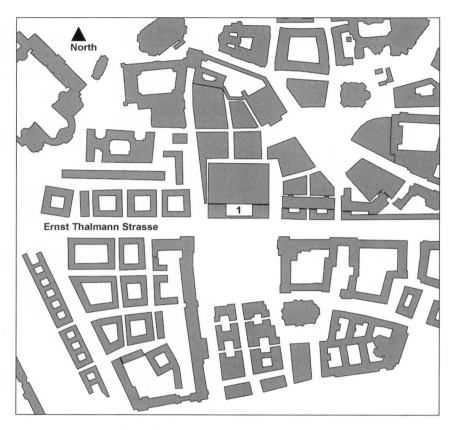

FIG. 2.18. *New urban plan of Dresden showing projected "Densification." Drawn by Mark Jarzombek.*

boards.[25] The task was made difficult by the grafting of the West German legal system onto the older systems that were partially grandfathered in, some even dating back to prewar days. Financial compensation to thousands of former property owners and their offspring also had to be undertaken.[26] Today, the old Socialist-era CIAM-styled (Congrès Internationaux d'Architecture Moderne) "civic center" has been transformed into a large and vibrant shopping district. It has a Burger King at one end and an enormous and well-supplied department store, Warenhaus Karstadt, at the other, with new bank buildings, shopping centers, tourist offices, ATM machines, and cinemas in between. From a contemporary planner's perspective, it is an unequivocal success. To integrate the Kulturpalast in this urbanization process, the planners decided to transform the building into a philharmonic and redesign it on the outside.

The attempt to disguise the former Socialist presence and deny its representational claims on the city extends even to the privileged position of the ground. To destroy the ground's unwanted symbolic memory, the city fathers called in urban archaeologists to explore the ruins buried beneath the streets. The result is yet another historiographic conundrum. The "history" of the city that is being uncovered—a history that goes down to the city's medieval layer—erases the historicity of rupture that was so important to the Socialists. It does so without having to admit its own strategy of rupture by submitting the argument that one is going back to the city's origins. But as valuable as that may be, it is not without political implications.

As fate would have it, the old Ernst Thälmann Strasse, now named Wilsdruffer Strasse after a village north of the city, separates the preservation district from the new commercial center. It is ironic that a street that had once represented the victorious annihilation of the past now survives as the city's most successful urban statement. Needless to say, Heinz Quinger's *Dresden und Umgebung* mentions neither the history nor the original name of this street.

We should reject at all costs Maurice Halbwachs's old-fashioned notion of a "collective memory" as some sort of generic, ontological marker bestowing meaning and significance to a culture. What remains of memory in a place like Dresden is a dialectical modernist proposition that is extracted only with difficulty and against the grain of various intervening historiographic ambitions. The recovery of "memory" is only possible if one acknowledges the traumatized, and traumatizing, temporal dislocations of the urban narrative. It is a narrative in which even nonaccidental omissions are regulated by history-producing visions that can be brought to light and challenged only by scholarship that looks behind the dynamics of the representational strategies out of which the urban consciousness is constructed. This brings us back to the question of memory and public space, for public space is the primary medium through which memory and its associated historiographical energy seeks its representation, and thus it is in the public space that the retrieval process works. To go to Dresden and focus only on the official discourses of therapy-in-public-space—the new commercial center "healing" the trauma of a failed Socialist economy, the Frauenkirche "healing" the trauma of the war, the State "healing" the trauma of the Holocaust—is to overlook the complex aporias of the city's own urban self-reflections. Attitudes to the *Trauender Mann,* to the film *"Das alte Dresden,"* and to Dresden's "new" archaeological history, are all part of the city's larger portrait. Though they might normally be considered to be at the periphery of urban history, they are, in actuality, the constitutive elements of the urban episteme. They are shaped by a dialectic that articulates presence and silences simultaneously.

It is not a traditional notion of dialectic of which I speak, one in which life is perceived as eternally trapped in a morass of history from which it can only extricate itself through the sublime temporalities of violence and rupture. Rather, it is a dialectic that inhabits the system in the form of confusions, proximities, anxieties, and fated overlappings that in itself constitutes the flesh and blood of modern urban life. The navigation process through this heterological system is the burden of the cosmopolitan self.[27] The irony, of course, is that the text against which that episteme articulates itself is something that no fiction writer could have imagined. Who, in the 1930s, could have believed that something like the Holocaust would take place? Who, even in the early 1940s, could ever have thought that Dresden would be totally destroyed in the war? Who could ever have thought that Dresden would be bulldozed down to the ground? And who, even in the 1980s, would ever have thought that the city would be part of a united Germany and that it would be rebuilt in the blink of an eye? Registering these fantastic events, the city becomes the locus of a memory to which no single person can ever have total access, for it only succeeds "as memory" when it challenges us to enter the shadows of our disparate modern subjectivities. What is needed, therefore, is an insistent deconstruction of the difference between fiction and reality that exposes the fateful illusions on which urban epistemologies are based.

In thinking of the city, one must resist reducing modernism to a negative that stands in temporal opposition to a revival of meaning, memory, and history. Instead, one must see the city as a transformational work-in-process that operates out of, and on behalf of, various modernizing and historiographic forces that have not one, but diverse articulations and presences. Their torts, both real and imaginary, require a compensatory probing and scholarly structure along which the narrations of trauma can surface and be "lived out."[28] A critical urban epistemology, therefore, must be distinct from the all too often encountered attempt to essentialize the urban narrative or to reduce its history to a linear formation; it would have to begin and end with this problem and thus with the city's ambiguous location in its representational history.[29] To use a phrase by Adorno, but changing his word *art* to my words *the city,* one can say that the city desires to be what has not yet been, even though everything that the city is has already been. Playing one end of this scenario off the other to expose the paradox of urban history is no doubt little more than a theoretical project, but it is a form of action in its own right. For only in perceiving of the city in this way, from the inside out as well as from the outside in, can we comprehend and respect the dialectical incompletion of the modern city. As a humanistic construct, the city may not be all that we hoped for, but, as an intellectual construct reflecting the geography of time, it is more than one could ever have imagined.

Notes

1. William A. Davis, "Dresden Builds a Future," *Boston Sunday Globe,* travel sec., March 5, 2000, M13. For a longer and more complete discussion see Mark Jarzombek, "Urban Heterology: Dresden and the Dialectics of Post-Traumatic History," *Studies in Theoretical and Applied Aesthetics* (spring 2001): 1–92; "Bellotto's Dresden: Framing the Dialectics of Porcelain," *Thresholds* 25 (fall 2002): 38–42.

2. Henning Prinz, ed., *Das Taschenbergpalais zu Dresden: Geschichte und Wiederaufbau der Sächsischen Thronfolgerresidenz* (Dresden: Landesamt für Denkmalpflege, 1998), 41.

3. The panels under the bridge were also a commentary on the *Fürstenzug,* an enormous one-hundred-meter-long wall mural on the side of the castle that is on the other side of the Elbe bridge and depicts the history of Dresden as a march of Dresden's nobility from ancient times to the late nineteenth century, when the mural was designed. The Nazi mural tries to point away from the contributions of the aristocrats to the more universal "aristocracy" of the

German nation. It was thus meant to represent the arrival of a new historical consciousness toward the city, one that purges and unifies at the same time.

4. The following quote was posted on the Web site of an organization called the "Friends of Dresden." Based in New York City, it was founded by Günter Blobel, professor of Cell Biology at Rockefeller University, in an effort to promote the city. Blobel donated a good portion of the money from his Nobel Prize to the organization. The "Friends of Dresden" has also made an effort to support the construction of the synagogue. See their Web site www.friends.dresdener.com.

5. There were some attempts at providing alternative designs. Helmut Jahn, a member of the "Friends of Dresden" Honorary Board, opened an exhibition about the Frauenkirche at Christie's new office in the Hancock Tower, Chicago. Jahn challenged the audience to participate in the building of a cathedral much in the way communities did in the Middle Ages.

6. The controversy, which peaked in 1990, is itself a complex one. See Jürgen Paul, "Eine Wiedergutmachung an Dresden: Die wiederhergestellte Kuppel der Frauenkirche gäbe der Stadt ein Stück Geschichte zurück," *Frankfurter Allgemeine Zeitung* 290 (Dec. 1990). In comparison, one can point to Manfred Sack, "Sterben und sterben lassen: Über den Umgang mit Ruinen und mit dem Verfall," *Die Zeit* 33 (Aug. 10, 1990). Christiane Hertel has discussed this controversy in detail in "Reconstructing Dresden," an unpublished essay that will be part of her planned book, entitled *Laocoon as Rocaille: Essays on Art and Critique in Eighteenth-Century Germany*.

7. Wieland Förster was born in 1930 in Dresden. He studied sculpture in Dresden from 1953–1958. He now lives in Berlin.

8. Peter H. Feist, "Denkmalplastik in der DDR von 1945 bis 1990," in *Denkmale und kulturelles Gedächtnis nach dem Ende der Ost-West-Konfrontation* (Berlin: Akademie der Künste, 1999), 194.

9. Ibid., 152.

10. John Soane, "The Renaissance of Dresden after 1985," in *Dresden: A City Reborn*, eds. Anthony Clayton and Alan Russell (Oxford: Berg, 2000), 110; John Soane, "Dresden: Its Destruction and Rebuilding, 1945–85," Ibid., 80, 83. Much of Soane's work, rooted in solid scholarship, constitutes an important contribution to our understanding of the history of the city. Nonetheless, Soane's obvious disdain for the Socialist period makes it difficult to accept the book as a way to "read" the current situation in Dresden. The book has a foreword by the Duke of Kent. Soane teaches at South Bank University in London, where a technical committee has been established for the purpose of managing the manufacture of the great Golden Orb and Cross. According to the Web site, "The Technical Committee will be tendering to the finest craftsmen in the country to ensure that the symbol of reconciliation between Britain and Germany is of

highest quality" (http://pisces.sbu.ac.uk/BE/CECM/german/dresden.html, accessed Mar. 22, 2000).

11. The film, which has since been recovered, was shown as part of the kick-off campaign for the rebuilding of the synagogue. Of the deported Jews, few survived Theresienstadt, where most were sent.

12. Leo Schlageter was an artillery officer during World War I. He had joined the Nazi Party, which was founded in 1920, at an early stage. His membership card bore the number 61. When the French occupied the Ruhr in 1923, Schlageter helped to organize resistance on the German side. He and his companions blew up a railway bridge for the purpose of making the transport of coal to France more difficult. For his part in the action, Schlageter, who was captured by the French, was condemned to death, but he refused to disclose the identity of those who issued the order to blow up the bridge. He was shot by a French firing squad on May 26, 1923. The renaming of Rathenau Platz to Schlageterplatz was, of course, a calculated move comparing his bombing of the bridge to the destruction of the synagogue.

13. Kurt Biedenkopf, "Construction of the Dresden Synagogue," in a speech delivered in 1997 at the first meeting of the Association of Sponsors. Here quoted from a 1996 brochure, "My House shall be called a House of Prayer for all Peoples," advertising the new synagogue.

14. Henry Landsberger, who was born in Dresden, and whose grandfather was the rabbi, has been instrumental in organizing the campaign for the new synagogue. Parallel projects are also underway in cities like Darmstadt, Ulm, and, of course, Berlin. The Dresden-Meissen Diocese raised fifty thousand dollars for the construction of the synagogue. The *Catholic News* reported that, in Dresden, "Today, we have a chance to do things differently and can dare to attempt to make amends."

15. The judges, under the chairmanship of Professor Karljoseph Schattner, originally awarded Wandel, Hoefer, and Lorch the third prize, with Livio Vacchini of Locarno and Heinz Tesar of Vienna coming in first and second respectively. Discussions with the Jewish Congregation changed the order.

16. See Jürgen Paul, "Dresden: Suche nach der verlorenen Mitte," in *Neue Städte aus Ruinen* (Munich: Prestel, 1992), 333.

17. Work on the new city center began in the 1960s, with several competitions being held to determine its final form. The Kulturpalast was inaugurated in 1969. For a good overview, see Ingolf Rosenberg, "Die Frauenkirche in der Dresdner Innenstadtplanung," *Dresdner Hefte* 23, no. 10/4 (1992): 63–70. For the contemporary Socialist perspectives, see G. Funk, "Wettbewerb für die Stadtbauliche und architektonishe Gestaltung der Ost-West Magistrale in Dresden," *Deutsche Architektur* 7 (1954): 240–24; O. Hempel, "Vorschlag für die Rekonstruktion des historischen Viertels um die Frauenkirche in Dresden," *Deutsche Architektur* 8 (1955): 107–71; G. Thümmler, "Die

Stadt Dresden, ein grosser Bauplatz," *Sächsiche Heimatblätter* (1959):
49–84. Gerhard Schill, "Eine sozialistische Grosstadt der DDR-Höhepunkt
der geschichtlichen Entwicklung Dresdens," *Jahrbuch 1974 zur Geschichte
Dresdens* (1974): 3–9; Gunnar Hartmann and Johannes Hunger, "Unser
erfolgreiches Aufbauwerk; Zur Entwicklung des Wohnungsbaues in der
Stadt Dresden seit der Gründung der DDR," *Jahrbuch 1979 zur Geschichte
Dresdens* (1979): 25–42; Dieter Möbius and Gunner Hartmann, "Die
städtebauliche und architektonische Gestaltung des Dresdener Altmarktes—
ein bleibendes Beispiel der Architekturentwicklung in der DDR," *Dresdner
Hefte* 4, no. 10 (1986): 48–57; G. Schuster, "Der Aufbau Dresden schreitet
voran!" *Deutsche Architektur* 3 (1989): 121–26.

18. Thälmann was idolized in party propaganda because of his loyalty to
Moscow. The history of the leftist movement during the 1920s and early
1930s is a complex one, driven not only by the differences between the
more moderate Socialists and the more strident Communists, but also by
the sometimes ambivalent politics of both. For a good discussion, see Istvan
Deak, *Weimar Germany's Left-Wing Intellectuals: A Political History of the
Weltbühne and Its Circle* (Berkeley: University of California Press, 1968).

19. It was designed by the firm Wolfgang Hänsch, Herbert Löschau, Heinz
Zimmermann.

20. See, for example, *Beginn eines neuen Lebens; eine Auswahl von
Erinnerungen an den Beginn des Neuaufbaus in Dresden im Mai 1945,*
Beiträge zur Geschichte der Dresdener Arbeiterbewegung 7 (1960).
The publications began in 1958.

21. The museum got the name in the nineteenth century when King Johann,
who ruled from 1854 to 1873, made it into a historical museum.

22. See Hans Nadler, "Beitrag zur Denkmalpflege in Dresden 1946–1952,"
Dresdner Hefte 28, no. 9/4 (1991): 8–22.

23. The restoration of the Zwinger was begun immediately after the war.
Despite the difficulty of undertaking such a project at that time, money
was found already in 1945. Work was completed in 1964. The fate
of Semper's Opera was less clear. Money was found, however, for its
restoration, starting in 1953. After undergoing several phases, work was
completed in 1985. The full ideological explanation of the Zwinger was
articulated by Hubert Mohr in *Der Dresdener Zwinger* (Berlin: Deutsche
Bauakademie, 1956). For Mohr, the Zwinger helps visualize an important
time in German history, when the bourgeoisie was attempting to liberate
itself from the strictures of absolutism. Though the Zwinger is indeed the
architecture of the aristocracy, we should see it not simply as a masterpiece
of a doomed feudal mindset, but rather as a site where the newly emerging
spirit of an industrially oriented bourgeoisie began to play itself out.
Daniel Poppelmann represents, according to Mohr, all that which is

"immortal" in the German people (p. 13). And it was for this reason that the German Democratic Republic invested so much money in the Zwinger's reconstitution.

24. For a not inaccurate but clearly pro-Socialist spin on the Socialist and Russian contributions, see Max Seydewitz, *Die unbesiegbare Stadt* (Berlin: Kongress Verlag, 1956).

25. The team was headed up by Professor Zech, from Munich, where he was the head of the City Building Department and emeritus professor at the Technische Universität of Munich. *Projektgruppe Stadtentwicklung Dresden,* as it was known, was answerable to a body of experts, the Lenkungsausschuss, which had representatives in it from both the city and the state, as well as from the Dresden Building Department. This body instructed the *Projektgruppe* with the duties of what to work on. Most often, these were tasks in the interest of the state, but within the area of the city of Dresden. The *Projektgruppe,* formed in the early 1990s, was always planned as a short-term institution. It ceased to function at the end of 1999. Professor Zech continued to represent the group for three more years.

26. The German government reported that approximately two million claims were filed with claims offices (Vermögensämter) in eastern Germany. In Berlin, approximately 310,000 property claims have been filed. Of these, approximately 150,000 claims were filed for the return of approximately 100,000 real-estate properties. From these, approximately two thirds have been decided. Thirty to fifty percent are given back, and the remainder were satisfied by restitution payments or rejected. See David Rowland, "Entschädigung im neuem Gewand," *Aufbau* (Nov. 22, 1996); "East German Claims Revisited," German American Chamber of Commerce (Nov. 4, 1996).

27. Important for me in this respect is Werner Flach, *Negation und Andersheit: Ein Beitrag zur Problematik der Letztimplikation* (Munich: Ernst Reinhart, 1959).

28. History, as presumed in the bourgeois world, does not think that it needs much in the way of this (from its perspective, "cynical") reflection, and it thus forces aesthetic practices to require of themselves a heavy dose of self-objectification so that they can be more easily identified and targeted for critique. (The figure of Peter Eisenman in Berlin comes to mind.) But once identified as "art," as something that can be bought and placed in the public domain, it begins to attach itself to the complexities of the historiography of its modernity.

29. This does not mean that the historian has to give up the principle of objectivity or the premise of critical action. But it does mean that, just as objectivity has to remain both grounded and ungrounded, the historian has to accept a degree of ambiguity between what he or she does as "an

historian" and the multiple locations of "history" in the political production. The synagogue project in Dresden, trapped in a similar in-between space, becomes the perfect metaphor for this problem. A figure of importance in this respect is Hans Gadamer, who, in studying Plato in *Wahrheit und Methode,* elaborates on the priorities of the question over the answer. I end with Adorno, however, because I feel that the idea of a negative dialectic more accurately frames the paradox of wanting to express something without being able to and of being able to express something without wanting to. His work reconstitutes the fragility of philosophical speculation, and by extension, the fragility of historical speculation.

chapter three

Designed Memories

The Roots of Brazilian Modernism

FERNANDO LARA

To the memory of Lúcio Costa (1902–1998)

*We must give Brazil that which it does not
have, and for that reason it has not lived until
today; we must give Brazil a soul, and for this
every sacrifice is grandiose, sublime.*
—Mário de Andrade, letter to Carlos
Drummond, 1924

Memory and Modernism

Memory and modernism do not appear to go together at first. Born to overcome the dominance of nineteenth-century neoclassicism, modern architecture reinforced the idea of rupture with the past, any past.[1] This position is not exclusive to architectural modernism. Modernity assumes that the present is a new era; it is not a continuation of the past, but rather it grew out of the rupture with past traditions.[2] As a universal concept, modernity should go hand in hand with local modernization. Nonetheless, the turbulent conflict between modernity and modernization gave rise to modernism.[3] Coming from plural and diverse roots, and committed to the ideas of modernity and modernization, modern architecture was supposed to have no memory, and no heritage. Yet by scratching the surface of rhetorical articulation, one perceives that memory was always there, if not in an active role, at least as the background against which the new ideas presented themselves. Memory has always been modernism's *alterity*,[4] or, that "other" against which one defines oneself by opposition.

This seems to be the case in Europe, where the past was identified with an unbearable social structure, and modernism promised a new (and better) social order. Italy is exemplary with regard to the role of memory as otherness, since having the heavier and most exuberant past, it generated the most radical avant-garde rupture: the futurism of Sant'Elia and Marinetti.[5] Perry Anderson's idea that modernism only flourishes where the modern and the traditional are in conflict would reinforce the role of memory as an alterity for the modern to come to existence.[6] However, in other places, the presence of past traditions has not been so dominant. In the Americas, our heritage was yet to be defined. While Frank Lloyd Wright was trying to blend modernism with the prairie tradition in search of an identity, Brazilians were doing something similar, giving memory a different role in the history of their modernism.

Brazilian Modernism Overview

Brazilian modern architecture is internationally known for the outstanding examples of free-form in reinforced concrete, built around the 1940s and 1950s, and labeled "anti-rationalist pioneers" by the architectural historian Nikolaus Pevsner.[7] To a lesser degree, Brazilian Modernism is also known for having achieved a level of popular acceptance by blending together the style of the modernist avant-garde with that of the traditional heritage.[8] This combination of international formal elements and local traditions also marks the foundations of the formal and symbolic achievements of Brazilian modern architecture.

In 1930, Getulio Vargas, the revolutionary commandant raised to the presidency, began a strong effort to increase both industrial and educational modernization. Regarding industrialization, the objective was to reduce the dependence on imported, manufactured goods and at the same time diversify Brazilian exports. At that point, the Brazilian economy, which was based on agricultural products, had dropped violently after the stock market crash of 1929. In education, the objective was to reduce illiteracy by providing elementary school for the masses and searching for the roots of "Brazilianess." One of the most intriguing characteristics of Vargas's government was the combination of an authoritarian regime with intellectual freedom.[9] In fact, many of the artists and intellectuals who had participated in the *Semana de Arte Moderna* in 1922[10] were now working for the new government. Their task was the formulation of a new Brazilian identity and the rediscovery of the country's culture.[11] This task was in tune with the apogee of nationalism during the 1930s, as described by historian Eric Hobsbawm.[12] More than searching for Brazil's heritage, these artists and intellectuals were constructing one specific memory that conveyed their own interests. This was done by collecting from among their many ancestors those who better fulfilled their future plans. I will explore this topic more deeply, but it is worth pointing out here that, since the 1930s, the Barroco Mineiro, or the artistic expression of the eighteenth-century mining society of Minas Gerais, has been the most disseminated example of past Brazilian artistic tradition.

But if this generation of early Brazilian modernists was constructing the past, it was also designing future memories. Lúcio Costa, a twenty-eight-year-old architect, was named director of the Brazilian School of Beaux-arts (ENBA) in 1930. Costa immediately began a radical reformation of the art and architecture curriculum, based on the Bauhaus structured method of architectural composition and on Le Corbusier's[13] theories about architecture, as synthesized in his "Five Points." Originally, the appointment of Costa was part of Vargas's strategy to strike a delicate balance between the progressive and conservative forces. But the resistance against Costa's reformation was so strong that an ideological war all but broke out.[14] Modernists and conservative academics battled for every competition and major commission through the 1930s, with Vargas playing a balancing act until the early 1940s, when the modernists became the dominant paradigm. From then on, Brazilian modern architecture was used to publicize ideas or signs of modernity. Rather than promoting the actual industrialization of the country or the development of mass production, the movement produced, instead, an *image* of modernization. Modernism could not wait for modernization and rather than creating an architecture for a new society or for a new social role of the arts, as stated by the Bauhaus, the Brazilian government was more interested in the social image it should acquire. The designed memory was being projected into the future to help promote the modernization that was yet to arrive.

The Avant-Garde Manifestations

Regarding the realm of the arts, modernity, modernism, and the avant-garde have specific definitions that may vary or overlap, but it is the relationship among them that is important to the understanding of twentieth-century art. In order to investigate the Brazilian avant-garde, I depart here from Peter Bürger's definition in *Theory of the Avant-Garde*.[15] According to Bürger, the autonomy of art is a category of bourgeois society, and the avant-garde opposes such autonomy by trying to integrate art into life praxis. It is interesting to note that the avant-garde proposition not only aims at integrating art into daily life, but also aims at building an absolutely new praxis, to be achieved by using art as a departing point.

Avant-garde ideas arrived in Brazil around the turn of the twentieth century, but until the 1920s, they only had an impact on some isolated painters and writers. The most celebrated event, which marks the starting point of Brazilian avant-garde, is the Semana de Arte Moderna, a week of exhibitions, lectures, and poetry, organized in São Paulo in 1922. From this period we can highlight the works of Oswald de Andrade on texts like *Manifesto Antropófago*[16] and the young female painters Anita Malfatti and Tarsila do Amaral. In those early avant-garde works we notice the adaptation of fauvist and cubist techniques to the understanding of the Brazilian society. This movement tried to resolve the apparently opposing forces of abstract internationalism and the representation of local identities. After the polemical introduction at the Semana, Brazilian avant-garde artists gradually began adapting the avant-garde to Brazilian reality and "Brazilianess."[17]

It is worth noting that while searching for the "Brazilianess," the modernist memory-making discarded other modernisms that were not aligned with the modernists' ideas. The whole tradition of art deco, for instance, was discarded from their designed tradition. Instead, modernists constructed other continuities, other roots. There were many different "Brazils" co-existing. The modernist project chose one and transformed that choice into *the* official memory.

Le Corbusier and the Avant-Garde Root

As early as 1925, Brazilian architects were already publicizing modern ideas, with two articles appearing in São Paulo's newspapers: one by Rino Levi, a Brazilian educated in Italy, in October,[18] and another by Gregori Warchavchik, a Russian immigrant, in November.[19] Levi and Warchavchik would be the first exponents of what contemporary historiography calls *Modern Architecture in Brazil* (made primarily with direct imported ideas), to differentiate it from *Brazilian Modern Architecture* (made under the Brazilian ideas and formal vocabulary). Rino Levi would become one of the main architects of the Brazilian Modernism, as would another Italian immigrant, Lina Bo Bardi. Warchavchik played an important role as Costa's partner for a while, and also as the first Latin American delegate to the CIAM (Congrès Internationaux d'Architecture Moderne), invited by Le Corbusier himself in 1929.[20]

At that time, Le Corbusier's visit remained rather unnoticed outside the realm of architecture schools, but after 1936, Le Corbusier would strongly influence Brazil, and, according to one of his biographers, Elisabeth Harris, the country would also strongly influence his works and thoughts. In 1936, Le Corbusier was invited as a consultant in support of the team of architects commissioned to design the new building for the Brazilian Ministry of Education and Health (MES). The invitation of Le Corbusier[21] helped support the canceling of the previous competition, since the winning design was considered by the government incompatible with the modern image that they were trying to establish.[22] From Le Corbusier's architecture, this early generation of Brazilian architects learned the "valorization of architecture as a plastic art, the preoccupation with formal matters, and the sensitivity to local conditions."[23] From the Bauhaus pedagogy, they appropriated the idea of conciliating the applied and the fine arts, synthesizing them all into architecture. Le Corbusier's immediate influence can be perceived when we compare two buildings designed by the Roberto brothers, the ABI (1936) and the Santos Dumont Airport (1937), the latter being much closer than the former to Le Corbusier's "Five Points of Architecture." The freedom of inquiry and the importance of experimental teaching were also acquired from the Bauhaus program, although the traditional historiography of Brazilian modern architecture reinforces the connections with Le Corbusier much more. As stated by Ruth Verde Zein and Carlos E. Comas in recent interviews,[24] the Bauhaus in general, and Mies van der

Rohe in particular, constituted strong influences, hidden by the architects themselves, and dwarfed by the Brazilian modernist historiography due to the ideological dichotomies of the time.

However, as stated by L. A. Passaglia,[25] we should consider the transformations on architectural pedagogy in order to understand the development of the early modernist generation in Brazil. Until 1930, the ENBA still adopted the nineteenth-century academic approach to architectural teaching, with a strong emphasis on classical figurative drawing. This was changed in the 1930 curricular reformation, and the early generation of Brazilian modern architects took advantage of both the strong domain of classical drawing as well as the new architectural freedom of avant-garde techniques.[26] The issue of memory combined with modernity has been ever present in the roots of Brazilian Modernism, either as a drawing process or as narrative rhetoric.

The SPHAN and the Baroque Heritage

With the task of cataloguing, protecting, and publicizing Brazilian historic and artistic heritage, the *Serviço do Patrimônio Histórico e Artístico* (SPHAN) was created by the Ministry of Education in 1937. Directed by Rodrigo Melo Franco, SPHAN included, among its consultants and collaborators, Mário de Andrade, Gilberto Freire, Joaquim Cardoso, and Lúcio Costa. Mário de Andrade is one of the most important Brazilian intellectuals of the twentieth century. Author of literary landmarks like *Macunaíma*,[27] he was one of the leaders of the Semana modernist group and one of the first to research the baroque architecture of Minas Gerais. Gilberto Freire is a well-known sociologist whose work revolutionized the study of racial relations in Brazil. Joaquim Cardoso was not only a poet and a historian, but also the structural engineer who gave mathematical coherence to the curved surfaces of Oscar Niemeyer's buildings.

Lauro Cavalcanti reminds us that other groups had different ideas for the office of preservation, but that the modernist group was better qualified and had a more sophisticated, cosmopolitan, and inclusive project of national memory and national identity than the conservative groups.[28] According to Carlos Eduardo Comas, what kept them together was the resistance they encountered, and the idea that, for their project to succeed, every battle was

FIG. 3.1. *Igreja de São Francisco de Assis,
Ouro Preto, 1770s. Photo by Fernando Lara.*

worth fighting.[29] Among all those intellectuals, no one had a larger role on the construction and intellectual articulation of Brazilian modern architecture than Lúcio Costa. Together, they all had in common their commitment to the Brazilian heritage, while projecting its appropriate future. But Costa was the one who translated those goals into architecture in a very effective way. In essays like "Arquitetura Jesuítica no Brasil,"[30] Costa elevated the Brazilian baroque to the status of a genius loci, more than a restricted spirit of time. Standing in defense of the baroque, not yet valued by modern critics and diminished by the Beaux-Arts academia,[31] Costa worked on transitions and continuations, rather than ruptures and breaks with the past. By doing so, he inscribed the baroque into the trunk of Brazilian "soul," presenting modern architecture as a natural continuation of the baroque axis. Memory was being used to imply continuation and identity rather than rupture or alterity.

SPHAN was also responsible for publicizing the nationwide myth of Minas Gerais as the site of Brazil's origin.[32] Home of the first Brazilian urban society in the eighteenth century, Minas Gerais was, according to Darcy Ribeiro, the knot that united the nation.[33] We should keep in mind that the Vargas government had overcome the rural elite, and when rewriting Brazilian memory, deliberately dismissed most of its accomplishments. When trying to anchor this new image of Brazil into the past, the eighteenth-century baroque of Minas Gerais (Barroco Mineiro) was selected as the safe choice for Vargas's nationalist ideas. The urban society of Minas Gerais had been the first to challenge the Portuguese with revolts in 1720[34] and 1789,[35] the latter, known as Inconfidência Mineira, being already part of the Republican imaginary. If the Republicans at the turn of century had already used the Inconfidência revolt and its leader, Tiradentes, as a mythological origin, the Vargas government reinforced the idea of Minas Gerais as the embodiment of the Brazilian past. Even intellectuals from São Paulo, like Mário de Andrade, used the Barroco Mineiro[36] as a Brazilian myth of origin, maybe due to the lack of other alternatives.[37] Reacting against the Beaux-Arts and their classical ideals, the Barroco Mineiro was the perfect candidate for fulfilling the need of an origin and fighting the academic establishment. Costa assumed the task of constructing this past,[38] and working on both edges, he used his modernity to support his preservationist ideas and used the past to legitimize the modernist project.

What is interesting to consider is how the search (or construction) of the past was done at the same time and by the very same people who represented the Brazilian avant-garde. As reminded by Lauro Cavalcanti,[39] the marriage between conservation and modernism in Brazil is quite singular. While Le Corbusier proposed the demolition of parts of old Paris and the Bauhaus banished the teaching of architectural history from the curriculum, their Brazilian followers were putting together concepts that seemed irreconcilable. Following this debate, the architectural historian Kenneth Frampton remarked that "the young Brazilian followers of Le Corbusier immediately transformed these purist components into a highly sensuous native expression which echoed in its plastic exuberance the 18th century Brazilian Baroque."⁴⁰ It is important to ask at this point who is represented by this baroque past, if anybody. More than representing or identifying with the aspirations of part of the Brazilian population (which varies a lot regionally), the baroque axis pointed to concepts of Brazilian independence, uniqueness, and mixed origins. One memory axis was being constructed (baroque-modernism) while another one was being denied (French academicism).

From the MES Building to the Ouro Preto Hotel

The denial of the classicist-academicist axis and the establishment of the baroque-modernist axis did not happen until many battles were fought. The Ministério da Educação e Saúde (MES) (Ministry of Education and Health) building represents the most publicized battle, due to Le Corbusier's participation. Its original traditionalist design was discarded, to be replaced by one of the first modernist high-rise structures in the world. Vargas maintained a twofold take on architecture through the 1930s. In 1935, one year before Le Corbusier's second and most important visit, Marcello Piacentini, chief architect of Mussolini's government, was invited as a consultant for some federal buildings.⁴¹ In 1937, at a competition for the Ministério da Fazenda (Treasury Ministry) building, a modernist design entry by Wladmir Alves de Souza was chosen, but later rejected, with the government commissioning a more classical building. Reflecting on those battles, Carlos E. Comas states that this constant competition pushed the modernist architects to the limits of formal, functional, and technical features, and became one of the major components of their success.⁴² But the role of memory and the relationship with the past stood out in what is considered to be the main and decisive battle fought and won by the modernist group: the Ouro Preto Hotel.

A commission was organized in 1939 for a hotel in the city of Ouro Preto, home of the most important baroque buildings in Brazil. SPHAN was responsible for the project, and the first architect chosen, Carlos Leão (himself a member of the MES team, ironically) presented a neocolonial scheme in accordance with the academicist ideas at that time. Niemeyer, also invited to participate, presented a modernist scheme. Since the neocolonial design of Leão had problems with its functional and topographical features, Lúcio Costa convinced Niemeyer to modify his design, adding a ceramic tile

FIG. 3.2. *Grande Hotel de Ouro Preto, 1940. Photo by Fernando Lara.*

roof (like the rest of the city) and wooden trellises instead of steel *brise-soleils,* shading devices that allow simultaneous light control and ventilation. Niemeyer's new design was accepted and built, and the Grande Hotel de Ouro Preto, not known by many, became a landmark on the history of Brazilian Modernism. By inscribing a modernist design in the heart of the main historical city of Minas Gerais, the modernist group accomplished a major task. Their modern project was once and for all tied to the glorious past and elevated to the same status, able to coexist and sharing the same spaces. Most of the conservative criticism on the lack of nationalism and the lack of tradition in modern architecture was neutralized by the materialization of the hotel in such a way that demonstrated the possibility of blending together modernity and tradition. It is important here to understand that the Ouro Preto Hotel building gave the modernist group the recognition they needed in terms of authority over both the past and the future.[43] The lesson was learned and the idea of blending the modern and the traditional was applied from then on.

Pampulha, Selected Avant-Garde, and Designed Heritage

The combination of modernist European avant-garde and traditional baroque heritage served as a conceptual basis for designers like Oscar Niemeyer, Luis Nunes, Carlos Leão, Mauricio and Marcelo Roberto, Afonso Reidy, and others. Through their designs, this generation tried to solve the conflict of nationalism versus internationalism, and avant-garde versus traditional heritage. At this point, Brazilian modern architecture was clearly seen as a combination of international modernism (mainly the plastic nature of Le Corbusier's forms) and local heritage. Two events marked the international publicity of Brazilian Modernism. At the 1939 New York World's Fair, the Brazilian pavilion[44] attracted the architectural media. But the Brazilian success of that summer was Carmen Miranda on Broadway, and Brazilian architecture would have to wait until 1942 to achieve fame. As part of the Good Neighborhood policy with South America,[45] an exhibition was put together at the MoMA, in New York. The exhibition, "Brazil Builds," showed works by Costa, Reidy, Levi, and mainly the young Niemeyer. His buildings under construction at Pampulha were on display, while the exhibition catalogue, divided into new and old buildings, highlighted their connection with the local baroque.[46]

Celebrated abroad as a step ahead of the functionalism and rationalism theories,[47] Brazilian Modernism acquired, at home, the status of a paradigm. Supported by the federal government, and adopted by the emerging sectors of the urban society as the desirable image, modernist architecture was spread all around Brazil through exhibitions, competitions, commissions, urban designs, and interior shows. Among these opportunities, a series of buildings was commissioned around Pampulha's artificial lake, in the city of Belo Horizonte. The city mayor, Jucelino Kubitchek (the president who would build Brasília fifteen years later), had known Niemeyer since the construction of the hotel in the neighboring city of Ouro Preto, and did not hesitate to give him these commissions following advice from Costa and Gustavo Capanema, the Brazilian minister of education between 1935 and 1942. (As minister of education, Capanema presided over SPHAN, where Costa worked.)[48] The designs of Capela da Pampulha, Casa do Baile, Casino, and Iate Clube became the paradigms for Brazilian architectural modernism for decades. A brief analysis of the buildings shows traces of the designed memories adopted and adapted by the modernist syntax, as it developed a more effective and impressive identity.

FIG. 3.3. *Capela da Pampulha, by Oscar Niemeyer, 1942.*
Photo by Fernando Lara.

At Capela da Pampulha, for instance, the walls and ceiling are not independent, as dictated by the modernist paradigm, but inseparable. Little ceramic tiles *(pastilhas)* cover its parabolic vaults, and a ceramic panel *(azulejo)* decorates the rear wall. The use of azulejos is part of a Portuguese heritage widely used on modernist buildings. The Casino completes the Pampulha complex that has since become the so-called "exuberant-paradigm" for Brazilian modern architecture. Its free-form canopy, supported by thin steel columns, and the continuous glass wall on the façade were exhaustively replicated from then on. Inside the cubic-shaped main volume, the ramp dominates functionally, and the round concrete columns punctuate the rhythm of the interior space. At the back, closer to the lake, an elliptical dancing hall is integrated with the main volume by another ramp, and its continuous glass wall brings the lake landscape inside.

FIG. 3.4. *Casa do Baile, by Oscar Niemeyer, 1942.*
Photo by Fernando Lara.

Frampton wrote that "Niemeyer's genius reached its height in 1942" at the Casino, where he "reinterpreted the Corbusian notion of *promenade archi-tecturale* in a spatial composition of remarkable balance and vivacity."[49] Segawa notes that "in Pampulha, Niemeyer (now working alone) produced an architecture further away from Corbusian syntax, for sure more mature and personal than his designs for the 1939 Brazilian pavilion or the 1940 Hotel in Ouro Preto."[50]

As a response to the contradictory forces that lie in their roots, these buildings try to resolve the conflict of local versus international references, representation versus abstraction, and industrialization versus artisan construction. Many of the requirements that formed the basis of European modern architecture were absent in this context. The new social programs that should have generated these buildings were absent; instead, the buildings

FIG. 3.5. *Casino (now art museum) at Pampulha, by Oscar Niemeyer, 1942. Photo by Fernando Lara.*

originated from governmental commissions for a church, a casino, and a dancing hall, and were more relevant to the nineteenth-century bourgeoisie than to the twentieth-century working class. The industrialization and mass production that should accompany modern architecture were also absent, and although the buildings presented a modern image, they were carefully handcrafted, despite the new materials used.

Frampton labels the Casino a "narrative building," an idea that very much reinforces the connection between modernism and the baroque in the Brazilian case. The image (or the narrative) overcomes the structure (or the content) that lies behind it. This creates a façade of modernity in which memories (or the past roots) are as important as future promises regarding the articulation of this identity. As perceived by Eduardo Guimaraes back in the 1950s, Niemeyer's formal exuberance would be copied and spread all around Brazil, but the same powerful concepts that were responsible for its success would cause the self-sufficiency that became its later downfall.[51]

The Role of Memory Design in Brazilian Modernism

In Brazil in particular, and all around Latin America in general, the relationship between modernism and modernization was different from that in Europe or North America. In trying to explain the rise of avant-garde movements in the context of little or no industrialization and social changes, the thesis defended by Garcia-Canclini,[52] among others, is that Latin America had an exuberant modernism with deficient modernization. Whether we agree or not with that position depends on our own assumptions: for some, the European path is the only possible model; others, however, acknowledge the plurality of different modernization developments. It is interesting to note that, despite the late modernization, Brazilian Modernism had a different attitude toward memory from the beginning. It is traceable to the path of Brazilian modern architecture, which, after an international Corbusian starting point, was turning more and more local, while at the same time achieving worldwide publicity. At the root of this transformation, and at the root of its success lies the role of memory. Such a role generated an axis that connects both the constructed past and the desired future. As Cavalcanti says, the Brazilian modernists played a double role as architecture's simultaneous biographers and visionaries.[53]

If, regarding the traditional, modernist avant-garde, the past is used as an alterity, as something to be opposed to, then the Brazilian case is singular for the use of memory in the construction of identity. Note that it is not every memory, but a carefully designed and chosen myth of origin. However, the use of memory as an identity rather than an alterity allowed the modern project to resolve many of the complex conflicts of the first decades of the twentieth century. Ancient and modern are put together, and whereas the modern project proposed a continuation with an older past—baroque—it successfully denied the importance of the Beaux-Arts ideals of the nineteenth century. Such articulation also joins together the international and the local in the debate for modernist architecture. In it, Barroco Mineiro represents the first phase of Brazilian architecture. The presence of the baroque rhetoric and the baroque narrative on the exuberant Pampulha buildings is also the result and the materialization of such intellectually designed identity. Both the acceptance (presence) and the denial (absence) of the baroque-modernism axis in the diverse, contemporary architecture in Brazil show the degree to which it has been rooted in the country's identity. Memory was designed and used to anchor the modernist project both in the useful past and the prospective future. One can deny it and regret the modernist project, but again, such memory will be there as an alterity, waiting for other identities to be constructed.

౿

Notes

The epigraph is from Mário de Andrade, *A Lição do Amigo: Cartas de Mário de Andrade a Carlos Drummond de Andrade* (Rio de Janeiro: José Olympio, 1982), translated by Fernando Lara: "Nós temos que dar ao Brasil o que ele não tem e que por isso até agora não viveu, nós temos que dar uma alma ao Brasil e para isso todo sacrifício é grandioso, é sublime."

1. Ulrich Conrads, *Programs and Manifestoes on 20th-century Architecture* (Cambridge, Mass.: The MIT Press, 1971).
2. Jürgen Habermas, "Modernity's Consciousness of Time and Its Need for Self-Reassurance," *The Philosophical Discourse of Modernity* (Cambridge, Mass.: The MIT Press, 1987), 1–11.
3. David Harvey, *The Condition of Postmodernity* (Cambridge, Mass.: Basil Blackwell, 1989).
4. The term *alterity* is used here as "other," or "otherness." In the Romance languages, alterity is everything that alters, something against which one stands and that defines it by contrast.
5. "Modern building materials and our scientific ideas absolutely do not lend themselves to the disciplines of historical styles. . . . Each generation will have to build its own city." Tommaso Marinetti and Antonio Sant'Elia, "Futurist Architecture," in *Programs and Manifestoes on 20th-century Architecture,* by Ulrich Conrads (Cambridge, Mass.: The MIT Press, 1971), 35.
6. Perry Anderson, "Modernity and Revolution," *New Left Review* (1984): 317–33.
7. Nikolaus Pevsner, "Architecture and the Return of Historicism," *RIBA Journal* (1961): 230–37.
8. Fernando Lara, "Modernity Adopted and Adapted: Heritage's Role in Brazilian Modern Architecture," *ACSA North-East Regional Conference: Modernity and Heritage* (Newport, R.I., Oct. 1997), 230–36.
9. Elizabeth Harris, *Le Corbusier–Riscos Brasileiros,* trans. Gilson C. Souza and Antônio P. Danesi (São Paulo: Nobel, 1987), 54.
10. Coincidentally organized in the same year that the Brazilian centennial of independence was celebrated, the Semana de Arte Moderna (Modern Art Week) was a kind of manifesto-exhibition that put together cubists,

fauvists, and futurists and gave those avant-gardists the first broad publicity in the newspapers and radio programs. What they had in common was their interest in both international modernism and the search for understanding and defining the Brazilian identity.

11. Regarding the role the intellectuals had in the construction of this new Brazilian identity, Daniel Pecaut supports the argument that the 1930s generation of Brazilian intellectuals focused on identity and the conflict between nationalism and cosmopolitanism. D. Pecaut, *Os Intelectuais e a Política no Brasil: Entre o Povo e a Nação,* trans. Maria J. Goldwasser (São Paulo: Ática, 1990).

12. Eric Hobsbawm, *Nations and Nationalism since 1780* (New York: Cambridge University Press, 1990).

13. Born Charles-Edouard Jeanneret, in 1887, in La Chaux de Fonds, Switzerland, Le Corbusier adopted his well-known pseudonym for his architectural work around 1920 and established a most influential practice in France that included art, architecture, and theoretical writings.

14. In 1931, Eero Saarinen and Frank Lloyd Wright were in Brazil as jurors for the Columbus Light Tower competition; the ENBA students went on strike to support Lúcio Costa. According to Elizabeth Harris, *Le Corbusier–Riscos Brasileiros,* 51, Saarinen stayed away from the polemics, but Wright, who publicly supported the students and Costa, was celebrated for taking a stance.

15. Peter Bürger, *Theory of the Avant-Garde* (Minneapolis: University of Minnesota Press, 1984).

16. The *Manifesto Antropófago* (Cannibalist Manifesto), published in 1928, was inspired by the stories of cannibalism among native Brazilians and used as a metaphor for the appropriation of European avant-garde. According to de Andrade, the *Antropófagica* attitude should exhibit the purest, most natural state: "Language with no archaisms. No erudition. The millenary contribution of error. . . . Against all the importers of canned consciences. World without dates. Unindexed. No Napoleon. No Caesar." (The *Manifesto Antropófago* has been widely published; see, for example, Pietro M. Bardi, *New Brazilian Art* [New York: Praeger, 1970].)

17. Pietro M. Bardi, *New Brazilian Art* (New York: Praeger, 1970).

18. Rino Levi, *O Estado de São Paulo* (Oct. 1925).

19. Gregori Warchavchik, *O Correio da Manhã* (Nov. 1925).

20. The first visit of Le Corbusier to Brazil and Argentina, in 1929, was due largely to the influence of Blaise Cendrars (Frederic-Louis Sauser). Cendrars, a French avant-garde poet, was a friend of Oswald and Mário de Andrade, in São Paulo, and had accompanied them to Minas Gerais in 1924. Back in France, he kept telling his friend Le Corbusier about the Brazilian avant-garde and *"anthropofagia,"* while writing to his friends in Brazil about the new ideas in architecture. Harris, *Le Corbusier–Riscos Brasileiros,* 19.

21. This fact calls our attention to the authoritarian attitude of the 1930s, when modernism was being imposed, but not without dubious meanings. In a letter to the Ministry of Education complaining about this decision, Arquimedes Moreira (the author of the rejected winning design) uses the expression "Communist modernists" to describe Lúcio Costa. At that point in Brazil, modernism was truly perceived as a left-wing proposal, although it was partly supported by Vargas's populist government.
22. Lúcio Costa, *Registro de uma Vivência* (São Paulo: Empresa das Artes, 1995).
23. David Underwood, *Oscar Niemeyer and the Architecture of Brazil* (New York: Rizzoli, 1994), 23.
24. Interviews with Carlos E. Comas, Porto Alegre, July 12, 1999, and with Ruth Verde Zein, São Paulo, July 9, 1999.
25. Luiz A. Passaglia, *O papel do desenho na formação do arquiteto* (Belo Horizonte: PUC-Minas, 1995).
26. Fernando Lara, "Designing with a Single Line," *Dimensions* 11 (spring 1997): 17–23.
27. Mário de Andrade, *Macunaíma: o herói sem nunhum carater* (São Paulo, 1937).
28. Lauro Cavalcanti, *As preocupações do belo: arquitetura moderna brasileira dos anos 30/40* (Rio de Janeiro: Taurus, 1995), 147.
29. Interview with Carlos E. Comas, Porto Alegre, July 12, 1999.
30. Lúcio Costa, "Arquitetura Jesuítica no Brasil" (Brasília: IPHAN, 1997). First published in 1941 in *Revista do Patrimônio Histórico e Artístico*.
31. The polemics about the baroque roots go as far back as 1989, with Haroldo de Campos's "O sequestro do Barroco na historia da literatura brasileira" (The Baroque Kidnapping of Brazilian Literary History), in which Campos denounces the continuing disappearance of the baroque from traditional historiography.
32. It is worth noting that both the minister, Gustavo Capanema, and the director, Rodrigo Melo Franco, of SPHAN were from Minas Gerais. In the Brazilian politics of the 1930s, Minas Gerais, joining forces with Rio Grande do Sul and the northeast, provided most of the support for the Vargas government against the economic leadership of São Paulo.
33. Darcy Ribeiro, *O povo brasileiro: a formação e o sentido do Brasil* (São Paulo: Cia das Letras, 1995), 153.
34. In 1720, the revolt, led by Felipe dos Santos against Portuguese control and heavy taxes on the mining region, was suffocated by the Portuguese police.
35. In 1789, a more articulated movement for the independence of Minas Gerais was denounced. The participants were all arrested and sent to exile in African colonies, except for Lieutenant Joaquim José da Silva Xavier, known as "Tiradentes," who was hanged in Rio de Janeiro and had parts of his dismembered body displayed in cities around Minas Gerais.

36. *Barroco Mineiro* is the name applied to the late-baroque manifestations of the state of Minas Gerais, Brazil, during the eighteenth century. Influenced early on by the Italian and Iberian baroque, it gradually evolved to a singular style due to its isolation and local resources. For an extensive analysis of Barroco Mineiro see works by Robert Smith, Germain Bazin, Mário de Andrade, Lúcio Costa, and Carlos Antônio Brandão.

37. In "Em torno da questão do barroco no Brasil," Guilherme Gomes Jr. proposes that intellectuals like Manuel Bandeira and Mário de Andrade were not at ease when dealing with the baroque as Brazilian in origin. However, according to Gomes Jr., that was part of their modernist paradox: to make a "deal" in order to construct a Brazilian identity that obligatorily would have a baroque "birth certificate." See Eliana M. M. Souza, ed., *Cultura Brasileira: Figuras de Alteridade* (São Paulo: Fapesp, 1996).

38. Maria Angelica Silva, *As formas e as palavras da obra de Lúcio Costa* (Rio de Janeiro: PUC-RJ, 1991), 18.

39. Lauro Cavalcanti, *Revista do Patrimônio Histórico e Artístico* (Brasília: IPHAN, 1997), 170.

40. Kenneth Frampton, *Modern Architecture: A Critical History* (New York: Oxford University Press, 1980), 254.

41. Harris, *Le Corbusier–Riscos Brasileiros,* 66.

42. Interview with Carlos E. Comas, Porto Alegre, July 12, 1999.

43. Cavalcanti, *As preocupações do belo,* 23.

44. Lúcio Costa had won the competition organized by the Ministry of Foreign Affairs for the Brazilian pavilion at the 1939 New York World's Fair. However, reflecting on his design and the runner-up entry by Niemeyer, Costa proposed that they work together to combine their entries into a third project that would be better than the previous ones. Together they designed the Brazilian pavilion for the 1939 New York World's Fair.

45. It is worth noting that Gustavo Capanema (Brazilian minister of education and culture) was a personal friend of Nelson Rockefeller, the major sponsor of the Good Neighborhood policy. This policy was a cultural effort, led by Rockefeller during World War II, that sought to bring the United States closer to its Latin American neighbors and to counterbalance German and Italian influence. The Good Neighborhood policy supported the creation of Walt Disney movies about Latin America; Carmen Miranda's performances on Broadway, and later Hollywood; and, in the case of architecture, the "Brazil Builds" exhibition at the MoMA in 1942.

46. Philip Goodwin, *Brazil Builds: Architecture New and Old, 1652–1942* (New York: The Museum of Modern Art, 1943).

47. Underwood, *Oscar Niemeyer,* 55.

48. Carlos A. C. Lemos, *Arquitetura Brasileira* (São Paulo: Melhoramentos, 1979), 147.

49. Frampton, *Modern Architecture,* 255.

50. Hugo Segawa, *Arquiteturas Brasileiras: 1900–1990* (São Paulo: EDUSP, 1998), 98.
51. Eduardo Guimaraes, "Niemeyer na Pampulha," *Arquitetura e Engenharia* 51 (Oct. 1958): 3.
52. Nestor Garcia-Canclini, *Hybrid Cultures: Strategies for Entering and Leaving Modernity* (Minneapolis: University of Minnesota Press, 1995).
53. Cavalcanti, *As preocupações do belo,* 176.

chapter four

Patrimony and Cultural Identity

The Coffee Plantation System—
Paraíba Valley, Rio de Janeiro, Brazil

MARIA de LOURDES LUZ and
ANA LÚCIA VIEIRA DOS SANTOS

*A*rchitecture represents the history, tradition, and culture of a specific community. By protecting the cultural patrimony, we are contributing to the rescue and consolidation of the community's social identity in its historical evolution.

Memory has a fundamental role both in the transformation and in the preservation of cultural manifestations. The built environment is an important mnemonic agent that makes visible the differentiation of places, informs us of how society appropriates space, and instructs us to behave appropriately. Without memory there is neither human present nor future. Memory works as biological-social instrument of identity, conservation, and development, allowing events to flow legibly. Without memory, change would create alienation and dissociation. We believe that the built environment is an expressive indicator of each society's modus vivendi. It furnishes elements for a better comprehension of the social group in which it was generated, and remains essential to the study of social life. Furthermore, as our investigation shows, the built environment provides a firm, supporting ground at times of rapid cultural change. Brazil is a melting pot of different cultures. From the first

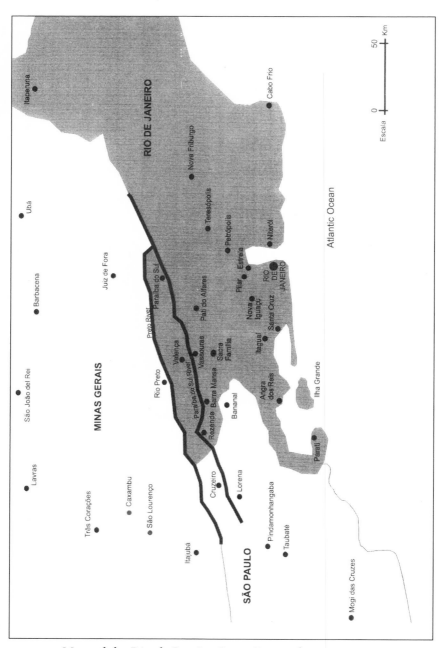

FIG. 4.1. *Map of the Rio de Janeiro State. Drawn by*
Maria de Lourdes Luz and Ana Lúcia Vieira Dos Santos.

days of colonization, when Portuguese, Native Americans, and Africans started to construct a new world, to the last hundred years, when immigration from Europe and Asia contributed to the building of the independent country, very different traditions, habits, techniques, and uses were brought together, constructing a new identity.

In order to introduce our architecture students to the concepts of memory, patrimony, and cultural identity, we turned our attention to the nineteenth century, when Brazil became an independent nation. It was a period of great social, political, and economic transformations, with important changes in the architectonic types established during the three preceding centuries. Through the study of traditional architecture, we explore the relationships between architectonic form and value systems, which signify deeper structures of society. These systems are responsible for differences between "cultures," and can only be apprehended through interpretations based on culture and social life. As we study the architectonic production related to sociocultural and historical contexts, we contribute to the redefinition and reaffirmation of regional identities, and to a better understanding of people in society.

Our research has focused on the coffee plantation system. Coffee formed the economic basis of the Brazilian Empire (1822–1889) throughout the nineteenth century, though with varying degrees of significance. The coffee plantations, concentrated in the Paraíba Valley during the early nineteenth century, became a symbol of the power and progress of the Brazilian Empire. By the second half of the nineteenth century, there were close to a hundred farms, many of which were abandoned later due to the shift of the coffee industry from the Paraíba Valley, in Rio de Janeiro, to São Paulo; the political and economic changes that culminated in the abolition of slavery in 1888; and the proclamation of the Brazilian Republic in 1889.

A Brief History of Brazil

In 1808, as Napoleon invaded Portugal, the Portuguese court moved to Rio de Janeiro. Rio became the capital of the Portuguese kingdom, and both Portugal and its colonies were ruled from there. In 1821, King D. João VI was forced to go back to Portugal, on account of the Porto Revolution. He left his son, D. Pedro, in Rio as regent. By that time, Brazil was not a regular colony any more, but a "united kingdom" to Portugal and Algarve.

The Brazilian Empire was founded on September 7, 1822, when the Portuguese prince, D. Pedro, declared Brazil an independent country that was also independent from Portugal. He became D. Pedro I, of Brazil, and called himself an emperor, not a king. Despite the name, Brazil was a regular monarchy and not an empire, as it did not have any colonies.

When the Portuguese court arrived in 1808, the coffee crop was quickly developing, and had already reached the Paraíba Valley. The sugar culture was in decline, and coffee quickly became the most important exportation product, especially between the 1840s and 1860s. In the 1870s, a new coffee plantation area began to develop in São Paulo. The fresh lands of São Paulo produced more coffee than the exhausted soils of Rio de Janeiro, where the crop had begun to decline. It is important to note that labor in São Paulo was based on free workers, mainly immigrants (Italian, German, Portuguese, and later, Japanese), while in Rio de Janeiro it was mainly slave labor. When slavery was abolished in 1888, Rio de Janeiro's coffee system collapsed, though the abolition of slavery was not the main cause of this collapse. The end of the Brazilian Empire came on November 15, 1889, when the country became a republic. Emperor D. Pedro II, son of D. Pedro I, left the country with his family, and finished his days in France.

Coffee remained the basis of the Brazilian economy until the 1940s, when we finally see the beginnings of the country's industrialization.

The Crop

Coffee dominated Brazilian exports from 1822 to the end of the nineteenth century, reversing the deficit caused by the decline of the sugar trade. Even after the institution of the Brazilian republic in 1889, coffee continued to form the foundation of the country's economy. The coffee culture took the "plantation" or "plantage" form, maintaining the traditional structure of the Brazilian economy, which was based on large properties, monoculture, and slave labor. Coffee is a more delicate culture than sugar cane, demanding good soils and mild temperatures. It takes four to five years to start production, so it needs larger investments of capital. It is a permanent culture, and requires more land to enlarge production. The great investment of capital required by coffee (long unproductive period, great extensions of land, and large number of slaves) rendered the activity impossible for the small proprietor.

By 1790, the crop was fully adapted in the Paraíba Valley region, located in the state of Rio de Janeiro. The success of coffee culture was due, in great part, to that location. It has a tropical climate, with temperatures ranging from 62°F to 95°F, depending on the season. That specific area is located in the Atlantic Forest, therefore having the typical vegetation of the tropical forest and its rich mineral soil. Coffee proved to be more profitable than sugar cane, which was the main resource before coffee, and the wealth coffee brought helped expand its cultivation. It was possible to find in the Paraíba Valley farms that cultivated thousands of plants. Some proprietors had several adjoining farms, with the size of each estate limited by the distance the slaves could cover on foot from the *senzala* (the slave quarters) to the plantation.

The coffee cycle was responsible for the development of both old and new cities and towns. The cities of Valença, Rio das Flores, Vassouras, Piraí, and Barra do Piraí are all located in this valley and were of great importance to Brazil in the nineteenth century. They flourished as coffee trade became more lucrative. The plantation owners were granted nobility titles because of the great power and prestige they exerted. The coffee barons became the third and last nobility of the country, after the sugar-cane landlords and the great mine owners. Coffee growers became part of the Brazilian social elite, enjoying the attendant life of wealth, nobility titles, and festivities. Their influence was directly proportional to the responsibility of administering a farm and its production. These properties were often so large that they extended beyond where the eye could see from a single vantage point.

The coffee production was exported through the Rio de Janeiro port, in the city of Rio de Janeiro, which is located about 120 miles from the region of the Paraíba Valley. In this same port, slaves arrived by the thousands.

The Slaves

Upon reviewing the country's history, it is interesting to consider Brazil as a country of slaves. For three and one-half centuries, four million African slaves were shipped into the country, playing a big part in the coffee expansion. Although the first phase of the coffee plantation expansion was based on the use of the labor force coming from the decline of the Minas Gerais mining cycle, the second and definitive phase of the coffee culture was dependent on the working hands of just-arrived African slaves.

Slaves were seen as a product that was highly commercialized: they were sold or bought, borrowed or traded, as well as inherited. During a specific period of slavery, even poor people were able to have their own slaves. Slaves were exposed as animals in the market, where the slave traffickers chose them by licking their skin to test for sweat, as opposed to shiny oil, and by examining their teeth and overall health condition.

Commercializing slaves was a lucrative but rather expensive business, not attainable by regular businessmen. The trader must have enough capital to invest in the acquisition or rental of ships, the purchase of articles for exchange with African tribes, and the purchase of insurance. Insurance was essential due to the high mortality rate of slaves during the trip from Africa to Brazil.

In general, the slaves' lives in South America were difficult, mainly because of the adversity of resocialization. It is important to confirm the context in which they were traded, and how they lived. The study of the buildings where they lived and worked may give us some clues about their incorporation in the new society. We know by now that slave families were common in the last decades before abolition. Slaves were often traded as a family (mother, father, and their children), as it was presumed that maintaining the family together would minimize slave escapes, suicides, and aggressive reactions, and provide better productivity for the lords.

Domestic slavery retained many aspects of medieval European slavery. Domestic slaves were preferably women and were directly subjected to the mistress of the house. They were cooks, wet-nurses, nannies, dressmakers, and so forth. Called *mucamas,* these domestic slaves worked in the house, keeping it clean and ordered, set the table and served meals, took care of the children, and helped the mistress of the house with her daily work. Mucamas were thus closer to their masters, occupying a special place in the slave hierarchy. These indoor slaves could be recompensed with affection and credibility from the lords and mistresses, receive religious and moral assistance, and also receive gifts that represented a higher status.

On the other hand, it is easy to understand the reasons for slaves wanting to escape from the lords. Separation from their family or simply the desire to be free could motivate an escape. Another main reason was the aggressive physical punishment. Violence pervaded all social relations. Based on an old Portuguese tradition, the landlord (the chief of the family) had the right to punish physically his wife, children, and followers. But at the same time, it was his obligation to protect these people, for whom he was responsible.

Escapes were sometimes massive, and always caused great worry for other lords in the region where it occurred. When fugitive slaves got organized, a *quilombo* was formed. We have some written documents about the quilombos and very few archaeological findings. Descriptions and pictures show us that the quilombo buildings were very similar to the senzalas, the slave quarters. The reproduction of spatial structures related to slavery in a situation of freedom (by the newly freed slaves) indicates that slaves had acquired a new identity during the captivity period.

The Plantation House

It is important to remember that the first decades of the nineteenth century were marked by the transference of the Portuguese court from Lisbon to Rio de Janeiro in 1808, which propitiated two significant cultural events. The first event was the arrival of the French Mission. Missing Europe's rich culture, King João VI brought painters, sculptors, architects, and other artists from France to enrich Rio de Janeiro's cultural atmosphere. The second event was the inauguration of the Imperial Academy of Fine Arts in Rio de Janeiro. Vale do Paraíba—the Paraíba River Basin region—was not far from the changes that took place as the Portuguese court arrived in Brazil.

The colonizers brought from Europe the urban life experience. In the nineteenth century, the neoclassical style was already fashionable in the imperial court, located at Rio de Janeiro. Paraíba Valley was tuned to what was happening in the Rio de Janeiro court. The tendency of the coffee barons was to copy and take back behaviors, customs, and values from their contact with the capital. The coffee plantation buildings suffered these influences, and many houses were rebuilt or remodeled to fit the new patterns.

The coffee complex may be divided into two worlds, one of labor, and one of habitation. It is the dwelling space that will hold our attention. There are two dwelling buildings in the coffee plantation: the "big house," where the masters lived, and the senzala, the slave quarters. Generally speaking, the buildings that composed the coffee plantation's complexes were distributed around a square area in which the coffee was dried. One side of the square was devoted to the big house, which was usually located on higher ground, overlooking the whole area, and thus enhancing the proprietor's status. On the other side were the slaves' houses (senzalas), cellars, and mills. This model of farm complexes was strictly followed in Brazil.

The farm programs included orchards, gardens, chapels, dams, aqueducts, deposits, workshops, engines, private tramway lines, and, when they were located by the railroad, they could even have a private platform to flow production. Thus, it is common to find descriptions that compare the farms to villages, on account of their size. These complexes were sometimes enclosed by a high wall that gave them the appearance of fortresses, with the highest point occupied by the owner's house.

The big house was central to farm life. The social areas were composed of adjoining rooms that always led to the main reception room. The fact that guest bedrooms were found in this area indicates the family's preoccupation with maintaining its privacy. Even though travelers could arrive at any time, with no previous notice, they were not perceived as invaders of the family privacy. On the contrary, their arrival and relationship with the owners of the house constituted a rare moment of sociability in the rural world. In fact, the barons were known for their hospitality. To travelers, the farm offered a cordial shelter, food, and a roof over their heads. With its concentration of wealth, the coffee culture also contributed to the transformation of social life in the large rural properties.

The dining room was the connecting point between the two parts of the house—the public and the private. This social area was the most important part of the residence, the part through which the outside world saw the family.

In the private part of the house, the rooms were modest and simple, with furnishings limited to the essential. The father's room was located in a way that allowed him to keep an eye on his children, primarily his daughters. The service area, which included the kitchen, pantry, food storage, and ironing and sewing rooms, was the exclusive domain of the women: these areas were shared by mistresses and slaves somewhat democratically. These rooms were connected to the kitchen garden, where there were vegetables, fruits, and farm animals.

In our research, we were able to verify the existence of three phases in the construction of the big houses. The first phase, from the last years of the eighteenth century to the first decades of the 1800s, produced the more rustic houses that distinguish the first period of occupation of the Paraíba Valley, when investments in habitation were small.

FIG. 4.2. *São Policarpo Plantation, the Big House. Photo by
Maria de Lourdes Luz and Ana Lúcia Vieira Dos Santos.*

The second phase of houses, built at the apogee of the coffee economy,
when fortunes were already consolidated, showcases greater investments in
the constructions, and better finishing patterns. At the beginning of the 1850s
we also observe the arrival of Portuguese carpenters, masons, and cabinet-
makers, as well as French artisans. For about three decades, the houses built
in the Paraíba Valley rivaled those of the court, based in Rio de Janeiro.

The third phase corresponds to the last days of the coffee period in Rio
de Janeiro, from the late 1870s to the abolition of slavery in 1888. It comprises houses on properties that, in many cases, did not plant coffee any-
more, and served primarily as vacation residences for the barons or were

used by their sons and daughters when they got married. This last phase is associated with a greater facility of transportation, as the railroads already went up the hills, permitting the arrival of more sophisticated building and decorative materials, as well as imported goods.

The spatial structure of the big house was based on aisles, a division that reflected the inhabitants' way of life, and communicated to visitors, servants, and family members the behavior expected of them all.

The "U" plan favored the existence of an internal court. It was in the back of the U that the social barrier point was located: the dining room. The dining room was also the space that linked together the other rooms, or aisles, of the house. On one side of the court were the service areas; on the other side were the bedrooms and rooms for the private use of the family (sewing and family rooms, etc.); over the dining room were the reception rooms. This internal court also allowed the existence of outdoor spaces that were not disturbed by the activities from outside the house, clearly defining "inside" life and "outside" life. Even if there were no street, it was necessary to isolate the house from the agricultural work, then considered "outside" life.

Neoclassic façades and richer interiors transformed the overall appearance of the big house, symbolizing high status and intimacy with the Rio de Janeiro court. But the internal disposition of rooms did not change, and the separation between public and private remained clear. This separation persists in the contemporary Brazilian house, which still has social, intimate, and service zones.

The Senzalas

Our research aims to provide a link between the different stages of the transformation of free people into slaves, their lives in the senzalas, and the built environment. We believe that social transitions have spatial equivalents that make them more clear.

Our study focuses on the current debate over the slave family and the political limits of slavery. Recent academic production in Brazil deals with the strategies that enabled the owners to keep control of the slaves, and enabled the slaves to survive the hard conditions of captivity. It is the person that the slave could never refrain from being, capable of adapting his necessities to his possibilities, that we are searching for in our reflection on the senzalas. In this picture of political struggle, new interpretations give new meaning to the senzala building, reflecting power relationships.

Unlike white people and slaves born in Brazil, persons caught in Africa *became* slaves and Africans during their captivity in Brazil, assuming, in other words, the identity of a slave and of an African. Our starting point was the apparent contradiction between the need for the depersonalization of the slave, on the one hand, and the maintenance of traditional African habits in the senzala, on the other hand.

When the early colonizers installed the sugar-cane plantations in the sixteenth century, they hurried to start the economic exploitation of the new colony. The simple transposition of European architectonic models to the tropics was not adequate for local conditions, so what prevailed at first in the construction of dwellings was the knowledge of the native population and of those brought with the colonization process. At first, the Portuguese did not use the dwelling spaces as an instrument of domination in their contacts with the native population and African slaves. They created the appearance of settlement models that did not entirely duplicate the European elite's patterns.

The building of the slaves' quarters was left to the slaves themselves, as that made construction quicker and less expensive. According to descriptions, these quarters looked like traditional African dwellings. In the nineteenth century they still had no windows, their doors were small, and their floors remained unpaved. Our research shows that these are common features in the African countries that supplied slaves to Brazil.

The pluralism of the first years of colonization was replaced by an order appropriate to the social and economic relations that emerged in the colony. As a result of the cultural contact between societies with different rationales, new dwelling forms appeared, which crystallized into models transmitted over decades without much reflection about their origins. We have assembled these models under the denomination of "contact architecture," and we are studying the effects of social changes on their architecture.

The comparative study of senzalas and traditional African dwellings allows us to perceive how Africa was re-created in Brazil. As we develop this study, we propose to look for the main formal and constructive characteristics in the countries that provided slaves to Brazil, looking for common elements that might have served as the basis for the Brazilian senzalas.

FIGS . 4.3 *(right)*
AND 4.4. *(below)*
Ponte Alta
Plantation,
the Senzala.
Photos by Maria
de Lourdes Luz
and Ana Lúcia
Vieira Dos
Santos.

The concept of interethnic contact allows us to comprehend the interaction of individuals carrying different *mentalités,* resulting in new cultural patterns and suggesting the examination of the social group dynamics before the contact. Knowing about each culture before the interethnic contact allows us to recognize how the resulting architectural models were derived from elements unique to each culture. As we saw, the spatial model of the senzala, based on African traditions, survived, contrary to what happened in colonies of other European nations, where houses of Western form and materials were imposed on the slaves.

We consider the senzala to be a traditional building, largely adopted throughout the Brazilian territory during the slavery period, and maintaining the characteristics acquired through habit with astonishing persistence of form and building technique. The longevity of the senzala allows us to consider it as one of the traditional architectonic prototypes of the Brazilian house. Isolated from the big house, the worker slaves' living quarters were built with mud walls and straw roofs, facing either east or west, in a long succession of square rooms. Each room accommodated four single slaves or a family of slaves. Verandas were common in the nineteenth century and served as social areas for the slaves. At the same time, the slave was introduced to the labor world regulated by the slavery system, and to the universe of the senzala, where the master's order was not the only order present.

Foreign travelers who visited Brazil in the nineteenth century bequeathed us with important documents on the daily life of the places they visited, offering unique descriptions of Brazilian culture, values, and habits especially important to a largely illiterate society that produced very little written documentation. Artists themselves, or accompanied by painters, they produced not only texts but also images of the visited regions. They were shocked by the minimal resources of the senzalas, in contrast with the big house. But the senzalas did not differ from the houses of small proprietors or free peasants, either in form or in building techniques.

We believe that the senzala's form provided the African slaves with mechanisms that helped them adapt to their social condition and survive. The appropriation of physical references from traditional African dwellings allowed the individual to adapt the environmental conditions to his or her primitive necessities (territory demarcation, spatialization of family structures, protection, etc.). The familiarity of the building form of the senzala helped compensate, in part, for the psychic chaos that confronted the new slaves. It provided them with an ordering schema that helped them maintain their integrity and provided for a social cohesion that permitted them to continue operating as social beings.

The memory of African cultural patterns in the senzalas certainly played an important role in the resocialization of newly arrived slaves. Through the re-creation of their domestic universe, the senzalas furnished these slaves with elements that helped them endure the cultural shock and the unfavorable conditions of captivity. The cultural diversity of slaves makes the senzala's form even more important, as the more differentiated the group is, the stronger the help of the built environment to the engendering of collective life and survival strategies.

If we put aside Western concepts and patterns of salubrity and comfort, we may look at the senzalas as a product of the contact of Portuguese and Africans, adapted to the latter's necessities. Even if the senzala were different from the slave's original house, he or she would have been able to find in the new habitat elements common to many African cultures, such as lack of windows, unpaved dirt floors, and building materials, mainly wattle and daub.

These elements must have played an important role in the psychological restructuring of individuals, helping their adaptation to the new condition, and, at the same time, providing them with means to resist the cultural patterns of the masters by maintaining aspects of African lifestyle. The abolition of slavery did not cause the extinction of the model created for the slaves. This dwelling type can be found today in the less-favored communities throughout Brazil, regardless of their ethnic origin.

The study of the senzalas leads us to the investigation of contemporary homes' service quarters, which are strongly related to the past existence of slavery. These segregated areas of the house have been changing for the past hundred years, as memory and habits from the slavery period fade.

Today, the coffee complexes are an endangered cultural patrimony, as the high costs of conservation have placed them totally under the auspices of private initiative. Our first goal was to make an inventory of the surviving buildings, an urgent measure for the preservation of the memory of the coffee cycle. The first results of the surveys indicated that the coffee complex spatially reflects the changes that occurred in the Brazilian society of the nineteenth century, providing rich information for its study.

Before they start working on this research, students are asked to read about Brazilian history and architecture. The surveys are done by the request of the estate owner, or by suggestion of the students, when they are acquainted with the proprietor. The students are well received by the owners, who always have many stories to tell. These stories are particularly interesting when the property has belonged to the same family since the nineteenth century, as family memories contribute to the reconstruction of a historical moment. The students produce plans, photos, and written descriptions of the present situation, and investigate the past of the property through research in public and private archives. This research has enabled the reconstitution of many original plans, which will be very useful in the event of future restoration.

The Paraíba Valley region is searching for new economic activities. Future development of the region points to the tourist potential of the ancient coffee farms. At present, there is a strong tendency to transform coffee farms into hotels, and many owners agree to receive tourist visits. Our work is of great interest to the proprietors, as we are gathering and organizing information about the estates at a fast rate. In addition, we are investigating the meaning of the spatial changes that the economic prosperity, brought by the coffee cycle, promoted in the traditional house. The Brazilian house is characterized by a persistence of form and territorial diffusion that some authors compare to that of religion and language. Our research shows that even though the size and external appearance of the house changed in the nineteenth century, internal distribution and functions remain unaltered. As individuals of different mentalités live together, memories from different cultures blend, producing new forms and functions, in a new cultural pattern.

The big house is not the Portuguese house, and the senzala is not the African house. The inventory of the coffee estates provides data that helps us understand how the multiethnicity of Brazilian society is expressed in the built environment. Memory has a fundamental role in the creation of new models, as selected features from each culture remain in the resulting building, making it possible for individuals of different origins to live and work together.

 ℅

Bibliography

Alencastro, Luiz Felipe, ed. *Império: A Corte e a Modernidade Nacional,* História da Vida Privada No Brasil, vol. 2. São Paulo: Cia das Letras, 1997.

Cardoso, Joaquim. "Um Tipo de Casa Rural do Distrito Federal." In *Arquitetura Civil II.* São Paulo: Editora da USP, n.d.

Florentino, Manolo, and José Roberto Góes. *A Paz das Senzalas.* Rio de Janeiro: Civilização Brasileira, 1997.

Freire, Gilberto. *Casa Grande e Senzala.* Rio de Janeiro: José Olímpio, 1964.

Graham, Sandra Lauderdale. *Proteção e Obediência.* São Paulo: Cia das Letras, 1992.

Lamego, Alberto Ribeiro. *O Homem e a Serra.* 2nd ed. Rio de Janeiro: IBGE, 1963.

Pires, Fernando Tasso Fragoso. *As Grandes Casas Rurais do Brasil.* New York: Abbeville Press, 1995.

Rocha, Isabel. "Arquitetura Rural do Vale do Paraíba Fluminense do Século XIX." *Revista Gávea,* no. 1: 55–56.

Toledo, Roberto Pompeu de. "À Sombra da Escravidão da Escravidão." *Revista Veja* 29, no. 20 (May 15, 1996): 52–65.

Vasconcelos, Silvio de. *Arquitetura no Brasil: Sistemas Construtivos.* Belo Horizonte, Braz.: UFMG, 1979.

Part Two

Literary Memory Spaces

chapter five

Memory Work

The Reciprocal Framing of Self and Place in Émigré Autobiographies

SABIR KHAN

Part One

In exploring the relationship of memory and space through a reading of émigré autobiographies, this chapter focuses not only on what one remembers but how one remembers it. In doing so, it stresses how the bearer of memory reconstructs the relationship between memories of spaces and the spaces themselves. Even though memory appears to be tied to time, the metaphors we use to understand its operations invariably invoke the spatial and the architectural: "layers excavated, veils lifted, screens removed."[1] Whereas a distancing in time and space sponsors memories, the act of remembering itself is predicated on disjunction, on a break in the flow of the present, and a dislocation between the memory and the one doing the remembering. It is no surprise, then, that memories, consciously recalled and reformulated, figure significantly in the refashioning of émigré identity.

The negotiation of self and place through the medium of memory is especially evident in émigré autobiographies. Autobiographical writing provides a framework for the émigré's interpolations of memory, experience, and language. This effort to render memory visible incorporates many architectural and cultural references into the autobiographical account. The manner in which émigrés reconstruct and re-present the passage of their lives reveals much about the terrain they passed through as well. Reading their life-stories for the ways in which a culture is spatialized and lived underscores this proposition. In their accumulation of everyday detail, as well as in their rhetorical strategies, autobiographical accounts represent a twofold transformation of lived life: first, the figuration into memory of experiences and sensations, and then the transmutation of that memory into a coherent narrative.

This chapter looks at two narratives of homecoming and leave-taking, in which memory enunciates spaces of extraordinary resonance, written by two South Asian women émigrés. Attia Hosain's autobiographical novel, *Sunlight on a Broken Column,* and Sara Suleri's memoir, *Meatless Days,* are interpretive and partial reconstructions of spaces that articulate with precision and nuance the domestic everyday, the space that is given over to women. Both Hosain and Suleri, in their ongoing effort to remember and rehearse their lives, approach "memory as practice," memory not as "unmediated natural fact" but rather as the culturally mediated "memory work" that comprises our memories *and* the uses to which we put them.[2] In their accounts we see how the "memory of the individual, precisely that which is often taken to epitomize individuality, draws upon collective idioms and mechanisms":[3] the culturally coded spaces of the *zenana* or the extended family, for example, or the more universal narratives of loss and migration, of letting go and putting to rest. The memory work undertaken in these autobiographical accounts both employs and reveals these culturally specific forms and norms.

As women twice dispersed, from both their familial and cultural milieux, as women living between and across disparate cultures, Hosain and Suleri weave complex narratives of identity out of displacement (the routes traversed) and location (the roots that bind).[4] In doing so, they enlist a range of culturally specific references to places and traditions in order to reenact the events of their lives, from the communal *charpai* (bedstead) on the verandah of the family home to the kitchen table in small apartments in American college towns. The domestic arrangements recounted in these texts articulate specific social and cultural milieux, the changing structure of domesticity, and the boundaries—spatial, social, and psychological—that define an individual's sense of self and her relationship to family, community, and society.

Both books are itineraries of the *self* that articulate their relationship to *place* through memory operations in order to come to terms with rerouting and rerooting. Both engage the dynamics of cross-cultural transactions, working the vein of "in-between-ness" with the ambivalent (and bivalent) perspective of the émigré. And both choose to keep the focus of their works intimate and domestic, even as the force of historical and public events washes over them. Taken together, these two books make for a culturally coherent pairing: they extend each other's stories farther back into the past and forward into different futures. In a sense, Suleri could very well be the modern Pakistani daughter of one of Hosain's Muslim characters who emigrated from Lucknow to Pakistan via England. Certain tropes and patterns remain strikingly constant even as their articulations vary: the relationships between women; between the home and the outside, "historical," world; and between domestic arrangements and their architectural accommodation.

Style, Language, and Self-Articulation

In the recalling and retelling of autobiography, the details of spaces, events, and people are rhetorically reconstituted. The critical effort on the part of the autobiographer in her memory work is to find an "enabling style," for "self-hood" is as much "a matter of style and rhetoric" as it is "historically produced and culture-specific."[5] The issue of style, of crafting an appropriate idiom for autobiography, is particularly central to Suleri's and Hosain's efforts at making sense of their lives and their social and cultural milieux. Straddling as they do different cultures, languages, social conventions, and geographies, theirs are not simplistic narratives of identity caught between the bipolarities of the modern versus the traditional, or the authentic versus the metropolitan. Their need to find their own voice, to reterritorialize their lives, gives their accounts a particular currency for those who work and live between, across, and at the margins of cultures. Their deracination, it seems, exaggerates their sense of belonging and of displacement, making their stories all the more vivid.

Carolyn Barros suggests that autobiographies are essentially "narratives of transformation" where "someone tells someone else something happened to me."[6] While transformation and change are operative metaphors in these books also, something else is going on as well. The subject of transformation is also a *questing* subject: not simply recording the facts of her life, but trying to take stock of and make sense of them as well. The authors return to old *haunts,* in the double sense of the word that conjoins memory and place. The haunting that marks these autobiographies is a result of these obsessive forays along the locus of one's memory and to a series of sites from the past and in the present.

These exercises in self-understanding—archaeological reconstructions of subjectivity and identity—are by necessity self-conscious. Self-disclosure and self-discovery are predicated on a distancing of the self from the subject of the autobiography. The point of view is neither singular nor fixed. The locus of enunciation in autobiography shifts constantly as the narrator, though apparently omniscient, is acutely receptive to the evolving and multiple voices a subject incorporates. The problem of autobiography's audience raises the rhetorical ante further, as the audience is by definition split, even splintered. Autobiographical narratives are stories told to strangers who will chance upon it, and to all the past ghosts and present characters that populate one's life.

The literary critic Naomi Schor suggests that detail carries within itself a bivalency that, culturally and historically, has been gendered as feminine: the detail is "bounded on the one side by the ornamental with its traditional connotations of effeminacy and decadence and on the other by the everyday whose prosiness is rooted in the domestic sphere presided by women."[7] The sheer specificity and particularity of detail give these accounts a rare phenomenological density. Whereas Suleri focuses on the domestic locations and locutions of the nuclear family, Hosain restages the extended, or joint-family, household. In both works, domestic detail serves contrasting yet complementary functions, indexing both the ornamental and the everyday. Whether implicit in narrations of domesticity or in a feminine aesthetics of remembering, this particular bracketing of the detail (between the quotidian and the ornamental) does point to a crucial aspect of memory formation: the way in which an autobiographer in her memory work constantly elaborates upon and amplifies the echoes of everyday events.

Both Suleri and Hosain write in English, employing an ornate, self-consciously literary, sensual, and somewhat overwrought style in their autobiographies. Hosain's allusive voice draws from the poetic idiom of *Lukhnavi* Urdu, with its vernacular treasure trove of aphorisms, proverbs, and burnished banter. Suleri works the particular frisson of living in two languages, shaping sentences and deploying idioms through which each language sounds out the other and the memory worlds that it harbors.[8]

Its transregional status within the Indian subcontinent aside, subcontinental writing in English signifies in other ways as well, marking, for example, the particular class and cultural status of those who write in it. While growing up "at home" in English, Hosain and Suleri were also acutely aware of how it set them apart from their surroundings. Writing their life-stories in English reiterates it as a sign of their being simultaneously at home and not at home, a marker of their status as insider/outsider both when growing up and as émigrés in England and America. While neither account maps tidily onto either "Western" or South Asian autobiographical traditions, the literary conventions of the language one is remembering in play a role in shaping memory.[9] In contrast to the genres for autobiographical expression in the Indo-Persian tradition, there is, for example, a palpable sense of agency in Hosain's and Suleri's accounts, a desire for the self-representation that autobiography, if not life itself, makes possible, especially for women émigrés.

Hosain and Sunlight on a Broken Column

Although *Sunlight on a Broken Column* is purportedly fiction, it maps very closely the cultural and historical contours of Hosain's life. Hosain's family was part of the feudal elite that managed to continue its cultural traditions while carrying on a limited though mutually beneficial commerce with the British ruling classes. By the time of Hosain's parents' generation, this cross-cultural and unbalanced commerce had produced a group of English-educated "technocrats," who served the bureaucracies of the Raj while continuing to assert their traditional feudal ties and profit from them. The social schisms produced by this cultural equivocation were exacerbated when Hosain's generation, born around the First World War, chose to apply the precepts of their English liberal education to question both the *noblesse oblige* of an increasingly bankrupt feudal society, and the legitimacy of British rule.

Some women from this class and generation were the first to be allowed to attend university. Hosain herself was the first woman to graduate from among the feudal families of Lucknow. While her intellectual horizons broadened, the field of action for women of her background remained circumscribed by the ubiquitous reach of tradition, social custom, and spatial protocol. Even as the fetters of the "*zenana* mentality" were loosened, the zenana remained the dominant spatial, cultural, and emotional frame.

(The *zenana,* from the Persian *zan*—woman—refers to the apartments of a house in which the women of the family are secluded. In spatial or architectural terms, it is the *underoon,* literally the "interior of the house"—the rooms around the inner courtyard, away from the public and the male domain of the house.)

It was only after Partition, in 1947, had sundered irrevocably a geography and a culture, and in the process, a way of life, that women like Attia Hosain were able to maneuver a space of their own, though at tremendous emotional cost. Both Hosain and her stand-in in her novel leave their family homes, exiling themselves to neutral environments. Hosain emigrated to England, where she worked as a broadcaster, actress, and writer. In 1953, she published a collection of short stories, *Phoenix Fled,* that detail episodes from the zenana. *Sunlight on a Broken Column* is her only novel, an account written across the distance effected by time and emigration.

Sunlight on a Broken Column is structured as an autobiography: a girl gives an *account* of her life that is also an *accounting* of herself as well. As she reimagines herself in place, she also attempts to understand her "subjectivity," her place in the world and the position from which she speaks. Hosain reconstructs *Ashiana* (literally, "nest," or "abode"), the house of her childhood, the typical sprawling compound of a Muslim joint-family in pre-Partition India. The first three sections of the book give a chronological description of her life in the house up to her marriage (in 1938), when she leaves Ashiana for her own home. The fourth section breaks and reverses the direction of the narrative flow, returning her to the house for a final visit, five years after Partition and the domestic dispersal that followed it.

This section takes the form of an extended inventory of spaces and events as she wanders, in real time, through the ancestral house, now half empty and partly tenanted by strangers. As she walks through the evacuated rooms, the echoing halls and tarnished mirrors play back and review her life, chapter by chapter, chamber by chamber, performing, as it were, an extended exorcism that readies her for her second, and final, leave-taking.

Whereas in the first three sections the house is her world, subtly shaping and demarcating her experiences, in the final section the house itself takes center stage; it becomes both the drama and the drama's decor. As she drives back through the gates of Ashiana, the shiver of memory produces a rush of emotions that leaves her nauseated. The sheer evocative power of spaces, and the memory of them, transforms the house into an animistic landscape, a stage just abandoned, with the uncanny presence of people who have just left the room, the echo of their footfalls not quite having died away:

> The silence in the house was more disturbing than the signs and smells of being uninhabited through the long summer and the season of the rains. It was not the peaceful silence of emptiness, but as if sounds lurked everywhere, waiting for the physical presence of those who had made them audible.[10]

Every object is both a fetish and documentary evidence, summoning up and summarizing her life: "My most private memories were contained by this house, as much a part of its structure as its every brick and beam."[11] Where memory fetishizes, history forces an objective distancing. The ancestral house becomes simultaneously a haunted burial ground and an archaeological site. After Partition, the house had been declared "evacuee property" and had been "allocated" to refugees from newly created Pakistan. The post-Partition cross-border bartering of property between evacuee and refugee, overseen by bureaucrats, had rendered the house, once so private and guarded, into mere real estate. The house that had formed her, where her subjectivity had come into its own cognizance, now was peopled with strangers and their belongings. The house, "having buried one way of life and accepted another" during Hosain's growing up, had now accommodated yet another.

The interweaving of memories of the house and its sensorial immediacy are crucial to Hosain's reconciliation with herself, with the "girl who haunted me." Unlike the straightforward recounting of the first three sections, the accounting of the final section invests the house with the weight of memory and the weathering of history.

Suleri and Meatless Days

Sara Suleri's memoir, *Meatless Days,* maps the domestic terrain of upper-middle-class nuclear families in post-Partition Pakistan. Suleri retraces herself through a series of houses in different cities where she lived with her sisters, her Welsh expatriate mother, and émigré Pakistani father. (Suleri's father had emigrated from India to newly formed Pakistan after Partition). With her journalist father constantly in and out of jail, Suleri's memories are of a "company of women" very different from the cloistered world of Hosain's zenana.

Yet the relationships, both spatial and familial, that she evokes and invokes are as complex and layered as Hosain's labyrinth. Whereas Hosain frames both the past and present through her ancestral home, the spaces of Suleri's childhood and adolescence constantly seep into her consciousness, reshaping and coloring her present American domicile.

Suleri moved to the United States in the late seventies to continue post-graduate work in English. She now lives and teaches in New Haven. *Meatless Days,* written ten years into her American sojourn, is her attempt to give her memories, and herself, the coherence of plot. Yet, as she herself acknowledges, character has a way of escaping the overdetermination that plot implies. "Daughter, unplot yourself; let be," her mother admonishes Sara, who responds: "But I could not help the manner in which my day was narrative, quite happy to let Mamma be that haunting word at which narrative falls apart."[12]

Suleri's memoirs renounce the clarity and obviousness of a chronological stocktaking. In contrast to Hosain's, they offer an alternate route through the spaces of memory and experience, an indeterminate itinerary looping back and forth in its search for "the sweeter peace of inadvertency and a world less heavy with the expectation of its ability to gratify" with answers.[13] Suleri conjures herself out of parables, allegorical tales, and apocryphal conversations that she reconstructs with and for her immediate family. The nine chapters that make up her book, each revolving around a character, draw upon submerged memories and recall, re-imagine, and re-choreograph scenes, in an attempt to re-member the people, events, and spaces of her life. Bodily metaphors are central to this task, even as she acknowledges the impossibility, the propriety, or even the necessity of a literal re-membrance. Perhaps even more evocatively than Hosain's, Suleri's memoir suggests that while specific spaces may disappear from ones' lives, they live on in the body's memory as it continually shapes itself after the physics of some long-forgotten moment.

The voice of Suleri, the post-colonial diasporic academic, is not the predominant voice in these accounts. Suleri's rhetorical use of everyday detail, and the daily give-and-take of relationships, enables multiple voices and registers to suffuse the spaces she describes. Her accounts startle us with the precision with which she locates the emotional resonance of material things in different cultural situations, as when she notes that for her American boyfriend, a "dining table was so markedly more of a loaded domestic space than was a bed."[14] Combing through the intimacies and cultural entanglements of domestic life, Suleri's memoirs reveal without exposing, and thus, "in a double sense, re-cover the lost."

Part Two

Autobiography, understood as both an object of *and* an apparatus for remembering, offers us a powerful way into the tangled web of memory and space. In the following section, I focus on a few of the many rich instances that these two émigré autobiographies offer. In the spirit of Hannah Arendt's pearl diver, who plucks forgotten fragments off the ocean floor and brings them up to the surface of the present, I am interested in the specificity and density of description that these fragments embody. A full historical or sociological reconstruction or explication is not intended. More narrowly, the sections that follow—on the zenana, *purdah*, and "mixed society" from Hosain; on the "company" of women, the domestic compound, and the gendered space of the mosque from Suleri—begin to trace a psychosocial glossary of subcontinental spaces through the filter of memory within the medium of language.

Selections from Hosain's Sunlight on a Broken Column
THE ZENANA

In precolonial *havelis* (urban residences), the zenana lay within the fabric of the house. During the colonial period, the havelis of the more established feudal families (such as Hosain's) developed an articulated spatial arrangement where the zenana was twinned with the free-standing bungalow, a type that itself had evolved during the early years of the colonial encounter. This grafting of a zenana on to the *bangla* (bungalow) produced a hybrid that reified, through overt spatialization, the class, gender, and cultural distinctions that marked colonial society. The two arenas, while part of a singular domestic regime, had distinctive spatial and social patterns. The public, male, and Westernized "front" of the house had a full complement of formal living and dining rooms, verandahs, front lawns, porches and driveways. The zenana rooms, however, were not articulated by specific function; the diurnal cycle of activities moved its inhabitants from interior halls to large verandahs and on to rooftops or courtyards.

Within this constellation, the zenana was an introverted world, fold-
ed in upon itself, the restrictions giving rise to a parochial dynamic: "Life
within the household, ordained, enclosed, cushioning the mind and heart
against the outside world, indirectly sensed and known, moved back into
its patterned smoothness."[15] The jealousies and frustrations in the "household of women were intangible like invisible webs spun by monstrous,
unseen spiders. And yet, without each other they had no existence" (251).
Hosain's descriptions of life in the house map with precision the spatial and
familial commerce between the two wings: "The day my [spinster] Aunt
Abida moved from the zenana into the guest-room off the corridor that led
to the men's wing of the house, within call of her [ill] father's room, we knew
that Baba Jan had not much longer to live" (14).

Hosain describes the screened corridor that links the "walled *zenana*,
self-contained with its lawns, courtyards, and veranda'd rooms, to the outer
portion of the house" and the old *baithak* (literally "sitting place") that united the two wings of the house where the closest members of the family, of
both sexes, could meet when necessary: "Into this vast room the coloured
planes of the arched doors let in not light but shadows" (18). Hosain describes
the zenana's daily activities, its social protocols, its inhabitants drawn from
an extended network of kinship and social obligations (widows, poorer relatives, and other dependents), and the punctuations in its rhythms marked by
festivals: religious and seasonal, but especially, the two events that transform
it temporarily, marriages and funerals. Marriage is what makes the world of
the zenana spin, both the reason behind the cloistering of women and the
emblem of escape, for it is the event that promises a liberation of sorts:

> The *zenana* stirred and vibrated with movement and noise as
> guests and maid-servants and children and groups of village
> women milled around, their voices raised and shrill with
> excitement. For every woman and girl there was an excuse
> to wear the richest of clothes and jewels. . . . the whole house
> spilled with gem-set colors and throbbed with the rhythm of. . .
> marriage songs . . . and the insistent beat of drums. . . . The elders
> were more curious about [the bride's] dowry . . . displayed in
> [the dowry room]. . . . The only quiet corner was [the bride's]
> room where she was kept in seclusion . . . [all the girls] wanted
> to sit and stare at the bride they would be one day. (113)

The spaces of the zenana are literally cut off from the world. The only views out are from the rooftop and the courtyard, from where one can get a glimpse of the day passing, the light changing, and the sun moving across the sky:

> During the rainy season we used to hang a plank on thick ropes, on the thickest branch of the tallest mango tree, and Zainab would sing the songs of the season, as we swung, with our dopattas streaming behind, high above the walls [of the purdah orchard], looking at the green world stretched out under purple clouded skies. (106)

One gets a sense of this framing from the genre paintings of sub-imperial and provincial courts, with their ever-present embrasures, lintels, arches, and screens. This spatial regime restricts the perspectives of the inhabitants even as it imbues the architectural elements with metaphorical resonance:

> My life changed. It had been restricted by invisible barriers almost as effectively as the physically restricted lives of my aunts in the *zenana*. A window had opened here, a door there, a curtain had been drawn aside; but outside lay a world narrowed by one's field of vision. (180)

PURDAH

The zenana indexes both a particular place and a particular view of one's place in the world. The spatial and cultural codes that governed the life of zenana women extended beyond the zenana itself through the notion of *purdah,* literally "curtain," "veil," or "screen," *covers* that carry with them connotations of secrecy, privacy, and modesty. In Urdu, it is idiomatically very resonant, with multiple phrases describing the subject and object of purdah, and the reciprocal actions of exposure and concealment. While *purdah* may refer to a specific material object (a curtain, for example), Urdu has other words that identify the articles of clothing that effect the operations it implies. More generally, *purdah* indexes a gendered sociospatial formation, a code of conduct, and a specific spatial regime for women.

Like the similar *chador,* literally "sheet," purdah is a central cultural trope. Phrases like *chador aur chaar-divaari* (literally "sheet" and "four walls") very precisely convey the culturally specific notions of the household, carrying within it the feudal understanding of chattel sequestered within defensible boundaries. Hosain's account gives a sense of purdah's multiple invocations. In an instance of its complex protocols, she describes how her aunts did not observe purdah from her grandfather's orientalist English friend, but were "careful that their voices, even the rustling of their clothes, were not heard" by his Indian friends and male relatives (35). Through this acoustical erasure of bodily presence, purdah covers over all evidence of the female body as a sexed object: husbands never speak directly to their wives when in the presence of their elders. And in the zenana, husbands visit their wives in the cover of night, leaving before dawn.[16]

As the colonial cross-cultural encounter produced its own etiquette for social intercourse, purdah began to take on new locutions. Hosain, for example, describes, with delicious irony, the "*purdah* parties" given by the spinster sister of the local Anglican priest:

> The sanctity attached to his profession—and the fact that the Governor attended his church—made it permissible for the highest born, most secluded Indian ladies to attend her *purdah* parties where she ardently established good relations between Indians and the English. So the wives of the Commissioner and District Officers balance their cups of tea, and teetered on the edges of gulfs of silence, with correct, polite smiles on their lips when language failed them, and the Ranis and Begums smiled back with warm unself-consciousness. (49)

MIXED SOCIETY

When Hosain's grandfather dies, her "westernized" uncle, now the head of the family, returns to Ashiana to live. Hosain describes the significant changes in the life of the household that ensued. The zenana was disbanded; spinster aunts were married off and the assortment of relatives relocated to the family house in the village. Because of her uncle's belief in the education of women, Hosain stays on at Ashiana to continue her education at a women's college. As her world opens up, she finds herself doubly estranged, distanced from both the zenana that formed her and the social protocols and "western trappings" of her uncle's milieu.

Her account manifests the self-conscious tensions of her generation as well as that of her uncle's as both negotiate between the social and spatial protocols of different cultures, each attempting to find their own balance. Hosain sketches out the problematics of becoming modern, while remaining traditional, through deft descriptions of cross-cultural transactions. Although she does not question the inherent contradiction, even fallacy, that underlies this complicated desire, she does provide vivid glimpses of its effect on the domestic sphere and, especially, on women. The awkward, halting, and stilted miscegenation is captured in a telling phrase. The new social and spatial protocols of "mixed society" forced open commerce not only between the East and the West but, for the first time, between men and women. While the material texture of the domestic domain changed with the sometimes abrupt accommodation of new fashions of dress, furniture, and architecture, the proprieties and rites of mixed society were not as easily assimilated.

Hosain describes "the gossip of women whose minds remained smothered in the *burqas* [veils] they had outwardly discarded, and the men who met women socially but mentally relegated them to harems and *zenanas*" (207). She describes the desire of husbands to bring their wives *out of* purdah, to be groomed by English lady companions, a transformation of "dutiful *purdah* girls" into "perfect modern wives" that literally reconfigures their bodies: "No more loose shapeless clothes, no more stooping and hunching of shoulders to deny one's body" (141).

This transformation also brings with it an entirely different social and material regime. Hosain describes the changes in the main house after the arrival of her "modern" Aunt Saira: different furnishings, a new corps of servants (lady's ayahs, valets, and butlers, instead of maidservants sent in from the village), new rituals (tea in the living room, formal sit-down dinners at the dining table instead of the nomadic *dastarkhans*—floor spreads—of the zenana), and a different hierarchy of public and private space (the sanctity of her uncle's study, the privacy afforded individual bedrooms as opposed to the flexible, common, and non-function-specific territory of the zenana). The shifting valencies that attach to material objects in cross-cultural commerce are illustrated in Hosain's descriptions of the "taste" in furniture across three generations: her grandfather's, Aunt Saira's, and her own.

Though her grandfather's rooms display an indiscriminate inventory of European objects in the spirit of a big-game hunter displaying hunting trophies, Aunt Saira's rooms are tasteful copies of contemporary English homes:

velvet curtains, linens, crystal and china services, and tasteful prints. Her uncle's study, for example, displays "Raphael's 'Madonna,' 'The Stag at Bay,' 'Dante and Beatrice,' 'Storm at Sea'" (108). The traveled, progressive, "smart set" among Hosain's own generation lives in houses in New Delhi that are "very modern and Western in appearance and convenience, very Indian and ancient in decoration" (295). Here the initial consumption, and later cooption, of Western objects and styles by the previous generations has been substituted by a Western "eye," with tradition transliterated according to a European aesthetics of recuperation. Tradition is reappropriated as heritage by these well-meaning nationalists, unwittingly setting into motion the process of its commodification as "ethnic" style.

Selections from Suleri's Meatless Days
THE COMPANY OF WOMEN

Although there was no zenana, or purdah, in the houses Suleri grew up in, it was a household of women, and it is the relationships among these women (her paternal grandmother, her Welsh mother, and her four sisters) that give her stories a particular South Asian sensibility. "Leaving Pakistan," Suleri says, "was tantamount to giving up the company of women."[17] Suleri's memoirs do not reduce all these women into some abstraction of "woman"; she does not "write" the subcontinental woman. Even as her account inevitably poses the question of her own position as a woman within a specific historical and cultural milieu, she insists upon crafting for herself her own "idiom for alterity." This is difficult territory and Suleri acknowledges it as such. She ventures: "There are no women in the third world" (20):

> The concept of women was not really part of an available vocabulary: we were too busy . . . living and conducting precise negotiations with what it meant to be a sister or a child or a wife or a mother. . . . Once in a while, we thought of ourselves as women, but only in some perfunctory biological way that we happened on perchance. (1)

Suleri's comments frame a warning against a singular reading of "woman" in cross-cultural encounters and, especially, in autobiographical narratives of identity that, by definition, pose and rehearse articulations of the self *against* both familial roles and conventional readings of what it means to be a woman, a third-world woman, a modern woman.

Although space is clearly gendered, it is in culturally specific ways. Even though the "Suleri" women are not cloistered away within a zenana, the space they occupy—the domestic everyday—is the one marked off for women. It is the private sphere of the household where "women are enabled to enter a community among themselves, as a vital collectivity."[18] Suleri describes another instance of a community of women: the walled-off, single-sex college for upper-class women. Kinnaird College for Women, on Jail Road, in Lahore, exemplifies the persistence of the zenana as a powerful, culturally specific, South Asian space, one that informs "modern" and colonial institutions as well:

> The college was indeed on Jail Road, as was the jail, and the race-course, and the lunatic asylum too. All those institutions looked identical, built out of the same colonial red brick in a style that suggested a profusion of archways and verandahs and enclosed gardens, highly walled. Massive thrice-locked gates dotted that potent street. . . . The hostels where the boarders slept . . . were intended by college rule never to be entered by a man, other than at best a father or at worst a sweeper. (47)

The inhabitants of Hosain's zenanas were literally unable to step outside, to look back at their confinement and its physical particularities. Because Suleri and, to a lesser degree, Hosain had the opportunity to move in and out of, and between, secluded zones, they are able to conceive of the delirious draw of such spaces. Suleri describes Kinnaird in the imagination of the citizens of Lahore and the "histrionic terror engendered by its secret locked-up space":

> To the city, after all, Kinnaird signified a magical arena containing a few hundred women of primetime marriage-ability in an architectural embrace. . . . And we who lived on the inside of that idea were caught in that curiously constricting position: we felt imprisoned in the very place we knew represented an area of rampant fantasy in the city's psychic life. Which was more real: we, Kinnaird, on the inside— or the little bits of fantastic longing that drove their traffic outside and around our walls? (48)

THE MASJID SYNDROME

The extended duration of an autobiography privileges a sedimented understanding of cultural commonplaces. In Suleri's account, the mosque is one such topos and she builds up a composite description that captures its multiple spatial, temporal, and cultural registers. For most South Asian Muslims, men and women, and whether practicing or not, the mosque punctuates their daily lives and the landscapes they inhabit to a remarkable degree: the calls to prayer that aurally mark the passing of the day; the calm interiors one passes by that periodically pulse with life, when men leave their houses to pray together in the house of God.

Although women may visit mosques, South Asian custom generally does not allow women to pray in mosques. The following anecdote indexes the various vectors—religious precepts, customary practice, gender distinctions, touristic consumption—that keep the mosque in play in the memories of émigré women like Suleri and Hosain. Suleri describes her interchange with the man at the gate of the Jami Mosque in Delhi:

> Muslim women are not allowed in the mosque between the hours of *maghrib* and *isha*, he told me, so "of course I am not a Muslim," I replied. "Then I'll never let you in," he told me smugly, "because I am the vice-imam." "Then of course I'm a Muslim!" I screamed back. "My grandfather was a Hajji, and my father is a Hajji—he's probably in there now!" It worked as a threat on him as well as it would have on me, and I strode in, undeterred. (81)

The degree to which the spatiality of mosques suffuses Suleri's sense of space cannot be accounted for by the centrality accorded to mosques in South Asian Muslim life. South Asian Muslim women, after all, rarely enter mosques after puberty: for them, the interiors of mosques are where their men go, from which they are absent. And for Suleri, a mixed breed growing up in a not particularly religious household, mosques would have been even more remote and unknown.

Perhaps it is precisely her outsider status that gives her entrée, allowing her to reimagine the space of a mosque and, in the process, inhabit it. "I used to think that it would be refreshing to live in a house that was shaped like a mosque, basing its center on empty space, with a long kitchen where the imam should pray and four turret bedrooms, one for each minaret" (80). Suleri the wayfarer (as tourist, as expatriate) articulates what the native intuitively experiences. She isolates with extraordinary precision the spatial essence of a mosque: space that is empty but is not a void; a "disinterested geometry"; a positive emptiness, one that resonates with the communion that is enacted there:

> If I must mimic the postures of the devout, I think I would
> rather go to a mosque for the odd half-hour and cool my head
> in its geometry of complete disinterest, which warns me that
> I better soon be gone before the courtyard is white with men
> and fallen angels. (80)

The unexpected equivalence she draws between the qualities of domestic spaces and those of mosques is startling until one recognizes the transmutations and conflations that memory produces:

> I always liked to see a vacant space intact—a room disinterested
> in seeming furnished—which surely shows the influence of
> growing up in houses built around courtyards designed in a
> world where people pray in mosques. I still miss it, the necessity
> of openness that puts a courtyard in the middle of a house and
> makes rooms curl around it, so that each bedroom is but a door
> away from the seclusion of the sky. (174)

Suleri's father's world-weary declaration (after his wife's death)—"Take me to a masjid; just let me live like a holy man"—and its subsequent absorption into the family's private idiom, illustrates the complexity of the mosque as a figure. Suleri's father uses it as a trope for renunciation, for leaving worldly concerns behind. His daughters, however, tuned to different cultural registers, hear instead the "preposterous" presumption implicit in his hyperbole: "For years we used the phrase, 'it's the old masjid syndrome', to characterize his, and our own, excesses of self-sorrow" (80).

THE COMPOUND
The word *compound* has a particularly rich set of spatial significations in Indian life. While the word's origins can be traced to different sources, a

derivation from the Malay *kampung* seems most probable. The type itself arose in the Malay archipelago, in the early eighteenth century, where it denoted the enclosed outposts and "factories" within which the mercantile and missionary activities of the colonial enterprise resided. The space of the "compound" has a ring of self-sufficiency to it, an expansive world, secure behind its four walls, very different from the stand-alone and fully exposed individual house of the Anglo-American suburbs. Originally, *compound* referred to the "enclosed ground, whether garden or wasted space, which surrounds an Anglo-Indian house."[19] Its more common usage implies a spatially coextensive relation between a house and the space that surrounds it, the two together as a single social, territorial, and affective unit.

Suleri reconstructs the emotional and physical landscape of the compound, specifically the single-family compounds her upper-class family lived in while she was growing up. Because her family moved with some frequency, the houses serve as the coordinates of another way of ordering eras and measuring history: "The family moved from the Fowler Lines house in Karachi to the 23-H Gulberg house in Lahore, and then to 9-T Gulberg, from where Papa went to jail, which moved us back to Karachi, and finally to London to live in Chiswick" (94).

Even though in its current suburban iteration the compound has devolved into little more than a big box penned in between four walls, arrayed along the arbitrary grids of anonymous subdivisions, in Suleri's accounts it retains the territoriality implicit in the feudal chaar-divaaris of Hosain's world. And whereas the joint-family has given way to the nuclear family, an extended community still inhabits these compounds: maidservants, cooks, night watchmen, "drivers," widowed grandmothers all move through and stake their claims to their portions of it.

Suleri's memoirs resurrect the structure of such a place, and of a day in that place: Dadi "painstakingly dragging her straw mat out to the courtyard at the back of the house and following the rich course of the afternoon sun"; Mother "in the garden after the ferocity of the summer sun watering the driveway . . . the heady smell of water on hot dust"; the sisterly intimacy of an afternoon "chitchat bed"; teatime with the whole family congregated on Papa's bed; reading on a monsoon verandah or on the lawn in the winter sun; asleep on a "sweet-smelling *nivar* rope bed" on the roof on a summer night.

Suleri's account is dense with the texture of lived space. From it we can glean the surfaces of an architecture placed directly in the path of everyday life. There are moments where Suleri choreographs an entire sequence, incorporating into the scene movements of the body, material artifacts, a voice, a setting, and the memory of it. It is in moments such as these that we see the full scope of autobiographical revisioning, the polish and gleam that is the handiwork of memory:

> Some holiday mornings I would not wake to the sound of my mother calling up my name but instead to the sound of her privacy with some piece of music. . . . There was always some filial obligation that she paid in the pleasure she took to sit down at his [her father's] piano, so when I stood at the top of the stairs and watched her play, I could see her spine swaying with loyalty. . . . I would slowly go down the stairs, measuring my steps to the weaving movement of her body. . . . She was paying a compliment to some lost moment of her life, and I felt startled to observe such privacy. (162)

Memory for the émigré is a constant ebb and flow between such willed forgetting and willed remembering. Suleri recalls how after a few years in her new home in the flat vastness of the American Midwest, and after the desolation following her mother's and sister's violent deaths, she woke up one morning to find that "my mind had completely ejected the names of all the streets in Pakistan, as though to assure that I could not return or that if I did, it would be to loss" (18). And she recalls her own grandmother's phrase, in response to the trauma of Partition and emigration and the rupture of memory and geography that it entailed: "The world takes on a single face" (6).

Yet the tenacity of our sense of place is such that it ensures its survival, attaching itself to sounds, to smells, and even to particular physiognomies. Memories of her family members evoke particular contexts, lending significance to their features: "And it is still difficult to think of Ifat without remembering her peculiar congruence with Lahore, a place that gave her pleasure. 'It's blossom-time and nargis-time', she wrote to me in her last letter, 'and what a lovely city it is—a veritable garden'"(181).

I would like to close by speculating upon the parallels between the effort of crafting an appropriate idiom for remembering and the designer's struggle to read and enunciate space. As the preceding discussion suggests, telling the story of a life is not a matter of simple narration. In the retelling, the space and time of a life are produced anew. "Time, as it were, thickens, takes on flesh. . . . Space becomes charged and responsive to the movements of time, plot, and history."[20] It is not just in the space of the literal descriptions but in their *literariness*—the architecture of the writing, the effort of facturing description—where the lessons lie. As designers we always move, however implicitly, from our own experiences of space, as we reimagine others. The designing "I" is a many-layered thing. In the course of our lives, in some aspect or another, we are all simultaneously "placed" and "displaced." The disassembling and reassembling of the autobiographical subject mirrors the design process; both are "inherently dialogic [in their] inevitable orientation towards *another*."[21]

Memory is not just a matter of inventory, a simple record of direct experiences. The work of memory is as discursive as it is culturally specific, as it works through language to shape and reshape itself. What these two autobiographies offer to the designer is a glimpse into the stylistics of memory, in how a subject narrates herself and her worlds. The style employed in articulating oneself is "inextricable from an implicit politics, from an intensely particular view of the world, for any particular person, and is itself a product of a unique nexus of class, race, gender, and other socio-cultural accidents."[22] Reading Suleri and Hosain brings home the centrality of rhetorical choice to constructions of the world, whether in the luminous world of memory or in the clear light of the everyday.

Notes

1. Paul Antze, "Forecasting Memory," in *Tense Past: Cultural Essays in Trauma and Memory*, by Antze (New York: Routledge, 1996), xi.
2. Ibid., xv.
3. Ibid., xiii.
4. James Clifford, *Routes: Travel and Translation in the Late Twentieth Century* (Cambridge, Mass.: Harvard University Press, 1997), 3.

5. Samir Dayal, "Style Is (Not) the Woman," in *Between the Lines: South Asians and Postcoloniality,* ed. Deepika Bahri (Philadelphia: Temple University Press, 1996), 256.

6. Carolyn Barros, *Autobiography: Narrative of Transformation* (Ann Arbor: University of Michigan Press, 1998), 2.

7. Naomi Schor, *Reading in Detail: Aesthetics and the Feminine* (New York: Methuen, 1987), 4.

8. See Richard Cronin, *Imagining India* (New York: St. Martin's Press, 1989), 4. Unlike the subcontinental narratives of Salman Rushdie, Hosain and Suleri do not explicitly problematize their writing in English. Rushdie, among others, self-consciously forges an idiom for an Indian English in order to legitimize its status both as a form of English (on par with "American" or "Australian") as well as an Indian language (on par with Hindi, Bengali, etc.). This strategy, for example, gives the autobiographical conceit of *Midnight's Children* a pan-Indian scope, drawing upon an understanding of English as the only "Indian" language that does not "confer on the [Indian] writer a regional identity," in the way that writing in Hindi, or Bengali, or Tamil, inevitably does.

9. See Barbara Metcalf, "What Happened in Mecca: Mumtaz Mufti's Labbaik," in *The Culture of Autobiography,* ed. Robert Folkenflik (Stanford: Stanford University Press, 1993), 154–56. Barbara Metcalf, in her study of Muslim pilgrimage narratives, suggests that biographical writing in Urdu and Persian emphasizes the givenness of "personality" over its chronological, and self-generated, development. Biographies, she says, are occasions "for showing contexts within which [personal] qualities manifest" themselves; in this scheme there rarely are "radical breaks in self-perception," epiphanies, or conversions. In Hosain's and Suleri's accounts, there is something of the anecdotal structure of *hikaayaat* ("tales") or *malfuzaat* ("table-talk"), genres that illuminate "a personality from different angles . . . like a prism, held up to the light of multiple contexts so that its constant characteristics are revealed."

10. Attia Hosain, *Sunlight on a Broken Column* (first published in Great Britain by Chatto & Windus, 1961; repr. New York: Viking Penguin, 1988), 275.

11. Ibid., 272.

12. Sara Suleri, (Chicago: University of Chicago Press, 1989), 157.

13. Ibid., 79.

14. Ibid., 37.

15. Hosain, *Sunlight,* 59. All subsequent references to this novel in this section are indicated in the text with a parenthetical page number.

16. During the extended rituals of the marriage ceremony, the twinning of objectification and erasure are enacted in the elaborate ceremony of "seeing" the face of the bride (the bride sits unmoving under a heavy

veil of flowers as guests come and part it to catch a glimpse of her face) and at the moment when the groom enters the zenana (after her siblings collect a "tariff") and sees the bride for the first time (under the cover of a sheet, and with the help of a candle and a mirror, the two exchange indirect glances).

17. Suleri, *Meatless Days,* 1. All subsequent references to this novel in this section are indicated in the text with a parenthetical page number.
18. Dayal, "Style," 225.
19. A. C. Burnell and Henry Yule, *Hobson-Jobson: A Glossary of Colloquial Anglo-Indian Words and Phrases, and of Kindred Terms, Etymological, Historical, Geographical and Discursive* (1886; repr. Calcutta: Rupa & Company, 1994), 240.
20. Michael Holquist, *The Dialogic Imagination* (Austin: University of Texas Press, 1981), 84.
21. Terry Eagleton, *Literary Theory: An Introduction* (Minneapolis: University of Minnesota, 1983), 117.
22. Dayal, "Style," 264.

∞

Bibliography

Ali, Meer Hassan. *Observations on the Mussalmauns of India.* 1832. Repr., Karachi: Oxford University Press, 1978. This edition first published in 1917.

Antze, Paul. *Tense Past: Cultural Essays in Trauma and Memory.* New York: Routledge, 1996.

Ashcroft, Bill. *Key Concepts in Post-Colonial Studies.* London: Routledge, 1998.

Bahloul, Joelle. *The Architecture of Memory.* Originally published in French as *La maison de mémoire,* in 1992. Repr., Cambridge, UK: Cambridge University Press, 1996.

Bahri, Deepika, ed. *Between the Lines: South Asians and Postcoloniality.* Philadelphia: Temple University Press, 1996.

Barros, Carolyn. *Autobiography: Narrative of Transformation.* Ann Arbor: University of Michigan Press, 1998.

Burnell, A. C., and Henry Yule. *Hobson-Jobson: A Glossary of Colloquial Anglo-Indian Words and Phrases, and of Kindred Terms, Etymological, Historical, Geographical and Discursive.* 1886. Repr., Calcutta: Rupa & Company, 1994.

Clifford, James. *Routes: Travel and Translation in the Late Twentieth Century.* Cambridge, Mass.: Harvard University Press, 1997.

Cronin, Richard. *Imagining India.* New York: St. Martin's Press, 1989.

Dayal, Samir. "Style Is (Not) the Woman." In *Between the Lines: South Asians and Postcoloniality,* ed. Deepika Bahri, 250–69. Philadelphia: Temple University Press, 1996.

Eagleton, Terry. *Literary Theory: An Introduction.* Minneapolis: University of Minnesota, 1983.

Ferozsons. *Ferozsons Urdu-English dictionary; Urdu Words, Phrases and Idioms with English Meanings and Synonyms.* Lahore: Ferozsons, 1980.

Folkenflik, Robert, ed. *The Culture of Autobiography.* Stanford: Stanford University Press, 1993.

Holquist, Michael. *The Dialogic Imagination.* Austin: University of Texas Press, 1981.

Hosain, Attia. *Sunlight on a Broken Column.* First published in Great Britain by Chatto & Windus, in 1961. Repr., New York: Viking Penguin, 1988.

Metcalf, Barbara. "What Happened in Mecca: Mumtaz Mufti's Labbaik." In *The Culture of Autobiography,* ed. Robert Folkenflik, 149–67. Stanford: Stanford University Press, 1993.

Nabokov, Vladimir. *Speak, Memory.* New York: Vintage Books, 1989.

Schor, Naomi. *Reading in Detail: Aesthetics and the Feminine.* New York: Methuen, 1987.

Seizer, Susan. "Paradoxes of Visibility in the Field: Rites of Queer Passage in Anthropology." *Public Culture* 8, no. 1 (fall 1995): 73–100.

Sharar, Abdul Halim. *Lucknow: The Last Phase of an Oriental Culture.* Trans. E. S. Harcourt and Fakhir Hussain. London: Paul Elek, 1975.

Suleri, Sara. *Meatless Days.* Chicago: University of Chicago Press, 1989.

chapter six

Memory and Diaspora in Tel Aviv's Old Cemetery

BARBARA MANN

*If I forget thee O exile, may my right hand
lose its cunning.*
—epigraph to *The Book of Tel Aviv
Street Names* (1944)

Part One: The Old Cemetery, Mourning, and Sites of Memory

A photograph of Achad Ha'am's funeral in 1927, in Tel Aviv's Old Cemetery on Trumpeldor Street: Amidst a group of people surrounding the fresh grave, the poet Ch. N. Bialik[1] eulogizes the ideological mentor of a generation of young eastern European Jewish intellectuals. Most of them look at the grave or one another. Some are in uniform, police or officials of some sort. Bialik is at the center of the photograph; he looks into the camera with an expression of fatigue and sadness—an eastern European Jew, wearing a heavy coat over a nondescript suit, with a modest cap on his head, standing by a freshly dug grave, in the dunes of the Trumpeldor Cemetery. More panoramic photographs of the ceremony show that the grave is located in the Cemetery's newer section, surrounded largely by sand, a few other graves, and some spare, newly planted shrubbery. The dark suits

FIG. 6.1. *Ch. N. Bialik eulogizes Achad Ha'am in the Trumpeldor Cemetery, 1927. Courtesy of the Historical Museum of Tel Aviv–Jaffa.*

of the crowd, their European dress, contrast sharply against the bareness of the place, the emptiness of the dunes, the dirt, the stone wall of the Cemetery looming in the background, the large, triangular stone of a mass grave strongly visible on the horizon. What is most affecting, however, about this particular photograph, is the result of a belated, surreptitious knowledge: Bialik stands in almost precisely the spot where he will be buried seven years later. His fatigue seems more than simply grief for his friend and mentor, almost a kind of surrender, an admission, but of what precisely? Is he simply tired of standing in the center of yet another photograph?

It is the nature of photography that the viewer often possesses some knowledge of the world outside the frame that those within the photograph lack. This is especially the case with photographs of historic events, where the retrospective knowledge of hindsight produces belated, unconscious judgments regarding the photograph's subjects, who themselves appear

FIG. 6.2. *General view of the Cemetery during Achad Ha'am's funeral. Courtesy of the Historical Museum of Tel Aviv–Jaffa.*

oblivious to future events. This photograph, however, disturbs this knowledge, and the viewer's sense of power, in that Bialik's fatigued expression seems almost a premonition of his death. The photograph of Bialik standing awkwardly upon his own "final resting place" profoundly unsettles the notion of death as "at peace." It also complicates the association contained within the Hebrew terms for graveyard—a "house of graves" *(beit-kvarot)* or an "eternal home" *(beit-olam)*—between the cemetery and home. The photograph links these two oscillating and unresolved relations—death as *not* rest/cemetery as *not* home. Its early Tel Aviv historical setting—and the centrally defining roles played by Bialik and Achad Ha'am in the creation of modern Hebrew culture—implicitly raises the contradiction of creating something that is at once radically new, and a home. In this, the Trumpeldor Cemetery is emblematic of Tel Aviv's own repeated and paradoxical attempts to be a "home" for modern Hebrew culture.

The Cemetery was founded during the 1902 cholera epidemic in Jaffa, when Ottoman officials prohibited burial of the dead within the city walls. Jewish community leaders requested an alternative and were granted permission to purchase land in what was then called "the Lands of North Jaffa." According to one story, the area consisted largely of shifting sand, and was difficult to cultivate because of these rough topographical conditions.[2] Legend also has it that sacred books were buried in a special grave and two "black weddings" were held at the site in an effort to gain God's favor and halt the epidemic.[3] Only five years later was the plan to build a modern Jewish neighborhood outside of Jaffa announced, a plan that led, in 1909, to the founding of Achuzat Bayit, the neighborhood that eventually became Tel Aviv. In essence, then, Tel Aviv began with its dead. In the words of one historian, "the city followed its graves."[4] That cemetery, known as "the Old Cemetery," is today situated at Tel Aviv's geographic center, a walled-in pastoral patch occupying prime real estate in a desirable location—an uncanny reminder of the city's distance from a diasporic home. Jewish tradition, however, insists on an intimate connection between the very idea of burial in "the Land of Israel" and homecoming—a motif stretching from the biblical story of the Cave of the Patriarchs to the contemporary desire of Jews living abroad to be buried in Israel. The Trumpeldor Cemetery has a unique relation to modern Hebrew culture's historical attempts to be "at home" in Palestine, being the resting place of key figures in early Hebrew culture, including Max Nordau, Ch. N. Bialik, Achad Ha'am and Meir Dizengoff.[5] It is, in other words, a virtual mapping of modern Hebrew culture. Ironically, however, the Trumpeldor Cemetery inverts the traditional relationship between burial and homecoming; the Cemetery's exposed location, and the fact that its existence predates the city itself, rendered it a constant reminder of *not* being at home, and of an instability at odds with the longevity of the diasporic Jewish cemeteries with which it was explicitly compared.

Therefore, another important dimension should be added to this narrative: that is, an understanding of the Old Cemetery as a "site of memory," in Pierre Nora's terms, as a place where "memory crystallizes and secretes itself."[6] Though Nora's specific context is modern French society, his formulation of the fundamental rift between history and memory has influenced a wide range of humanistic studies. Whereas history has conventionally been seen as dependent upon, even an extension of memory,[7] Nora sees history and memory as fundamentally irreconcilable, the former even responsible for destroying the latter.[8] For Nora, memory was once local, communal, organic, spontaneous, at once connected to tradition and an imperceptible part of daily life; it was affective, magical, sacred, and absolute. History, on the other hand, is monumental, imposed, constructed, invented, oriented toward the future and the idea of progress; it is intellectual, secular, prosaic, and relative.[9] The industrial age's destruction of what Nora argues were once "authentic" environments of memory led to the production of "sites of memory." These sites include actual commemorative places, such as memorials, monuments, and museums, as well as archives, state-sanctioned holidays, calendars, and other forms of textual representation. Nora views the rise of both historiography and an acutely historical consciousness as further evidence of the gap between modernity's present self and the past: for example, as peasant culture dissolved, the discipline of social history appeared to catalogue its disappearance.

Although we may quibble with the potentially idealized nature of Nora's once-authentic and now irretrievably lost memory, as well as the necessarily debilitating effects of history, his essential distinctions are both provocative and valuable. Memory's power as a stable, coherent concept that seems to preserve aspects of the past is in fact enhanced by its apposite construction, that is, the passage of time and the concept of history. That this is true for the Old Cemetery becomes particularly clear when you consider its location—the center of Tel Aviv's hectic, ever-metamorphosing downtown. Yet suggesting that a graveyard functions as a site of memory might seem a bit axiomatic, what with its abundant and transparent mix of spatial parameters and textual cues. If this were so, then the Old Cemetery would naturally function as a kind of outdoor museum, a mnemonic space through which the visitor moved and activated images linked to a collective memory.[10] One famous example of an urban cemetery functioning in such a fashion is Paris's Père Lachaise, memorialized in Balzac's novels. This mini-neighborhood of the dead, sprawling over a hill to the east of the city center, even has its own Metro stop.[11] Numerous volumes extol the history of the site, the record of which extends back to the year 418.[12] Père Lachaise's authority is thus constituted both discursively, in canonical literary works and historical studies, as well as geographically, on the urban grid.

The degree of authority stemming from these European cemeteries is hardly the case for Tel Aviv's Old Cemetery, which contains no less significant a gathering of local heroes. The Cemetery receives scant, almost cursory, mention in most standard written accounts of the city, including local histories and guides in Hebrew, as well as tourist guidebooks in English. My own informal survey of pedestrians in the streets surrounding the Cemetery, conducted over a number of years, revealed that most people don't know where it is or who was buried there. I myself come to the Cemetery, and to Tel Aviv as a whole, as a relative outsider, having lived in the neighborhood for four years, from 1988 to 1992. In my frequent visits to the city since, I have returned to the Cemetery, observing the minimal changes in landscaping and the occasional new grave. In contrast to the surrounding, rapidly escalating skyline, it sometimes seems that the Old Cemetery on Trumpeldor is the only spot in Tel Aviv that remains static and relatively untouched. This is not to argue against change, and in favor of a kind of fossilized, "nostalgic" view of the city's origins; neither am I expressly interested here in defending or attacking plans for the city's development as a cultural and economic center, or the preservation of its older neighborhoods. However, *from its inception,* Tel Aviv's sense of itself as a city has been characterized precisely by these two sensibilities—nostalgia and outsiderness. Literary and artistic expression in the city has even capitalized on the creative tension between the two: nostalgia for the founding vision of Tel Aviv as an intimate "Garden City" by the sea[14]—an express rejection of the crowded Jewish quarters of the Diaspora's urban centers—mingled with ambivalent memories of the cultural and social achievements of these metropolises—a feeling of outsiderness in a place where, for much of the city's history, most of its inhabitants were born elsewhere.

Not only is the Cemetery itself virtually ignored, but once inside, it is not an easy place to find your way around in. Though landscaping in the main areas is maintained, there is no map at the Cemetery's entrance, nor a brochure detailing the "who's who" or providing an official history.[15] The visitor is left to wander freely among the graves, following the path where there is one, treading carefully between the stones where, more often, there isn't. The lack of a didactic context is at noticeable odds with the overtly historicized and landmarked nature of so much of the Israeli landscape; this is perhaps because many of the famous personalities buried there are already overly inscribed elsewhere in the national collective memory—in educational curricula and in the numerous streets and buildings named after them. Perhaps one can hardly expect the Cemetery to become a kind of leisure park or touristic site like American urban cemeteries, given the centrality of mourning in Israeli society. Yet other Israeli cemeteries attract both touristic and local

FIG. 6.3. *Panoramic view of the Trumpeldor Cemetery today, near the center of Tel Aviv's downtown. Photo by Barbara Mann.*

attention, Mount Herzl being the most salient example (more on this subject in "Part Two: The Text of the Cemetery").[16]

The relative lack of public or literary discourse about the Cemetery on Trumpeldor Street is emblematic of Tel Aviv's difficult relationship to its past. For example, since the closure of the Municipality Museum, the city has no museum devoted exclusively to its own history, effectively erasing from the space of the city any institutionalized symbolic representation of its past. (The collection housed in the former Municipality on Bialik Street near the Cemetery has been closed for a number of years and there are no definitive plans regarding its renovation.) Even the official material handed out by the tourist information desk at the Municipality devotes only a single page to several important sites in the history of Tel Aviv, focusing mainly on the city's current nightlife, shopping, and beachfront activities. Recently, with the ninetieth anniversary of the city's founding, numerous exhibits, a spate of glossy volumes on the city's distinctive architecture, as well as vigorous public debate

FIG. 6.4. *A plaque describing the Trumpeldor Cemetery's historical significance— "The First Cemetery," in Hebrew and in English—discarded in a corner next to burial stretchers. Photo by Barbara Mann.*

regarding preservation and the quality of life in the city are a welcome indication that Tel Aviv has begun to recognize the degree to which its past must be productively integrated into its present.

Still, the enigma of the Cemetery remains untapped. On the one hand, we might say that the Old Cemetery thus functions as a site of memory only *in potentia,* as a kind of structuring absence, whose boundaries may define and enclose an important part of Israeli history, but whose actual presence and significance have yet to be addressed. On the other hand, the Cemetery has in a sense leaped over, or skipped, the more obvious, explicit processes and signs of commemoration and memorialization, arriving directly at what is perhaps the ultimate function of a site of memory, that is—*forgetting.*

What precisely is at stake in this forgetting, and what happens when we allow the Cemetery's own fragmentary textual history to remember? Memory speaks in unpredictable and uncontrollable ways. In giving voice to the Cemetery's textual history, I seek to understand what is unmanageable about the site, and the experiences buried and forgotten within.

Part Two: The Text of the Cemetery

A review of early documents relating to the Cemetery, and an examination of its tombstone inscriptions, augments its potential as a site of memory. For example, a short article from 1922 views the Cemetery as deserving of preservation and upkeep. In conjunction with another piece about tree planting in the city, Y. Segel, Tel Aviv's municipal gardener, urges protecting the graves from the surrounding sands with tamarisk trees. In this way, the "remnants of the past," which characterize the graves' iconic motifs, making the Cemetery worthy of the title *"beit kvarot yehudi antik,"* (ancient Jewish cemetery) may be preserved. Segel also warns against the imposition of "modish" cement gravestones,

> those enormous, clamorous stones, decorated with all kinds of
> irrelevant ornaments, like pictures, photographs of the dead
> beneath a glass frame on the gravestone, and all other sorts of
> customs lacking in taste or tradition, which spoil the cemetery's
> quiet, innocent appearance, lovely in its simplicity.[17]

Segel wishes to maintain the Cemetery in a manner reflecting the values of the community it serves: simplicity, hygiene, respect for the past, and a connection to Jewish tradition.[18] Though photographs were a relatively new addition, tombstone portraits of the dead were not, and can be found on graves in older Jewish cemeteries as well. The attachment to tradition, and the puritanism regarding visual expression, may seem surprising given Tel Aviv's secular aspirations. However, this antiornamental view is in keeping with Tel Aviv's strongly minimalist, modernist cultural sensibility, which found expression in urban planning and architecture as well as in literature.

Segel's article expresses no explicit concern for the Cemetery as a site that could bolster Tel Aviv's meager historical foundations. However, aesthetic discriminations regarding tombstone styles are at the heart of the first study to champion the Cemetery as a historical site, a volume that remains the only comprehensive study of the cemetery—*Sefer Beyt Ha-kvarot Ha-yashan* (*The Book of the Old Cemetery;* 1939). This rare volume contains a biographical listing of everyone buried in the Cemetery (3,758 at the time of printing), complete with tombstone inscriptions, a statistical breakdown according to gender, age, and year of death, and photographs of some of the more elaborate tombstones. In the extensive introduction, editors Zvi Kroll and Zadok Leinman distinguish between the various groupings of graves in the Cemetery—the famous and the anonymous; newer mass graves and the older, less orderly sections; children; and cholera victims—distinctions that remain helpful in navigating one's way around the Cemetery.

Kroll and Leinman particularly emphasize the stylistic differences among the various "generations" of graves. The placement of the Cemetery's earliest graves—those who died during the cholera epidemic in Jaffa—is disorderly and nonsymmetrical. Their tombstones, typical of Jewish cemeteries of the East, are laid flush to the earth, often covered by marble engraved with biblical verses or devotional acrostics. Despite their haphazard arrangement, and their structural "primitiveness," these stones, according to the editors, demonstrate a "stylistic unity" that is authentically rooted in a specifically Jewish version of the local. Their appreciation of the stones' native qualities parallels views expressed by early Hebrew painters in Palestine, who looked to ancient synagogue mosaics as a model for a new, authentically Hebrew art, in opposition to what they perceived as a diasporic Jewish sensibility. The Cemetery's newer tombstones, those constructed since 1922, stand upright, in the style of European cemeteries. "Modernization," according to the editors, has "overcome" these graves; the text upon their stones is "repetitive" and "empty of content."[19] The editors also comment on the brevity of the newest inscriptions, often consisting of just a name and years: "Of course this is the taste of the new generation, at the bottom of which is a desire to be free of the repetitiveness of the accepted formula."[20]

These distinctions between the earlier and later graves point to the ideological investment of the editors' judgment, an evaluation rooted in their conception of iconic and textual authenticity; the modernity of the later graves is viewed as empty and meaningless, and connected specifically to the Diaspora. Ironically, however, the editors measure their own efforts against the example of European Jewish cemeteries; the main line of scholarly inquiry followed by studies of those cemeteries concerns the broken, aging grave-stones, and their chief methodological challenge lay in a traditional Jewish realm—textual interpretation, that is, "deciphering" the writing upon the stones, thereby establishing the nature of the Jewish community in which these scholars lived and died. Those studies sought to demonstrate a coherent con-tinuity throughout the generations of Jewish dead. However, the editors of the *Book* declare:

> Research alone is neither fitting nor sufficient in regard to the Old Cemetery in Tel Aviv, whether because of the brief span of its exis-tence—though called the "old" cemetery, it is only 38 years old—or due to the impoverished content of the gravestones. The place lacks the antiquities of the distant, unknown past and even the passage between periods is not palpable.[21]

The idea that no majestic, historical process may be decoded in the Old Cemetery—even the passage from period to period is not palpable—was perceived as a complementary mark of Tel Aviv's newness. The relative shallowness of Tel Aviv's roots is its attraction: there is a touch of defen-sive pride in the editors' insistence on the need for a method unlike that used to study Jewish cemeteries in the Diaspora, and in their proclamation of the "impoverished" state of their own cemetery. Instead of the grand genealogy of European graveyards, the Old Cemetery's noteworthy are figures from the present,

> [the] builders of the city of Tel Aviv. . . . The impression of their deeds and activities . . . are still greatly felt in the atmosphere of our time—as if they were still with us, living and working. . . . The history of their lives and actions is the gravestone of a living generation which we knew, and to whom the connection is still unsevered.[22]

History, the record of events over time, is described as an ossified artifact—a gravestone—that can be tangibly observed in space. The feeling that the dead are "still with us" deflects attention from actual grave markers: the fresh memory of their deeds obviates the need for extensive tombstone

FIG. 6.5. *Zdunska-Wola Memorial: a piece of Jerusalem in Tel Aviv.*
Photo by Barbara Mann.

inscription. This paucity of textual inscription in the Cemetery as a whole, its stylistic minimalism, distinguishes it from diasporic Jewish cemeteries.[23]

Despite the *Book*'s modernist preference for "the stone itself," the Trumpeldor Cemetery is characterized by a jumble of styles. With the exception of certain cross-cultural motifs—the candelabra, the charity box, Sabbath candles, or a pair of hands raised in blessing—Jewish funerary iconography seems to be more connected to local, ethnic, or national context than to any set of legalistic dictums.[24] However, visiting the Cemetery today, one can't help but notice one enormous stone that does not fit any of the editors' categories, and seems to violate the uneasy aesthetic coexistence achieved among the disparate gravestone styles.

Towering above its eastern section, it is the Cemetery's most textual stone: a large rectangular monument built in memory of people who died far from Tel Aviv, and whose ashes were brought to Israel—the Jewish community of the Polish town of Zdunska-Wola.[25] Erected in 1950 by a group of Holocaust survivors, the reflective black marble slab with raised gold lettering is surrounded by a low wall of white marble, upon which are engraved the names and familial connections of the victims, entire families with ten and twelve children. Buried in this spot are ashes brought from the crematoria in Chelmno to Israel by Zelig Frankel, a native of the town. The stone's main text is a series of rhymed couplets describing the virtue of the victims, the brutality of their death, and their commemoration by survivors. The stone's monumental presence disrupts the cemetery's horizon, which otherwise stretches out at a fairly even height and in an almost uniformly pale gray and sandstone palette. This physical disparity highlights the incongruity of the stone in this setting—its dense and lyrical text, as well as the people and event it commemorates.

Generally speaking, shoah memorials in Israel may be understood in relation to the national narrative of *"shoah ve-g'vura"* (shoah and heroism), which emphasized the redemptive building of the Jewish state in the wake of the destruction of European Jewry. Jerusalem provides the most instructive example of how shoah and heroism are linked together in an urban space, where the Holocaust Museum *(Yad Vashem)* is located immediately next to Mount Herzl, an enormous military cemetery containing the graves of Israeli prime ministers, including, most recently, that of Yitzhak Rabin. Together with religious sites such as the Western Wall and the Old City, these civic-sacred sites—Yad Vashem and Mount Herzl—reinforce Jerusalem's special status in Jewish and Israeli history. Indeed, Yad Vashem and Mount Herzl often host national ceremonies, and are visited jointly, and in didactic sequence, on touristic itineraries.

The meaning of shoah memorials is generated largely by the landscape within which they are situated.[26] Israeli shoah memorials often represent the discontinuity of the shoah vis-à-vis the Israeli landscape, what might be called, after Momik, the child narrator of David Grossman's *See Under: Love,* its essential "Over Thereness." This "elsewhereness" of the shoah is a constitutive force in the form and shape of its Israeli commemoration. Thus Israeli shoah memorials generally, and Yad Vashem in particular, "build Europe within Israel."[27] However, although in Jerusalem the shoah is commemorated through these state institutions, its presence is more palpable as a matter of daily experience in Tel Aviv, where a higher percentage of the residents are survivors. In a sense, the monumental nature of the Zdunska-Wola Memorial "builds Jerusalem in Tel Aviv." Its inclusion in the Trumpeldor Cemetery troubles the degree to which this kind of memorialization of the shoah is a "natural" element of the Israeli landscape.[28] At the same time, it points to the difficulty of assimilating the trauma of the shoah to the triumphal narrative of "the first Hebrew city."

The Zdunska-Wola Memorial, and the events that it represents, may also be understood in relation to another important distinguishing feature of the Trumpeldor Cemetery vis-à-vis Israeli cemeteries generally. The Trumpeldor Cemetery has no military section, and contains few of the conventional markers of heroism and national sacrifice associated with death and mourning in Israel.[29] The presence of both shoah and *g'vura* (heroism) are thus quite muted in the Trumpeldor Cemetery, an exceptional quality indicative of the different ways in which Tel Aviv and Jerusalem mark and memorialize history.

Though constructed years after the *Book*'s publication, the possibility of the Zdunska-Wola Memorial was anticipated by its editors. Kroll and Leinman refer to events unfolding in Europe as the context for a morbid logic: just as Jewish life in Palestine is meant to commemorate, or even substitute for Jewish life in Europe, so this spot marking Jewish *death* honors the European Jewish dead.[30] Although they envision the Cemetery as a future landmark that will serve as a stable, bounded site of memory, the *Book* itself will also serve as a bulwark against forgetting, "come the day that no one will remember [Tel Aviv's] youth, her founding and the process of her growth."[31] In the closing paragraphs of their introduction, the editors plead with the public to maintain the Old Cemetery, and not to allow it to fall into disrepair. In a remarkably self-aware moment,[32] they imagine the future preservation of the Trumpeldor Cemetery as precisely the type of cultural landmark that Tel Aviv needs. No longer necessary as a functioning cemetery—a new site having been built in 1932 in *Nachalat Yitzhak*—the Old Cemetery, Tel Aviv's most "precious archives" (Kroll and Leinman 1939: xiii), should however be maintained in some fashion, because it represents the only authentic historical claim to roots that Tel Aviv can make, slim as it may be. Perhaps they imagined a role for it akin to that of the Old Jewish Cemetery in Prague, whose "characteristic, unique and wholly inimitable atmosphere . . . often nourished by the dramatic destinies of deceased inhabitants of the ghetto, soon found a place for itself in numerous myths, legends, literary works and paintings."[33] In this scenario, the Cemetery functions as an inert presence, a site that can be referred to in coherent,

FIG. 6.6. *Mass grave for victims of 1921 disturbances, including Y. Ch. Brenner. Photo by Barbara Mann.*

stable fashion, and inserted whole cloth into a variety of cultural discourse. To the relatively minimal extent that the Cemetery figures in subsequent discourse about Tel Aviv, this is in fact the case; the same set of legendary circumstances and anecdotes appear in almost standardized formulation. The Cemetery has become a kind of limited trope, offering a conveniently monumentalized version of the city's founding. Indeed, walking through the Old Cemetery today, it seems that select elements of Tel Aviv's history, and by extension, the history of modern Hebrew culture in Palestine, have been physically preserved. The dead carry on a kind of impossible postmortem conversation amongst themselves, an idealized version of history, in which Y. H. Brenner and his "comrades" still lie together in a *kever achim*, or mass grave, literally a "grave of brothers."[34] Their collective martyrdom is almost a rebuke to the social gathering of single stones marking the cultural pantheon clustered together in one section of the yard, including the Cemetery's most celebrated occupant, the poet Ch. N. Bialik.

The streets surrounding the Old Cemetery are another material signification of these permanently dialoguing relationships. Many of the street names repetitively map and reinforce the Cemetery's inner memorializing process[35]—again (to borrow Nora's terms) a kind of "secretion of memory," this time not a "hiding away" but an "emission" or "discharge." Walking down Trumpeldor, one encounters the poet Saul Tchernichovski, which runs into Bialik, and eventually Brenner, with his unlikely companion, the British General Allenby. The link between these urban signs and cultural memory is even more explicitly framed in the book cover of a recent biographical history of the period, depicting the fictional meeting of Brenner, Bialik, and Agnon streets. This whimsical street corner illustrates a canonical moment in Hebrew literary history, the product of a retrospective gesture. It also, however, hints at the volatility of this moment, in that it marks an *intersection,* a place where traffic meets and passes. Its very status as a fixed location is defined by movement through and around it. Similarly, though the Old Cemetery may be perceived as a relatively static site, the memory that fixes it is essentially a symbolic tool shaped by the concerns of the present.

Part Three: On the Corner of Bialik and Tchernichovski— The Cemetery as Literary History

Poetry relating to the Cemetery also treats it as an archive, though of a different order, as a dynamic repository of *literary* history. Instead of the stable, bounded site of memory envisioned by Kroll and Leinman, the Cemetery in poems by Avot Yeshurun and Dalia Rabikovitch is a site that destabilizes history, upending the notion of history as a linear progression, especially an unequivocal narrative of redemption. Yeshurun's and Rabikovitch's appreciations of the Cemetery-qua-archive may be illuminated by referring briefly to Michel Foucault's conception of the archive. For Foucault, "analysis of the archive involves a privileged region: at once close to us, and different from our present existence, it is the border of time that surrounds our presence, which overhangs it, and which indicates it in its otherness; it is that which, outside ourselves, delimits us."[36] Like Freud's uncanny, the archive's fundamental strangeness is dependent on its proximity and familiarity. The Cemetery is thus a kind of "shadow" site, *apart from* and *a part of* the city, underpinning its psychic structure, preserving those less assimilable elements

FIG. 6.7. *Bialik meets Tchernichovski. Photo by Barbara Mann.*

of its history. If the Cemetery is *this* kind of memory site, its literary history also tells how memory is produced and meaning invested, a process necessarily informed and circumscribed by cultural context.

Yeshurun's and Rabikovitch's poems recognize the Cemetery's pliability, its fundamental uncanniness. In their poems, the Cemetery symbolizes an ambivalence toward the "forgotten" diasporic past, as well as an explicit awareness of what Tel Aviv effectively effaced from the Palestinian landscape.[37] The uncanny's doubling effect is immediately apparent in Yeshurun's "Lullaby for Nordia Quarter." Born in Poland, Yechiel Perlmutter immigrated to Palestine as a young man, in 1925, and adopted the name Avot Yeshurun ("the fathers are looking at us") after the publication of his first volume, in 1942. Many of his Tel Aviv poems describe the psychic rift created by the separation from his family. In one lyric from *The Syrian-African Rift* (1974), the poet speaks directly to Tel Aviv, attempting to recover in the city the landscape of the *shtetl* he has left behind:

FIG. 6.8. *The Pantheon: Gravesites of Achad Ha-am, Bialik, and Nordau. Photo by Barbara Mann.*

I walked in you in the town I left
In your city, in my town.
My city that's behind your back,
and myself me, toward you I heft.

And in the city I have no funerals except of
Achad Ha-am, Bialik, Nordau[38]

The poet tries to compensate for his lack of personal memories in his new home, first by creating a "history of footsteps,"[39] then by placing Tel Aviv as a kind of palimpsest over the shtetl where he was born. The palimpsest is a spatial-mental structure that represents the uncanny's contiguous laying-over of the familiar—"the town I left"—and the strange—Tel Aviv. For Yeshurun, funerals of the Old Cemetery's famous occupants represent the culmination of his attempt to "walk in [Tel Aviv] in the town [he] left." The poet claims these highly public funerals as his own private history, the only past to which he has immediate, tangible access. Yeshurun bemoans more than his own dearth of memories; it is also the city itself that lacks a past: "Tel Aviv holy city, you have no / lullaby. Yesterday, it was."[40] Tel Aviv has no lullaby, implying that it never had a childhood, because it was built so quickly—"yesterday, it was." The poem describes a problem endemic to any fledgling national enterprise, that is, the lack of convincingly authoritative cultural roots. However, this historical poverty is grasped as a virtue constituting Tel Aviv's "holiness," as opposed to the solidly historical resonance of the archetype of Jewish urban holiness—Jerusalem. Moreover, Yeshurun's poem admits the presence of exile in Tel Aviv, including, or especially, the Cemetery's uncanny quality, embracing it along with the city's "poverty." This uncanny version of the Jewish past is all the poet has access to. The poem enacts the way in which personal memory impinges upon the collective narrative, revealing its inadequacy. If the editors of the *Book* believed the Cemetery could somehow replace European cemeteries, and their symbolic significance, this poem of over three decades later knows the trauma was too enormous. The poem describes an ultimately irredeemable loss, one for which the collective narrative can offer no compensation.

A more recent poem by Rabikovitch also uses Bialik's grave as a touchstone:

"The Poet's Hope"
What is it with you
young poets
that you write so much about poetry,
and the art of poetry
and the use of materials
so that,
heaven forbid,
the poet's silence shouldn't come
and devastate you.

After all, you've got a cure
which drives away all sorrow:
sitting leisurely at the morning table
covered with a slightly faded oilcloth
and gazing mournfully at the window pane,

until afternoon approaches.
And if you are seized by a sleepiness, don't drive it away,
and don't take lightly the taste of honey and butter.
And don't make of it poems or poetry
and don't make any craft
and if you have any joy,
hide it away for many days,
lest the eye should view it.
For why are you afraid, my dear,
to seize the horns of the poem as it slips away,
and poke its ribs
like a lone bedouin boy hurries
his tarrying donkey?

After all, the only good that will grow from this,
the best of all possible worlds,
is a single grave they'll dig/negotiate for you,
after great efforts at the mayor's office,
in the cemetery on Trumpeldor Street
sixty meters away
from Bialik's grave.[41]

Like much of Rabikovitch's work, the language is deceptively simple—beginning with the casual slang of the opening line. According to the first stanza, poetry about poetry is the last resort before writer's block, "the poet's silence," an unmistakable allusion to Bialik's infamous long poetic silence once he settled in Tel Aviv. The bedouin boy—a shepherd—is, of course, the "Ur-poet," his tarrying donkey an oblique reference to a messianic age. His appearance also signals the moral failure of the "young poets," whose weakness of spirit is implied in their fear of "seizing the poem by the horns," as a person of principle would seek sanctuary at the altar, as in the Hebrew expression, "to seize the horns of the sanctuary." The poem's ingenious construction "to seize the poem by the horns" recalls the expression "to seize the ox by the horns," which further alludes to the afterlife, ox meat being a mythically honored dish. The poet is finally imagined as a kind of Job, whose friends acquire a relative place of honor for him, the reference to Job 40:30 in line thirty carrying the double meaning of "dig" and "negotiate."

Despite an implicit promise of the world to come, the poem ultimately maintains that the most a poet can hope for is a permanent resting place sixty meters distant from Bialik's grave. The Old Cemetery is envisioned as the physical arena in which relations between a literary center and its margins are marked, and *re*-marked, as time passes and canonical "intersections" shift within changing cultural and political climates. The number sixty recaps the poem's fluctuating stance vis-à-vis the "headstone" of Hebrew literary authority. How close to the center *is* sixty meters? What constitutes a place of honor in a graveyard that no one visits? On the one hand, sixty is associated with Solomon's temple, sixty *amot* being one of its chief measurements. But sixty also brings to mind expressions such as "a small bit in sixty," that is, a minor element of minimal influence, and "one out of sixty," meaning "a small portion of." Most significantly, however, the number sixty marks the distance Hebrew poetry has traveled since Bialik's death, in 1934, neatly translating temporal measurement into spatial quantity—years into meters—a transformation that alludes to the Cemetery's own spatialized rendering of time's passage. Whereas Bialik and the other cultural figures buried in the Cemetery are now thoroughly dispersed within Israeli culture, the Cemetery itself seems to resist this kind of dissemination, representing instead an encryption of modern Hebrew culture's beginnings. With this ossification, the desire for memory that is the desire for roots expressed in 1939 in the *Book of the Old Cemetery* comes full circle, the anxiety of a budding modernist metropolis replaced by a postmodern shrug of ambivalent recognition, in Rabikovitch's ironic formulation, "the best of all possible worlds."

Acknowledgments

For their patience and expertise I am grateful to Nili Varzerbaski, Tel Aviv Historical Archives; Batia Carmiel, Tel Aviv–Jaffa Municipality Museum; Ayelet Eilon, Society for the Protection of Nature, Tel Aviv Branch. Thanks also to audiences at the Association for Jewish Studies Conference, Boston, December 1996 and the ACSA Conference at Washington University, St. Louis, October 1998.

Notes

The epigraph is from *The Book of Tel Aviv Street Names* (Tel Aviv: Ha-m'avir, 1944). On the title page, below the date and place of publication, is the inscription: "Five years since the destruction *(chorban)* of European Jewry."

1. Achad Ha'am ("one of the people") was the pen name of Asher Ginsburg (1856–1927), whose writings are considered the foundation of cultural Zionism. Ch. N. Bialik (1873–1934), the "Hebrew national poet" who moved to Tel Aviv from Berlin in 1924.

2. A. Remba, *Israel Rokakh: The Mayor of Tel Aviv* [in Hebrew] (Tel Aviv: Masada, 1969), 27–28.

3. In a "black wedding," two orphans were married in the hope that God would therefore look favorably upon the charity of the community, thus easing the epidemic. See Shlomo Shva, *Ho Ir, Ho Em: The Romance of Tel Aviv-Jaffa* [in Hebrew] (Tel Aviv: American Israel Fund and The Tel Aviv Fund for Art and Literature, 1977), 222–24.

4. Zvi Kroll and Zadok Leinman, eds., *Sefer Beyt Ha-kvarot Ha-yashan (The Book of the Old Cemetery)* [in Hebrew] (Tel Aviv: Private publication, 1939), vii.

5. Max Nordau (1849–1923), philosopher, social critic, and co-founder of the World Zionist Organization; Meir Dizengoff was the first mayor of Tel Aviv, a position he occupied until his death, in 1936.

6. Pierre Nora, "Between Memory and History: *Les lieux de mémoire,*" *Representations* 26 (spring 1989): 7.

7. See David Lowenthal, "How We Know the Past," in *The Past Is a Foreign Country* (New York: Cambridge University Press), 185–259.

8. Nora, "Between Memory and History," 8.

9. Ibid., 9–10.

10. According to the story of Simonides's invention of the art of memory, people "must select places and form mental images of the things they wish to remember and store those images in the palaces, so that the order of the places will preserve the order of the things." Cited in Frances A. Yates, *The Art of Memory* (Chicago: The University of Chicago Press, 1966), 2. See also M. Christine Boyer, *The City of Collective Memory* (Princeton, N.J.: Princeton University Press, 1994), 129–202.

11. The cemetery on the Mount of Olives in Jerusalem most approximates the sprawling, city-like feel of Père Lachaise. See Meron Benvenisti's study of Jerusalem's cemeteries, *City of the Dead* [in Hebrew] (Jerusalem: Keter, 1990), 56–85.

12. For a short history, see *Plan et Histoire Du Père-Lachaise* (Paris: Éditions Vermet, 1996).

13. See Citor Rybár, *Jewish Prague: Notes on History and Culture; A Guidebook,* trans. Joy Turner-Kadecková and Slavos Kadecka (Prague: Akropolis, 1991), 279–93.

14. See Ilan Troen, "Establishing a Zionist Metropolis: Alternative Approaches to Building Tel Aviv," *Journal of Urban History* 18, no. 1 (Nov. 1991): 10–36.

15. The Society for the Protection of Nature runs occasional tours. See also Shlomo Shva's survey of the Cemetery's pantheon, "Where are the living in Tel Aviv?" [in Hebrew], *Davar Ha-shavua* (July 25, 1986): 18–19.

16. See Maoz Azaryahu, "Mount Herzl: The Creation of Israel's National Cemetery," *Israel Studies* 1, no. 2 (fall 1996): 46–74.

17. *Tel Aviv Municipality Bulletin* [in Hebrew], vol. 4 (July 1922): 25–26.

18. For a discussion of the cemetery as a reflection of societal values, see Randall H. McGuire, "Dialogues with the Dead: Ideology and the Cemetery," in *The Recovery of Meaning: Historical Archaeology in the Eastern United States* (Washington, D.C.: Smithsonian Press, 1988), 435–80.

19. Kroll and Leinman, *The Book,* x.

20. Ibid., xii. Plans for the design of Theodore Herzl's tomb in 1952 were characterized by a similar tension: the desire for a more populist simplicity won out over monumentality. See Azaryahu, "Mount Herzl: The Creation of Israel's National Cemetery," 51.

21. Kroll and Leinman, *The Book,* xvi.

22. Ibid.

23. A volume on Vilna's cemetery views textuality as the ultimate memorial: "For memorial in a book is more valuable than that engraved in stone, which will one day be spoiled, while that which is written in a book will last forever." David Magid, *The City of Vilna* [in Hebrew] (Vilna: Ha-almana ve-ha-achim ram, 1900), ix–x.

24. See Arnold Schwartzman, *Graven Images: Graphic Motifs of the Jewish Gravestone* (New York: H. N. Abrams, 1993) for beautifully photographed examples.

25. The first ashes from the death camps were brought in 1947. See Don Handelman and Lea Shamgar-Handelman, "The Presence of Absence: The Memorialisation of National Death in Israel," in *Grasping Land: Space and Place in Contemporary Israeli Discourse and Experience,* eds. Eyal Ben-Ari and Yoram Bilu (Albany: State University of New York Press, 1997), 85–128 (here 122).

26. See James Young, *The Texture of Memory: Holocaust Memorials and Meaning* (New Haven, Conn.: Yale University Press, 1993).

27. Handelman and Shamgar-Handelman, "The Presence of Absence," 109.

28. The major shoah memorial in Tel Aviv, Yigal Tumarkin's monumental inverted steel triangle, *Shoah and Redemption* (1975), is located in Rabin Square, in front of the Municipality Building.

29. The grave of Dov Sterngelz, a member of the *Etzel* (a prestate military group) who died in 1946, is a rare exception; it bears the conventional military marker and inscription.

30. Kroll and Leinman, *The Book,* xix.

31. "For the living—to the dead" [in Hebrew], *Moznayim* 10 (1940): 325.

32. One of the editors, Zvi Kroll, is himself buried in the Cemetery.

33. Rybár, *Jewish Prague: Notes on History and Culture,* 289.

34. Y. H. Brenner (1878–1921), an influential writer and ideologue who lived in Palestine from 1909 until his violent death in 1921, during the Jaffa riots of that year.

35. See Maoz Azaryahu, "The Power of Commemorative Street Names," *Environment and Planning D: Society and Space* 14 (1996): 314–30.

36. Michel Foucault, *The Archaeology of Knowledge,* trans. A. M. Sheridan Smith (New York: Pantheon Books, 1972 [1969]), 130.

37. For a discussion of Tel Aviv and the Palestinian past, see my "Modernism and the Zionist Uncanny: Reading the Old Cemetery in Tel Aviv," *Representations* 69 (winter 2000).

38. Avot Yeshurun, "Lullaby for Nordia Quarter," in *The Syrian-African Rift* [in Hebrew] (Tel Aviv: Siman Kriah, 1974), 33–34.

39. Michel de Certeau, "Practices of Space," in *On Signs,* ed. Marshall Blonsky (Baltimore: Johns Hopkins University Press, 1985), 129.

40. Yeshurun, *Syrian-African Rift,* 34.

41. Dalia Rabikovitch, *The Complete Poems So Far* [in Hebrew] (Tel Aviv: Ha-kibbutz ha-meuchad, 1995), 318–19.

chapter seven

Housing the Symbolic Universe in Early Republican Turkey

Architecture, Memory, and "the Felt Real"

CAREL BERTRAM

From the work of Aristotle to contemporary semiologists, or even through self-reflection, we understand that the world is comprehensible not through its things or its places, or even because of the people who inhabit or have inhabited it, but by the meanings we have assigned to them. This is especially true for our understanding of the world of the past, which is only accessible through the meanings that have come down to us through memory. It is memory that transports the symbolic importance of objects, places, art, or language. But memory is a malleable carrier, one that allows objects to be remembered differently according to the needs of specific groups in specific situations or times; thus it is memory that allows places or objects to take on emblematic value or to become the centerpiece of a group's collective identity.

The "Turkish house" is just such a memory-symbol, an image that has operated in the Turkish symbolic universe in order to make the past meaningful to the present. The memory of the "Turkish house" has become a carrier of group meaning, in fact, the carrier of specific emotions that needed a place to reside during a tumultuous period of Turkish history.

FIG. 7.1.
A street of "Turkish
houses," Tokat,
Turkey. Photo by
Carel Bertram, 1993.

The period of time when Turkey was becoming Turkey, that is, the early
years of the Turkish Republic, during the 1920s and early 1930s, was a time
of severe changes, when the Ottoman Empire, with its religious associations,
was being dissolved and a new, secular ideal was being forged under the leadership of Kemal Atatürk. In the early Republican period, an image of "the
Turkish House," both in text and in the way that it was depicted visually,
emerged as a sign that encoded what was felt to be at risk in this changing
universe, and thus it became a memory-image charged with carrying old,
outdated, or even forbidden ideas into the present, and even into the future.

Although the "Turkish house" became a central image in the symbolic universe of the Turkish Republic, it is actually a house type of the
Ottoman era that was no longer being built by the time of the establishment
of the Republic of Turkey in 1923.[1] Therefore, the "Turkish house" is really an Ottoman house that was brought into the Turkish period from the

FIG. 7.2.
A "Turkish house,"
Yorük, Turkey. Photo
by Carel Bertram, 1993.

past. Thus, one could argue that there is no such thing as "the Turkish House," only an Ottoman house that was renamed. This renaming is, of course, important, but also important is the fact that this "Turkish House" had a very real visual form, and thus was easily imaged.

Before the nineteenth century, Ottoman towns in Anatolia and the Balkans were characterized by a variety of local styles and materials, but the late eighteenth century saw the beginning of a homogenization in housing types for most of the empire. At this time, mud-brick housing in most of Anatolia and the Balkans was replaced by timber-framed houses of four basic categories: the *konak,* or mansion; the *kiosk,* or suburban garden mansion; the *yali,* or waterfront house; and the *ev* or *hane,* the small family house. Most were made of wood and shared several common architectural characteristics, including living quarters above the ground floor with street-facing rooms cantilevered over the street, and with windows arranged in

FIG. 7.3. *The Hazeranlar Konak, now a museum, Amasya, Turkey.*
Photo by Carel Bertram, 1993.

rows along the façade, protected by wide eaves. By the nineteenth century, even the interiors shared a common spatial organization, especially that of the Ottoman room, the *oda*. The oda was the central module of the house, as it was the living space of a nuclear family within the extended family of the household. Its rows of sash windows facing the street were lined on the inside with built-in bench seating; this and its decorative wooden ceilings, wooden cabinets, and tile fireplaces were a form exported from the capital to become the standard of the provinces. Wherever the Ottomans went, from Sarajevo to Damascus, these very similar houses appeared.

But to the extent that these were wooden houses, they were continually ravaged by fires, and were continually replaced by new wooden buildings. This was only true until the end of the nineteenth century, however, when they were no longer rebuilt, for they were no longer suited to the new demographics, economics, and lifestyle needs of a growing and Westernizing nation. Instead, the old wooden houses were left to decay or were subdivided for immigrant families, or replaced with concrete apartments. Eventually,

FIG. 7.4. *An old man dreams that his past can still be found in an old "Turkish house." From Ismail Gülgeç, "Hikâye-i Istanbul [An Istanbul Romance]," Istanbul 17 (1996): 119.*

only a few old houses represented the urban past, clustered in small enclaves or bravely isolated and restored as museums, hotels, or restaurants. Clearly, then, as a mental image in the twentieth century, the "Turkish house" owes its survival not to architectural practice but to *memory*.[2]

This memory is very much alive in modern Turkey, but in a specifically symbolic way. For example, in the Turkish imagination of the late twentieth century, the "Turkish house" seems to appear whenever the words *Turkish, history, national*—or even *old*—find themselves together. The Turkish History Foundation's Publishing House has used the house as its logo, and it is the subject of a recent cartoon in which an old man dreams that his lost past can still be found in a Turkish house. It is also the subject of the drawing of a middle-school girl, who used it to depict a perfect future. The "Turkish house" has thus become a site in the Turkish imagination, endowed with symbolic resonance not only in autobiographical memory and in shared memory, but most particularly in collective memory.

These terms, *autobiographical, shared,* and *collective memory,* must

FIG. 7.5. *"My Ideal Future," award-winning drawing by a middle-school girl in Istanbul. From UNICEF,* The Environment and Youth: Youth Painting and Literature Competition [Çevre ve Biz Gençler: Gençlerarasi Resim ve Yazin Yarasmasi] *(Ankara: ISKI, 1992), 16.*

be differentiated when discussing how images become part of a symbolic universe: autobiographical memory is what real people remember from their own lived experience. Shared memory refers to events that are autobiographical in nature but are also experienced communally, such as great fires, earthquakes, or even "going to the movies in the 1950s." Collective memory, however, is something altogether different, at least as it has been theorized by Maurice Halbwachs, for collective memory has no autobiographical component at all.[3] In collective memory, people do not remember events or places directly. Their memory is stimulated by inherited stories, narratives, or depictions that lead to a type of "second-generation" memory effect, such as those of the young cartoonist above, who could never have lived in a "Turkish house," or the young girl who drew a landscape of houses of a type she probably had never lived in either.

I have been careful to distinguish among these types of memory because I am interested in how a group, rather than an individual, "remembers" the built world of a past that it considers its own. Furthermore, I am interested in how historical groups, who are no longer here to be interviewed, imagined a group past. But as we have no way of returning to the past for anthropological information, I rely on contemporary discourses as they appeared in novels and stories. Literature, of course, has its own biases and reference groups, and the literature that I examine here involves an elite metropolitan population, both in terms of authors and audience. Nonetheless, I would argue that novels provide a unique opportunity to enter the "Turkish house," a place that has been culturally and historically closed to scrutiny. Furthermore, by staging dramas of personal life, novels may be the major arena in which places can take on a symbolic resonance for a large group; this is especially true of historical novels, which choose their settings carefully. Thus, I argue that, when set in the "old Turkish house," historical novels reflect how the writer and his or her milieu thought about the houses of the past.[4] Novels, then, are makers and carriers of memory and of memory images.

I propose that the image of the "Turkish house" began to emerge as a player in memory in the first decades of the new Turkish Republic, in fact, just at the time that it was disappearing on the ground. Novels from this period suggest that at this time, when the spiritual values of the past were openly challenged by the new Republican values of secularism, Westernization, and modernism,[5] the "Turkish house" became aligned with the contested spiritual values of the past—and with an Islam that the past represented. We will see that in contemporary novels and stories the "Turkish house" took on an iconic power that was grounded in the *emotional charge* of these spiritual values, representing a spiritual universe that had no space in the present.

The Emergence of the "Turkish House" as a Spiritually Symbolic Space of Collective Memory

In the late-Ottoman period, a spiritual universe that integrated religion and government needed no specific symbolic space. The symbolic universe of Islam was large and flexible, with room for ongoing interpretations and reinterpretations of one's religious vision and core values. Every space held that potential: not only the mosque, but also the house, neighborhood, palace, and the Sufi lodge. Language, literature, script, dress, codes of behavior, and almost every other area of cultural production similarly reflected the symbolic and spiritual universe of Islam. But by the mid-nineteenth century, Westernization had begun to erode many of these symbolic spaces, and with the formation of the new Turkish Republic, they became politically charged representatives of the old order, an order said to be in need of reform, or even one that should be totally discarded. Mustafa Kemal's new, Western ideals insistently repressed public forms of older Islamic life styles and replaced them with idealized versions of Westernized life. Religious schools were closed, Sufi lodges outlawed, and dress codes that had identified religious practices, revised. The Arabic alphabet, which had tied the reader to the larger Islamic world, was replaced by the Roman one, which was both secular and Western. Clearly, the older frames of reference had no *public* place of expression. But I suggest that these publicly contested values did not disappear, in part because they were given a new, but *private,* representational space, and that was the memory-image of the "Turkish house." The *image* of the house was readily available, as it had already become an image in the rhetoric of nationalists who appropriated the Ottoman house as a symbol of "Turkish" history. In this way, a building that was intrinsically Ottoman was being nationalized, and was begun to be called the "Turkish" house. But the appropriation of the Ottoman house as a symbol of a modern national identity (as a vernacular example that anticipated the "Western" architectural ideals of light, ventilation, warmth, and hygiene)[6] did not take root. Rather, what made the image of this now "Turkish house" survive in the Turkish imagination was just the opposite: its association with the spiritual world that a nationalist rhetoric was working to erase, that is, a spiritual world that still "felt real." I will use only one of several literary examples to suggest how the "Turkish house" came to represent these "felt real" spiritual values of the past.

Fatih-Harbiye

In 1931, Peyami Safa wrote the novel *Fatih-Harbiye* at the height of the institutional changes that characterized the first decade of the Turkish Republic.[7] The novel itself takes place about six years earlier. Fatih is a

FIG. 7.6.
Beyoğlu, with buildings
from the early twentieth
century. From the cover
of Arkitekt/Yaşama
Sanatı, *issue 403 6/93.*
Photo by Enis Özbank.

neighborhood in the heart of Istanbul's historic peninsula that was (and remains to this day) a symbol of the religious and social heritage of the Ottoman East.[8] Harbiye is the farthest extreme of the area called Beyoğlu, an area on the north side of the Golden Horn, an area that has long been the site of a Westernized, or European, lifestyle.

In the novel *Fatih-Harbiye,* the heroine, Neriman, lives with her father, Faiz Bey, their trusty servant, Gülter, and their cat, Sarman, in an old wooden house in Fatih, clearly described with all its visual attributes. It has an upper floor (a *cumba*) that protrudes over the street, a central room upstairs (a *sofa*), and a stone-floored entry area below (a *taşlık*). When the front door closed, "the old wooden house shook and the window-panes rattled."[9] Everything about this house resonated with a warmth from the past:

In this *mahalle* (neighborhood), in this house, with this gas lamp, this old man, and this worn out plaster, with this crooked cornice and these frayed satin curtains, surrounded by the aroma of this newly polished moldy wood, Neriman saw that a person could be happy, and she remembered the cheery days that had been spent in this house.[10]

Neriman's father, Faiz Bey, is a retired government official who used to work in the ministry of education. Although not a musician, Faiz Bey plays the *ney*[11] for his own enjoyment, and he spends his evenings reading *rubaiyats* and *gazels* (Ottoman, Persian, and Arabic poetic forms, often with religious themes); his favorite topic of conversation is Sufi literature. Faiz Bey, a lover of "alaturka," or Eastern music, has a developed intellect and a religious sensibility.

His daughter, Neriman, is a girl who wears black dresses and covers her head with a black scarf.[12] She is also grounded in the high culture of "the East," for she studies the *oud*[13] in the Department of Classical Turkish Music at the National Music Conservatory, the *Darü'l-Elhan,* in Shehzade-bashi, a neighborhood near Fatih.[14] Neriman is thus a conservative girl, but one who leads a modern life, symbolized by her education in a modern conservatory. Her sweetheart of several years, Shinasi, studies *keman-je*[15] at the Music Conservatory. Shinasi is a young man from Neriman's own mahalle and milieu; he is also a talented musician whom Neriman's father loves as if he were his own son. In fact, the father and prospective son-in-law are very much alike. When Faiz Bey described Shinasi to others he would say:

He is silent and virtuous, with extraordinarily good manners and honorable by nature, and he has a compassionate heart. He has great emotional intensity, he plays the kemanje, and not only that, his name will be famous among the famous. When I listen to him I weep. I am enchanted by this boy.[16]

Thus, although their world is the mid-1920s, that is, during the very first years of the new Turkish Republic, Faiz Bey and Shinasi are depicted as men who are grounded in pre-Turkish, *Ottoman* Oriental culture.

Neriman is the perfect soul mate for Shinasi, partly because of the

FIG. 7.7. *Young women* oud *students at the Darülelhan,*
Istanbul, 1926. Istanbul Ansiklopedisi, *557*
(out of print; publisher no longer exists).

affinity between Shinasi and Faiz Bey, partly because she "grew up in a pure Turkish environment,"[17] and partly because she is studying the oud, which is not only an Oriental, or local, instrument, but the perfect partner to the kemanje. Because of their connection at the Conservatory, we understand that Shinasi and Neriman play classical Turkish music together, a music that is tied to a non-Western tradition and that has many affinities with religious history and religious feeling (although it has a strongly secular audience as well). Shinasi and Neriman are thus the perfect couple, alike in their interests and in their upbringing. Because "they both looked like sister and brother and husband and wife,"[18] the reader is primed to believe that they are destined to bring the best of the culture of their past into their shared future.

But the future that is imagined for this young couple is disrupted when Neriman becomes interested in the fancy shops and Westernized life of Beyoğlu, which is not merely at the other end of a tram ride, but also a place that makes her look at her own life differently:

Neriman got off at Beyoğlu. Just like most people who live in a genuinely Turkish neighborhood, she felt as if she had made a big trip. Fatih was off in the distance—it was far away. The distance wasn't even an hour by tram, but it appeared to Neriman as long as the way to Afghanistan, and she considered the difference between these two quarters as great as that between Kabul and New York."[19]

Not only is Neriman mesmerized by the Western life of Beyoğlu, but when she comes home to Fatih, she begins to look at it disparagingly.

Darkness falls on these *mahalles* early. Neriman couldn't bear being at home at this hour of night. Even the little things she had never noticed before were now becoming important to her. She stretched out on the *minder* [cushion on the floor]. She was looking at the darkness that thickened in the small openings of those window grills [*kafes*] that brought night early to the room. The small rectangular holes were losing their sharp contours and becoming circular. The white tulle curtains darkened. . . .

At this time, everything darkens and fades, and every living thing cowers. . . . Thin smoke from the kitchens spreads through the entire street; [there is] a light odor of coal and oil [and then] the call to prayer from the minarets of Fatih.[20]

Neriman's sense of oppressiveness is part of her imagination, a misreading under the influence of Beyoğlu, which had for so long been associated with lights, nightlife, vitality, and entertainment. In her memoirs, written in the years that this story takes place, the famous Turkish author Halide Edib (Adivar) recalled a Beyoğlu that inspired what were called "hat and ball longings," that is, the desire to go out with a hat rather than a head scarf, and to attend dances.[21]

Neriman's interest in Beyoğlu, and the West that it represents, is sparked when she meets Majit, a young man who is studying violin in the Western, or "alafranga," music section of the Conservatory. Enthralled by Majit's Western worldliness, Neriman begins to take secret trips to Beyoğlu, to sit with Majit in the Beyoğlu salon of Maxim's, to wear makeup, and to drink cocktails. Majit soon loses interest in the violin,[22] and under his influence, Neriman decides to stop her oud lessons because they are so "alaturka." She does not lose her interest in music, but considers entering the alafranga section of the Conservatory.

Her trips to Beyoğlu and her new affection for Majit challenge and confuse her feelings for Shinasi. She is not merely attracted to another man, but to a man who represents the antithesis of everything Shinasi stands for and everything that the two of them have in common. Because of her attraction to the things of the West and her love of her father and Shinasi, Neriman is undergoing a deep crisis, "a secret interior, spiritual struggle," which she desperately tries to sort out in her mind.

> In Neriman's eyes Shinasi was the family, the *mahalle*, the old and the eastern, while Majit was the new, the west, and along with this he represented mysterious and attractive adventures.[23]

Neriman, in fact, is undergoing the deep, spiritual crisis of her contemporary Turkey. Lost in a reverie in which she tries to define the two cultures that are tugging at her soul, she has an epiphany:

> Neriman thought and suddenly understood why Easterners loved cats so much and Westerners loved dogs. In Christian houses there were lots of dogs, in Muslim houses lots of cats,—because Easterners resembled cats and Westerners resembled dogs! Cats eat, drink, lie down, sleep, give birth. Their life is spent on a cushion and passes in a dream; even if their eyes are open, it's as if they are dreaming; they are languid, lazy and day-dreaming creatures who can't stand work. Dogs are vigorous, swift, and bold. They do useful work—a lot of useful work. Even when they are sleeping they are wakeful. If they hear even the slightest sound, they jump up and bark.[24]

When Neriman's father comes home, she bursts at him with her new intelligence:

> "Look!" she said. "Gülter is sleeping and so is Sarman . . . [and] they're not the only ones who are sleeping! *All of Fatih is asleep!*"[25] (emphasis mine)

This is a turning point in the story, for her wise and kind father understands her spiritual dilemma and gently offers another interpretation to what his daughter sees as a great East-West divide.

> There are some men who sit and think from morning to evening. They have a *hazine-i efkar*, a treasury of ideas, I mean they are rich on the side of thought. Then there are some men who work on their feet from morning till night, for example peasants . . . but the work that they do consists of laying four bricks on top of each other. At first people may appear lazy, but really, velakin! they are hard-working. Other people appear hard-working, but really, *velakin!* the work they do is weak. This is because one's work involves mental endeavors using the spirit, while the other's work is physical and uses the body. The spirit is always great, the body destitute. The difference between what they do is because of this.[26]

Faiz Bey seems to have summarized the East-West divide, but in fact it is his daughter who has made this false dichotomy. Faiz Bey recognizes only a division between the spiritual and the material, placing what appears to be the hard work of material progress in an inferior position to the intellect and the soul. He has resorted to this dichotomy in order to show his daughter that one must be careful not to be seduced by appearances and lose sight of the emotional, the spiritual, or the intellectual; it is these that comprise the symbolic universe that makes up his emotional identity and his religious vision.

It is this deep, spiritual universe, given weight by Faiz Bey's paternal authority, that becomes the legacy of the past, a past that is harbored in these old houses. The family father—in this Turkish novel, at least—is the force that holds domestic life together, but always from love, and always with a firm footing in the transcendent values that stand for a life-world of a Turkish-Islamic religious tradition inherited from the recent Ottoman past. Faiz Bey and the house that supports his worldview are exemplars of an Eastern spiritual-intellectual universe that holds the key to putting the West and Westernization into a meaningful perspective. The kind father, in his old house, is clearly associated with the finest aspects of the past that are in danger of being sacrificed to the uncritically accepted modern. Faiz Bey may avoid a polemic of Islam and religion because this polemic could only be

FIG. 7.8. *A house near Fatih, Istanbul. Photo by Walter Denny, 1989.*

expressed in code words, such as *East,* due to the nationalist-Kemalist insistence on the rational and the secular;[27] but Faiz Bey's *house* can become a space for a positive association with the spiritual by couching his spiritual universe in terms of the private, the domestic, and the remembered.

In fact, in *Fatih-Harbiye,* the details of this spiritual past are fleshed out with stories that take place inside the remembered konaks and houses of the past. In another moment of internal despair, Neriman asks the family retainer, Gülter, to tell her stories about her (Neriman's) childhood. These stories show that the life of the mind and the spirit, which was to be the antidote to an uncritical acceptance of Westernization, was becoming attached to the houses of the past; that is, these stories show how the memory of the spiritual life of the past was beginning (in 1931) to be associated in the present with the old "Turkish house."

> Your grandmother always had a book in her hand. Now, what history book was it? . . . You can be sure it was one of the great ones. . . . Wait, it's on the tip of my tongue; Hah! It was Naima's

> *History.* [Your grandmother] knew Arabic, and Persian
> too. . . . She would read to us and explain it. That konak
> [emphasis mine] was really a school.[28]

The role of the family father, the old house, and the values of "the east"
come together when they are reiterated later in the novel, when Neriman
confronts a "friendly ghost of the past" who inhabits an old wooden konak
in her neighborhood. Neriman and Shinasi used to pass this konak every
day as they walked home from the Music Conservatory.

> Every part was run down, the windows had lost their rectangular-
> ity, the eaves had lost some of their planks, the zinc cladding had
> fallen in; . . . this *konak* was in such ruins that even a three year
> old child could push it down. . . . [But] there were still curtains on
> the windows;—yet was any one inside? And if there was, who?[29]

Over the years Neriman and Shinasi would imagine that there was an old
man inside who was watching them, and each time they walked by, they
would add to their story about him, until he felt entirely real.

> He had a long white beard, the cap [*takke*] that he put on
> his bald head was plain and simple; he sat to the right of the
> *shahnish*,[30] by the right-hand window, and fiddled with his
> prayer-beads, his lips always mumbling a prayer. He would think,
> but he wasn't thinking about people or work; he had large ideas
> about the world, about humanity, about God and death. When
> he heard a footstep on the street, his trembling head would
> look out the window behind the grills, and when he would see
> Neriman and Shinasi walking by, he would shut his eyes and
> pray that they were happy.[31]

But when Shinasi and Neriman walked by this old konak during the
tense period of Neriman's "inner struggle," when she was struggling with
her "hat and ball longings," Neriman was

> caught up with a strange feeling, as if she had heard a footstep in
> the house; then she thought the door opened and she thought she

saw the image of the old man on the threshold. He still had his prayer-beads in his hands, [but] this time his face was as white as his beard and his night cap; and he asked with eyes that tried to conceal a deep, sad, astonishment: What has happened, children? What happened to you?[32]

This ghost of the konak wants Shinasi and Neriman to be together as before, when there were no threats to the continuation of traditional life's promise of spiritual peace. This vision is so disturbing to Neriman that she faints in Shinasi's arms.

Eventually, Neriman resolves her spiritual dilemma, boards the tram back from Harbiye, and returns home to Fatih, making a spiritual return. She even returns to playing the oud. In the last few pages of *Fatih-Harbiye*, Shinasi, Neriman, and Faiz Bey go back to their own houses among the other sleeping houses of Fatih, and fall into a sleep of relief. Because Neriman's decisions have been made correctly, in favor of "Eastern," or Islamic, values, in favor of the right music and the right spouse, and because the men have done their job of telling her what is right, everyone falls asleep easily, and with a good conscience.

I have already shown how Faiz Bey had reinterpreted the sleep of the cat, changing the association of sleep from one of laziness to one of spiritual depth. The sleep of the cat had allowed Neriman to voice the new Turkish Republican stigmatization of the East, a stigma that Neriman had connected to Fatih in particular, when she bemoaned that "All of Fatih is asleep." But her father's reinterpretation of the sleep of the cat as the sleep of the spiritually attuned tells us the real meaning of the ending, in which all of Fatih falls asleep *in their old Turkish wooden houses*. The final scene that is framed by the sleeping houses of Fatih and the falling into sleep of the protagonists suggests that the rupture with the past and its spiritual offering has been healed, at least for tonight *and at least at home*. Falling into sleep within these welcoming, sleeping houses means that the rupture with the past can be healed at a spiritual level because the old houses offer a place to experience mentally the wholeness and safety associated with the pre-Republican life.

Fatih-Harbiye is one of many literary venues in which a spiritual dimension is called forth in memory and assigned to the "Turkish house" in the first decade of the New Republic. It is in the old "Turkish house" in

Fatih that Faiz Bey has discussions with Shinasi about Sufi literature, and where he reads the classics of Eastern religious literature, the Mesnevis of Celaleddin Rumi, the poetry of Sa'di, the philosophy of Omer Khayyam and Al-Ghazzali,[33] and where he can enjoy "alaturka" music. Faiz Bey's house, like Neriman's grandmother's clean konak, is a "treasury of ideas," a hazine-i efkar. The old house is the repository of the spiritual strength of the East with all its connotations of correct moral behavior. To a great extent it is the treasury of insight and ideas of Islam in its broadest sense. This remembered spirituality does not refer to an individual's private religious beliefs or convictions, but to the higher moral authority of the Islamic system, a symbolic universe of interrelationships and morally defined behavior, supported by a rich intellectual tradition. It is a symbolic universe that connects everything, even one's internal world, to a larger system, where a carefully articulated order, mediated by the great Islamic thinkers and artists, is brought home by the family father.

Memory and Emotion

I would like to return now to the two important concepts of memory and emotion, because it is their linkage that gives the "Turkish house" its iconic value. I have argued that books like *Fatih-Harbiye* invest the memory-image of the "Turkish house" with those spiritual aspects of the past that had no other place to congregate. *Memory* is a player in *Fatih-Harbiye* because, although the novel appears to be taking place in the present (as it deals with the Kemalist rupture of the present),[34] in reality, the intact neighborhood and life-world of the old houses to which Neriman chooses to return do not exist.[35] These are the neighborhoods that were deteriorating as they were abandoned for the new and the modern.

Nonetheless, the reader, whether or not he or she shared a memory of such a house, shared an understanding of that life-world, and thus the "Turkish house" as the symbolic repository of spiritual values that have their origin in the pre-Republican world could easily take on that emotional charge. Whether or not *the house itself* was part of the autobiographical or shared memory of the reader, the spiritual values that it represented in the early Republican years were quite real, and resonated emotionally. At the moment of the most extreme secularization, an image of the wooden "Turkish House," which was coming into the public consciousness in political speeches as an icon of a "common Turkish ancestry," was also used as a marker of a remembered spirituality, with a positive emotional charge. The *constructed* memory of a shared architectural past became the carrier of a *real* memory of a once-intact world of spiritual values.

In this model, memory, as emotional charge, has an explanatory force that differs from metaphors of memory as "construction." This understanding forces a new evaluation of the boundaries imposed on autobiographical, shared, and collective memory. Constructed memory is collective memory as we discussed above; it is a collective idea that has no autobiographical base. It is founded on social narratives that are handed down by a social group in the process of defining and legitimating its origins. In the case of Republican Turkey, political narratives developed about the "Turkish house" as "the place where our grandfathers lived." This led to a belief that, since they were the dominant domestic form in Istanbul and Anatolia, all Turks had at least one ancestor who had lived in one,[36] and thus all Turks were bound by a common architectural heritage. This belief overlooks both the actual demographic data and the complexity of the Turkish heritage.[37] However, I do not maintain that all Turks came to think that there must have been a wooden Turkish house in their own history. Rather, I am suggesting that the use of the "Turkish house" as an icon of a collective past was successful because the *emotions* that it represented were a part of their history, and thus felt to be real.

Constructed memory has an agenda, as Hobsbawm and Ranger point out in *The Invention of Tradition*.[38] National and collective "traditions" operate like sites of memory, taking on a symbolic meaning and becoming political capital. The "Turkish house" might be considered a constructed site of memory in this way, for it took on national importance as a symbol of a shared identity that did not exist. It might also be seen as a construction of an ideal religious past experienced by no one. In other words, constructed models and invented traditions have an implicit sense of the counterfeit.

But we are talking about a different model of memory. Our discussion of *emotional memory* and the "felt real" is not concerned with finding objective reality or the ways that reality has been misstated or misappropriated. Emotional memory addresses something that is *always genuine*, and it is this genuine emotion, perhaps hidden within *all* memory sites, that accounts for their power and longevity.

Daniel Goleman has shown how the mind has two ways of knowing, one emotional and one contextual (and thus more conscious and aware), and that each has its own ways of remembering.[39] While the details of this theory go beyond this chapter, the concept of *emotional memory* is worth investigating. Emotional memory explains that certain events take on the weight of memory because they are emotionally charged. For instance, you remember the dress you wore on your first date, but not every dress you wore on every date.

> Lacking emotional weight, encounters lose their hold. One loses recognition of feelings, or feelings about feelings. The amygdala is a storehouse of emotional memory, and thus of significance itself; life without the amygdala is a life stripped of personal meanings.[40]

A concept of the emotional mind introduces an alternate epistemology, for alongside the part of the mind that searches for an "objective reality" is a part that identifies the "*felt* real"; this adds another dimension to perceiving, remembering, and interpreting events, and thus to the investing of images with meaning.

Thus, when we look at the emotional charge that surrounds the image of the "Turkish house," emotions of the "*felt* real" of spiritual life, the role of the family and the patriarch, and the emotions associated with the new,[41] we begin to understand that these memories *are* autobiographical even if memories about a house that holds or frames them are not. Emotions that are triggered by the image of the "Turkish house" are not emotions of nostalgia, desire, or longing for a *lost place*, but emotions that relate to the real, lived, ongoing life of the reader/viewer. The image of the "Turkish house" represents a shared emotional past not because those who imagine/remember it all lived in one, or even had a grandfather who did, but because Faiz Bey and Neriman's spiritual symbolic universe was/is indeed shared with the reader. The image thus becomes a bridge between autobiographical memory and collective memory. It is a conduit that signals that the desires of the past exist in the present, and so it can help us identify these desires and feelings.

Fatih-Harbiye presents a moment when the "Turkish house" was invested with emotions that were alive from the past, but were in jeopardy, or at least involved in a crisis of legitimization. The fact that the "Turkish house" persists in the Turkish imagination today, however, speaks perhaps as much to the longevity of this crisis of legitimacy as to its resolution. But by giving these emotions a site in the imagination, the image provided a place for the "felt real" of the spiritual world of the present to be reexperienced in the heart, and to have a voice in interpreting the present.

I believe that this explanation, although experimental, helps explain the popularity of the image of the "Turkish house" in the recent past, and allows us to investigate the meaning of its emotional charge today. More work must be done, however, in order to show that this persistence is rooted in the early years of the Republic. I suggest that it is, but certainly the connecting chain of events and associations is complex. For example, the emotions associated with the "Turkish house" at a time when identity building was a vital activity of a secularizing state may differ from those forty years later, when the old house became the centerpiece of a conservation and restoration movement, which began among the leftists and leftists-turned-liberals in the 1970s.[42] The rhetorical positions of the different groups who have allied themselves with the image of the "Turkish house" must be explored; certainly this image is now used in a variety of cultural and political contexts, including the fact that, recently, all things "Ottoman" have become a big image industry. Yet I believe that the association of this house with a shared memory of wholeness, begun in the early twentieth century, continues to this day. When we look at the cartoon of the old man entering a dilapidated "Turkish house" and imagining the world of the past, we can understand some of the warmth and safety that the cartoonist has felt in his own family life, and how he connects his spiritual universe to the past, perhaps even to his grandfather. This might also explain why the middle-school child from Istanbul chose the "Turkish house" to represent her ideal future.

Nonetheless, images of "the past" must always be investigated with sensitivity to changing ideologies and to contemporary populations. In the early Republican period, images were used conspicuously in an attempt to forge a common past. The "Turkish house" today remains an icon of that past, but the limits, contents, and ownership of the past are again in flux and subject to manipulation.[43] For example, since 1998, a row of "Turkish house" façades has been used as a centerpiece of Istanbul's celebration of Ramadan. Are these the symbols of a shared life-world with links to the spiritual past that was "felt" by Peyami Safa and his successors? Or are these images an attempt to associate Istanbul with a newly religious view of the Ottoman past? The desire of the municipality may be penetrated, but the

FIG. 7.9. *A street of Turkish house façades: celebration of Ramadan, Sultan Ahmet, Istanbul. Photo by Carel Bertram, 1998.*

way that these houses resonate with a new Istanbul population of villagers remains to be investigated. Their autobiographical and shared memories rarely contained a "Turkish house," but their collective memories, it appears, certainly will.

But what will this image mean? The Turkish-style houses that newly Istanbul-ized Anatolians see today are either the "restored" wooden houses of the fabulously wealthy or the decaying structures housing the very poor. Do these real structures enter the imagination, or does the *image* of the house have a life of its own, built, for example, on images in Turkish novels, films, and children's books? Those images, I believe, are part of the legacy of its positive associations with a felt spiritual wholeness, a legacy that remains a part of a contemporary symbolic universe. For this reason I believe that the image of the "Turkish house" will continue as a powerful memory site, and continue to be welcomed with approval and with familiarity within the larger Turkish landscape of urban apartment houses.

Notes

1. Not all Ottoman-period houses fit this typology, and not all are made of wood, but the Ottoman house in the Turkish imagination does fit this typology, and therefore I am surrounding it with quotation marks, making it the "Turkish house." The definitive work on the structure of Ottoman Turkish houses is Sedat Hakkı Eldem, *Türk Evi Osmanli Dönemi* [Turkish Houses in the Ottoman Period], vols. 1–3 (Istanbul: Türkiye Anit Çevre Turizm Değerlerini Koruma Vakfi, 1984); for the (Ottoman) Turkish room, see Önder Küçükerman, *Turkish House in Search of Spatial Identity* (Istanbul: Türkiye Turing ve Otomobil Kurumu, 1978). For an extensive bibliography, see Perihan Balçı, *Türk Evi ve Biz* (Istanbul: Türkiye Tarihi Evleri Korunma Derneği Yayınları, 1993).

2. I am grateful to Tracy Lord and Engin Akarı for their critical reading of this chapter.

3. Maurice Halbwachs, *On Collective Memory*, ed. and trans. Lewis A. Coser (Chicago: The University of Chicago Press, 1992).

4. For a discussion of several novels that carry the collective memory of this house, see Carel Bertram, "The Turkish House: An Effort of Memory," Ph.D. diss., University of California, Los Angeles, 1998.

5. For a discussion of the development of secularism in Turkey, see Niyazi Berkes, *The Development of Secularism in Turkey* (Montreal: McGill University Press, 1964).

6. Bertram, "The Turkish House."

7. Peyami Safa, *Fatih-Harbiye* (1931; Istanbul: Otüken Yayınevi, 1976.

8. Halide Edib wrote in her memoirs that "Fatih, as the center of great theological colleges *(medresses)*, was always opposed to Westernization. Great mutinies in Turkish history were led by the eminent Hodjas [religious leaders] and the theological students at Fatih, and these mutinies put forth the religious pretext, their usual war-cry being, 'We want Sheriat,' meaning the holy law." H. Edib (A.), *Memoirs of Halide Edib* (New York: The Century Company, 1926), 276.

9. Safa, *Fatih-Harbiye*, 23.

10. Ibid., 45.

11. The ney is a reed flute played in slightly varying forms from Morocco to Pakistan. In its traditional form it is made from the Arundo Donax plant, the same as used to make oboe reeds.

12. Safa, *Fatih-Harbiye*, 12.

13. The oud is the twelve-stringed (two strings per note) ancestor of the lute.

14. The Darü'l-Elhan was established in 1914 as an arm of the Darü'lbedayi, the Istanbul Municipal Theater. The purpose of the alaturka section was to revive interest in, and to spread, classical Turkish music. Namik Kemal's son, Ali Ekrem (Bolayir) Bey suggested it be given the archaizing name "Darü'l-Elhan" ("the House of Melodies") as opposed to the Westernized name, *"konservatuvar."* See G. Paçag, "Darü'l-elhân," in *Istanbul Ansiklopedisi* (Istanbul: Kültür Bakanlığı ve Tarih Vakfi'nin Ortak Yayınları, 1993) and N. Özcan, "Darülelhan," in *Islam Ansiklopedisi* (Istanbul: Türkiye Diyanet Vakfi Islam Ansiklopedisi Genel Müdürlüğü, 1986).

15. The Kemence (kemanje) is a three-stringed Middle Eastern lute with a long neck, played with a bow. Because of the long neck, it is held vertically, resting on the player's knee.

16. Safa, *Fatih-Harbiye*, 55–56.

17. Ibid., 57.

18. Ibid., 56.

19. Ibid., 30.

20. Ibid., 40.

21. Edib, *Memoirs of Halide Edib*, 229.

22. Perhaps the author has chosen the violin for Majit because it is the Western counterpart of the Kemence played by Shinasi.

23. Safa, *Fatih-Harbiye*, 58.

24. Ibid., 46.

25. Ibid., 47.

26. Ibid., 295–96.

27. I have discussed the family father *(aile reisi)* as a major code for and memory site of the Ottoman spiritual macrocosm in Bertram, "The Turkish House." See also Nüket Esen, *Türk Romaninda Aile Kuruma* (Istanbul: Boğaziçi Üniversitesi, 1997), who analyzes thematically the Turkish novel in the Republican period.

28. Safa, *Fatih-Harbiye*, 77.

29. Ibid., 66–67.

30. This is the projection of the "sofa," or central room, of the upstairs, making a type of "cumba."

31. Safa, *Fatih-Harbiye*, 67.

32. Ibid., 68.

33. Celaleddin Rumi (d. 1273) was a mystical poet and the eponymous founder of the Mevlevi or "whirling" Dervish order. A Mesnevi is a poetic form that Rumi brought to perfection. Sheik Sa'di of Shiraz (1213?–1292?) was a Persian poet known especially for "The Orchard" (1257), a verse collection illustrating Islamic virtues, and "The Rose Garden" (1258), a collection of stories, anecdotes, poems, and maxims (see Şükran Kurdakul, *Şairler yazarlar sözlügü* [Istanbul: Bilgi Yayınevi, 1971], 31). Omer Khayyam was a Persian poet, mathematician, and astronomer famous for his Rubiyats,

a rhyming poetic form. Abu Hamid Muhammad Al-Ghazzali (d. 1111) remains even today among the best known of mystics and scholars who gave a deeper ethical dimension to the fundamentals of Islamic belief.

34. In fact, the Music Conservatory's Eastern Music Department was closed in 1926, about the time that alaturka music disappeared from the radio due to unofficial sanctions.

35. See Peyami Safa, *Cumbadan Rumbaya* (Istanbul: Kanaat Kitabevi, 1936); Halide Edib (Adivar), *The Clown and His Daughter* (London: George Allen and Unwin, 1935); and Edib, *Sinekli Bakkal* (1936; Istanbul: Atlas Kitabevi, 1984) for other examples of a heroine choosing to make a spiritual return to the old house and neighborhood.

36. Ahmet Turan Altıner and Cüneyt Budak, *Konak Kitabı* (Istanbul: Tepe İnşaat Sanayı, 1997).

37. Perhaps it is impossible to have a collective memory that does not have a hidden hegemony to unify it. One wonders how it could be otherwise, when defining a Turkish collective memory assumes that "Turks" exist as a collective. For this reason alone, collective memory is in the service of national unity in a population of "Turks" who may privately consider themselves to be Kurds, Laz, or Georgians, not to mention Armenians, Greeks, or Jews, and each of whom carry around their own separate memories and versions of history and its causes.

38. Eric Hobsbawm and Terence Ranger, eds., *The Invention of Tradition* (Cambridge, UK: Cambridge University Press, 1983).

39. Daniel Goleman, *Emotional Intelligence* (New York: Bantam Books, 1997).

40. Ibid., 20–22.

41. See Bertram, "The Turkish House," for a discussion of novels, such as *Fatih-Harbiye*, as a method of imagined socialization and way of dealing with change.

42. I am grateful to Engin Akarlı for this example.

43. I am grateful to Tracy Lord for her assistance with and support of my closing arguments.

ꙍ

Bibliography

Altıner, Ahmet Turan, and Cüneyt Budak. *Konak Kitabı/The Konak Book.* Istanbul: Tepe İnşaat Sanayı, 1997.

Balçı, Perihan, ed. *Türk Evi ve Biz.* Istanbul: Türkiye Tarihi Evleri Korunma Derneği Yayınları, 1993.

Berkes, Niyazi. *The Development of Secularism in Turkey.* Montreal: McGill University Press, 1964.

Bertram, Carel. "The Turkish House: An Effort of Memory." Ph.D. diss., University of California, Los Angeles, 1998.

Edib (Adivar), Halide. *Memoirs of Halide Edib.* New York: The Century Company, 1926.

———. *The Clown and His Daughter.* London: George Allen and Unwin, 1935.

———. *Sinekli Bakkal.* Istanbul: Atlas Kitabevi, 1984. First edition 1936.

Eldem, Sedat Hakkı. *Türk Evi Osmanli Dönemi* [Turkish Houses in the Ottoman Period]. Istanbul: Türkiye Anit Çevre Turizm Değerlerini Koruma Vakfi, 1984.

Esen, Nüket. *Türk Romanında Aile Kuruma.* Istanbul: Boğaziçi Üniversitesi, 1997.

Goleman, Daniel. *Emotional Intelligence.* New York: Bantam Books, 1997.

Gülgeç, Ismail. *Hikâye-i Istanbul* [An Istanbul Romance]. *Istanbul* 17 (1996): 117–20.

Halbwachs, Maurice. *On Collective Memory.* Ed. and trans. Lewis A. Coser. Chicago: The University of Chicago Press, 1992.

Hobsbawm, Eric, and Terence Ranger, eds. *The Invention of Tradition.* Cambridge, UK: Cambridge University Press, 1983.

Islam Ansiklopedisi. Vol. 8, N. Özcan and H. Ayhan. Istanbul: Türkiye Diyanet Vakfi Islam Ansiklopedisi Genel Müdürlüğü, 1986, s.v. "Darülelhan."

Istanbul Ansiklopedisi. Vol. 2, G. Paçag and H. Ayhan. Istanbul: Kültür Bakanlığı ve Tarih Vakfi'nin Ortak Yayınları, 1993, s.v. "Darü'l-elhân."

Küçükerman, Önder. *Turkish House in Search of Spatial Identity.* Istanbul: Türkiye Turing ve Otomobil Kurumu, 1978.

Kurdakul, Şükran. *Şairler ve yazarlar sözlüğü.* Istanbul: Bilgi Yayınevi, 1971.

Nora, Pierre, ed. *Realms of Memory: The Construction of the French Past.* European Perspectives Series. New York: Columbia University Press, 1996.

Safa, Peyami. *Fatih-Harbiye.* Istanbul: Otüken Yayinevi, 1976. First edition 1931.

———. *Cumbadan Rumbaya.* Istanbul: Kanaat Kitabevi, 1936.

Sumner-Boyd, Hilary, and John Freely. *Strolling Through Istanbul.* Istanbul: Redhouse, 1972.

UNICEF. *The Environment and Youth: Youth Painting and Literature Competition* [*Çevre ve Biz Gençler: Gençlerarasi Resim ve Yazin Yarasmasi*]. Ankara: ISKI, 1992.

chapter eight

Storied Cities

Literary Memories of Thessaloniki and Istanbul

ELENI BASTÉA

*I am beginning to believe that we know
everything, that all history, including the
history of each family, is part of us, such
that, when we hear any secret revealed . . .
our lives are made suddenly clearer to us,
as the unnatural heaviness of unspoken truth
is dispersed. For perhaps we are like stones;
our own history and the history of the world
embedded in us, we hold a sorrow deep within
and cannot weep until that history is sung.*
—Susan Griffin, *A Chorus of Stones*, 1992

On the Memory of Place

*S*ocieties guard and control their memories and the transmission of their histories: they invent traditions, imagine communities, construct their sites of memory. I have been trying to understand how societies record and transmit the history of the built environment. Is it true that stones, buildings, and streets hold within themselves the history of a place and its people? And if that history is indeed embedded in the stones, is it revealed to the current inhabitants and visitors?[1]

Studies on the sites of memory *(Les lieux de mémoire)* have begun to define how states construct places of national memory—both literally and figuratively—in order to forge a sense of common history, culture, and purpose. Imposed by the government or the intellectual elite, national invented traditions and places of commemoration have thus been used to support the aims of the nation-state, both on the cultural and political fronts.[2] What I aim to bring into the study of memory and place is the focus on the individual actor—writer, architect, local inhabitant—who is inevitably part of the larger nation-building myth, but who is also able to resist or question this myth.

I have chosen to focus on Greece and Turkey in part because of my own cultural attachment to the region and knowledge of its history and architecture. Both places share a common architectural heritage that dates back to the periods of the Roman, Byzantine, and Ottoman Empires. They also followed surprisingly similar steps in adapting Western architectural designs to the local building conditions in order to modernize their cities and create distinct national identities. While respecting the unique perspectives, important differences, and local cultural heritage of each region, I am interested in studying how individuals have come to view their local architectural heritage, a heritage that reflects a rich historical and cultural amalgam. I do not aim to reconstruct an idealized, romanticized past, but rather, to forge a foundation that helps engender an informed, current dialogue for the present and the future. I am also trying to visualize a locus for comparative studies of modern Greece and Turkey, and more broadly, Southeastern Europe, a direction whose significance reaches far beyond the academic stage set.[3]

In this chapter I will concentrate on the role of literature in describing and engendering the memory of place. Specifically, I will examine representative literary works on the cities of Thessaloniki and Istanbul. Both Thessaloniki and Istanbul are marked by long and uninterrupted urban histories. Until the early twentieth century, both cities were inhabited by a multiethnic population that left its mark on both the built and the cultural landscape of each city. Thessaloniki was incorporated into the Greek kingdom in 1912. Istanbul became part of the Republic of Turkey in 1923. Since then, both have been fairly homogeneous ethnically, each proudly showcasing its nation's achievements.

In part as a result of the parallel nation-building projects, few contemporary literary works about Istanbul and Thessaloniki reflect each city's complex historical past, concentrating, instead, on the ethnic homogeneity of the present. In addition to the inevitable impact of contemporary foreign currents on local literary production, other reasons for this evident historical amnesia may be attributed to the writers' personal childhood memories, and to the successful nation-building project of each country that was constructed on the premise of ethnic and cultural homogeneity. Can we find a reflection of their past histories in the postliberation literature of each city?

Thessaloniki

Thessaloniki is the second largest city in Greece, with a population of approximately 750,000. Founded in the fourth century B.C.E., it served as a major administrative and commercial center during the Byzantine and Ottoman periods. An important port, with extensive railway connections with central Europe and Istanbul, Thessaloniki became the second largest city in the Ottoman Empire, and its "window on Europe." In 1912, the Greek army succeeded in capturing Thessaloniki and the surrounding regions from the Ottomans and incorporating them into the Greek kingdom.

Let us take a closer look at the city's population in 1913, as reflected on that year's census by the new Greek administration. Of the 157,889 inhabitants, 61,439 (38.91 percent) were Jews, 45,867 (29.05 percent) were Muslims, and 39,956 (23.31 percent) were Orthodox Christians.[4] There were also French, English, and Italian merchants. Newspapers were produced in Spanish, Greek, Turkish, Armenian, Serbian, Vlach, and French and continued to be published in these languages well after 1912. Thessaloniki was the center of the Internal Macedonian Revolutionary Organization and the center of activities of the Young Turk movement (Committee on Union and Progress), whose aim was to modernize the Ottoman Empire. It was also the birthplace of Mustafa Kemal Atatürk (1881–1938), founder of the Turkish Republic.[5]

Most Jewish families lived in the flat, downtown area, while the Muslim population lived in the Upper Town, and the Christians lived in some of the downtown sections, near the churches, and along the Byzantine-era city walls to the east. Architecture reflected not only the inhabitants' diverse backgrounds

FIG. 8.1. *Thessaloniki Harbor. Photo by Mark Forte, 1990.*

and socioeconomic standing, but also contemporary stylistic influences. Traditional Balkan domestic architecture coexisted with the international neo-classicism of most new governmental buildings. Roman remains; early Christian basilicas; late-Byzantine churches, synagogues, and mosques; covered bazaars; and Turkish baths revealed the city's complex historical past and accommodated the spiritual and secular lives of its people.[6]

In 1917, five years after the incorporation of Thessaloniki into the Greek state, a major fire destroyed most of the tightly built downtown area, dealing a major blow to the prominent Jewish community living there. The Greek government ignored the preexisting patterns of land use and undertook the redesign of the downtown according to the latest methods in modern town planning. The spatial modernization of Thessaloniki was intended to cement the Greek presence in the city and signal a new beginning. A planning committee headed by the French architect Ernest Hébrard completely redesigned the downtown area, introducing a central north-south civic axis that linked the Upper Town with the sea. Hébrard envisioned Thessaloniki as an international city of the future, capable of being connected with all points of the

FIG. 8.2. *Thessaloniki, Fountain Square. Notice the Roman Arch of Galerius in the background, surrounded by modern apartment buildings. The fountain is a reconstruction of the one originally built in 1889, containing some parts from the original structure. Photo by Eleni Bastéa, 2000.*

globe by means of advanced communication systems. Although this vision may not be obvious on the plan, the regular blocks and broad boulevards clearly reflect planning principles inspired by Baron Georges Haussmann's planning for Paris (1853–1870), the City Beautiful movement, and contemporary colonial designs.[7]

The implementation of Hébrard's design proceeded slowly, as it had to consider the rights of landowners, the accommodation of newly found antiquities, and the extraordinary political and military events that followed World War I. Between 1919 and 1922 the Greek army was leading an expansionist campaign in Asia Minor, in an attempt to incorporate Smyrna (Izmir) and its surrounding areas into the Greek state. This campaign proved disastrous for Greece, indelibly inscribed in Greek memory and history books as the fall of Smyrna and the Asia Minor Catastrophe. From the Turkish perspective, the

FIG. 8.3. *Alaca Imaret Mosque area, Thessaloniki. The fifteenth-century mosque is now used for art exhibits and cultural events. Notice the lone house (now destroyed) from the late Ottoman period and the surrounding apartment buildings from the 1960s and 1970s. Photo by Mark Forte, 2000.*

liberation of Izmir led to a successful end of the War of Independence and the establishment of the Republic of Turkey in 1923. Greece and Turkey signed a peace settlement with the European powers, the Treaty of Lausanne (July 24, 1923), which stipulated the compulsory exchange of minority populations between the two countries. More than 1.2 million Christian Greeks from the former Ottoman Empire immigrated to Greece, and about 380,000 Muslim Turks left Greece and settled in Turkey.[8] Thessaloniki experienced drastic demographic changes: most of the Muslims left their homes and immigrated to Turkey, while approximately 92,000 Christian newcomers had to be resettled in the capital of the New Lands.[9]

Immediately after 1922 we witness the unfolding of a wide-ranging cultural crusade with three primary goals: 1. the cultural integration of refugees (a highly diverse group in and of themselves) in the Greek state;

2. the incorporation of northern Greece into an uninterrupted Greek historical narrative that stretched back to the time of Aristotle and Alexander the Great; and 3. the vigorous cultivation of the area's economic, agricultural, and artistic resources. The establishment of the University of Thessaloniki in 1926 and the institution of the annual Thessaloniki International Fair, also in 1926, signaled the progressive intellectual and commercial forces dominating the newly acquired territories.[10]

Let us now examine the role of literature in this national reconstruction project.

According to the general state objectives at the time, the new literature that was written in and about Thessaloniki after 1922 was expected to incorporate the city into the contemporary Greek imagination and express the new experiences that were specific to the region. Whereas the architects reshaped Thessaloniki into a modern Greek city, the writers, most newcomers to Thessaloniki themselves, were charged with composing new literary landscapes about Greek Thessaloniki. Did the new literary works engage in the national effort to hellenize Thessaloniki? Were the energetic and rather successful efforts of the state and local authorities to "cultivate" Thessaloniki, both commercially and culturally, reflected on the written page?

Some of the literature in the 1920s did, indeed, refer to Thessaloniki as "the bride of the Thermaic Gulf," an imaginary city in the manner of the poet Constantine Cavafy's Alexandria.[11] Soon, however, the tone changed, as we can see by examining a major literary movement that flourished between 1930 and 1940 and became known as the School of Thessaloniki.

The School of Thessaloniki represented the work of a fairly close-knit group of writers who lived in Thessaloniki, though they were not necessarily *from* Thessaloniki. They published mainly works of experimental prose, and produced the modernist literary journal *Makedonikes Imeres* [Macedonian Days] (1932–1939). Best known among its members were Stelios Xefloudas (1898–1984), Alkiviadis Giannopoulos (1896–1981), Giorgos Delios (1894–1980), Petros Spandonidis (1890–1964; first editor-in-chief of *Macedonian Days*), Nikos G. Pentzikis (1908–1992), and the women Anthoula Stathopoulou-Vafopoulou (wife of the poet Yorgos Vafopoulos) and Zoi Karelli (Pentzikis's sister).

Considering its name, one might have expected that the School of Thessaloniki produced works filled with specific references to the local urban and social environment. In fact, exactly the opposite was true. Beginning with the first work to be associated with the School of Thessaloniki, Xefloudas's *Ta tetradia tou Pavlou Foteinou* [The Notebooks of Pavlos Foteinos] (1930), the movement became known for its *lack* of place specificity, local color, and recognizable social and historical settings. What emerged, rather, was a gloomy, introverted, and troubled relationship of the writers to their environment. Their works reflected the authors' *private* sense of loss and rootlessness, ignoring the nationalist propaganda described earlier. In a poem by Spandonidis titled "Saloniki! Saloniki!" that was published in *Macedonian Days* (September 1932), the city is described as "chaos city." The speaker, as a citizen of "chaos city," has a chaos within himself, as well.[12]

Instead of local references, we find most of the works permeated by a strong sense of cosmopolitanism. Their characters travel to Italy, France, and other foreign, exotic places. This is due in part to the fact that many of these authors had lived abroad for a period of time. Furthermore, the orientation of the School of Thessaloniki was decidedly modernist and open to foreign currents. *Macedonian Days* was the first journal in Greece to publish Kafka in translation. It also published translations of works by Rainer Maria Rilke, Thomas Mann, André Marlaux, Marcel Proust, Katherine Mansfield, Virginia Woolf, as well as works by Turkish, Bulgarian, and Albanian authors.[13]

What characterized the School of Thessaloniki was the search for one's self and the cultivation of one's inner world. This was articulated in the long interior monologues of the School's experimental novels. Athenian writers attributed this concentration on the "inner man" to the geography and climate of Thessaloniki, with its foggy, cloudy days, and rainy skies. Indeed, some of the works from the late 1930s present Thessaloniki as a place of trial, pain, illness, and disillusionment.[14]

As a native of Thessaloniki myself, I can attest to the gloomy predilection born out of the climate. What I found puzzling in reviewing the work of the School of Thessaloniki, however, is the absence of any references to the city's sites and multiethnic society. Despite the destruction from the 1917 fire, Thessaloniki had retained a strong architectural color that reflected its long and rich history. And while most of the Muslims had departed by 1923, the legacy of the Ottoman past was and still is apparent throughout the city. Furthermore, the Jewish community continued to maintain a strong presence in the city, despite the catastrophic effects of the fire.

It is possible that Greek writers refrained from writing about "old Thessaloniki" because the city was not "Greek" enough, precisely because of its strong multiethnic, pre-1923 profile. As Hercules Millas has pointed out in his work on Turkish novels, Turkish nationalist writers systematically discredited Pera—the most Westernized neighborhood of Istanbul—as a debased place, whereas the antinationalists systematically wrote about Pera in a positive way.[15]

Although writers may have been influenced by the state's nationalist propaganda in selecting appropriate settings for their novels, their own childhood memories of place must have also played a role in their literary creations. For example, Yorgos Ioannou, a younger member of the School of Thessaloniki, described a different city. Born in Thessaloniki in 1927, of refugee parents from eastern Thrace, Ioannou became the city's chronicler. He wrote about Thessaloniki's infamous neighborhoods, its Byzantine past, the German occupation, and the expulsion of the Jews. He criticized the provincialism of Thessaloniki and the arrogance of Athens. He titled one of his essay collections *I protevousa ton prosfygon* [Refugee Capital] (1984).[16] The term stuck on the city, working-class Thessaloniki, "mother of the poor." Most of his essays were narrated through the eyes of a young man, intent on rescuing the profound and ephemeral moments of his life from the wells of forgetfulness. "I liken my own body to this city," he wrote. "It is, after all, my birthplace."[17]

☙

I have pursued this thread of inquiry regarding regional literary production in Thessaloniki in order to examine the following, much broader question: How does built space enter into our personal and historical consciousness? My assumption has been that studying representative literary works will provide us with a rich and articulate reflection of the built environment on the memories of the writers. Although we do not expect a published work to represent directly the thoughts of "the man on the street," it should introduce us to the general sentiments of the time. Why, then, did a whole generation of writers remain oblivious to the physical testimonies of the past, while their successors, Ioannou and his followers, never tired of recording the life of their struggling city? Why do buildings reveal their past to some of us and not to others?

We can begin to address these questions by examining the role of memory in writing. Recent research on memory supports what we all know from personal experience: our most vivid memories come from our childhood. Moreover, we cannot recall past events and experiences without the help of a narrative structure. This narrative structure—a connecting glue made up of family stories, school events, national myths—helps us to make sense of the isolated events and experiences stored in our mind. Our memories would remain an amorphous mass were we not able to give them form, shaping them into a coherent narrative. Images and events stored in our memory are not etched in stone, as was previously believed, but are subject to a selective, continuous recasting that reflects our current experiences and preoccupations.[18] Memory of place, I believe, works in a similar fashion. We revisit our earlier experiences, adjust them, edit them, alter them, or suppress them. We experience architecture through our body but we process and narrate that experience through our mind.

These findings help explain the absence of place-specific references in the literature of the School of Thessaloniki. As some of the writers were not originally from Thessaloniki, they could not conjure nostalgic images of their childhood in that city. For those who were born and raised there, the years between 1912 and 1922 brought such drastic disruptions of the political, demographic, and economic fabric that a return to the city of their childhood might have been utterly impossible, if not unbearable. Perhaps the destruction of everything familiar drove them to willful forgetfulness. Perhaps they sought refuge in the international currents of modernism. Cosmopolitanism became their surrogate country.

Yorgos Ioannou was about thirty years younger than most other members of the School of Thessaloniki. As he came of age, the family and national narratives that help us make sense of our surroundings were stronger and more coherent. Although a son of refugees, like most of the Greeks in Thessaloniki, he could claim his roots in that city and draw from his memories in his writings.

Istanbul

Istanbul, capital of the Ottoman Empire, underwent major modernization projects in the nineteenth century, stemming from the Tanzimat reforms and the triumph of the sultan Mahmud II over the conservative opposition. Since the 1830s, European visitors could reach the city by steamship. The first

FIG. 8.4. *A view of old Istanbul from the mouths of the Bosphorus and the Golden Horn. Photo by Mark Forte, 1998.*

bridge across the Golden Horn was built in 1838. The European railroad extending to Istanbul was begun in the early 1870s, and the underground tunnel joining Galata to Pera was completed in 1873. Electric lighting was introduced in 1912 and electric streetcars and telephones in 1913 and 1914.[19]

In 1908, the city was occupied by the army of the Young Turks, who deposed sultan Abdül Hamid II. During the Balkan Wars (1912–1913) Istanbul was nearly captured by the Bulgarians. Throughout World War I the city was under a blockade. At the conclusion of the Armistice (1918), Istanbul was placed under British, French, and Italian occupation, which lasted until 1923. With the victory of the Nationalists under Mustafa Kemal Atatürk, the sultanate was abolished in 1922. After the signing of the Treaty of Lausanne, in 1923, Istanbul was evacuated by the Allies. On October 29, 1923, Ankara was proclaimed the capital of the new Turkish Republic.[20] Today, Istanbul is a continually expanding modern metropolis of approximately ten million inhabitants.

As with Greece, the Turkish Republic began its own nation-building project, which would now serve an ethnically homogeneous population.[21]

FIG. 8.5. *Istanbul, view toward the sea, overlooking fifteenth-century Ottoman baths, Sultanahmet area. Photo by Mark Forte, 1998.*

Whereas before the war, one out of every five persons living in present-day Turkey was non-Muslim, after the war, only one out of forty persons was non-Muslim.[22] As the theoretician of Turkish nationalism Ziya Gökalp (1876–1924) argued: "Nation is a group composed of men and women who have gone through the same education, who have received the same acquisitions in language, religion, morality and aesthetics. . . . Men want to live together, not with those who carry the same blood in their veins, but with those who share the same language and the same faith."[23]

How, then, were these dramatic political, demographic, and economic changes reflected on the urban literature about Istanbul? Throughout the twentieth century, Istanbul has been the setting of numerous novels, memoirs, and semiautobiographic works of fiction. Among them are the memoirs of Halide Edib (Adivar), *The Turkish Ordeal: Being the Further Memoirs of Halide Edib* (1928);[24] Aziz Nesin's *Istanbul Boy* (1966);[25] Irfan Orga's *Portrait of a Turkish Family* (1950);[26] and Maria Iordanidou's *Loxandra* (1963);[27] the novels by Ahmet Hamdi Tanpinar, *Huzur* (1949),[28]

FIG. 8.6.

Istanbul, the "Bahçekapı" area, at the intersection of Hamidiye and Mimar Kemalettin Avenues, located between Eminönü and Sirkeci, on the historical peninsula. Notice that the city's Western architecture character is also interwoven with Turkey's national history. The ornate domed building to the left (along Hamidiye Avenue) is the "Fourth Vakıf Hani"—Office Building for the Ministry of Endowments (Vakıf Administration). The architect, Kemalettin Bey, after whom one of the streets is named, was the leading designer of the Ottoman revivalist "National Style," which flourished after the Young Turk revolution of 1909. The long construction dates of the building (1916–1926) coincided with Istanbul's occupation, the War of Independence, and, finally, the Republic. Its main façade is along Hamidiye Avenue, named after Sultan Abdül Hamid (reigned 1876–1909), whose tomb is on the other side of the avenue across from the Vakıf Building. Photo by Mark Forte, 1998.

FIG. 8.7.
Late Ottoman-era houses in the predominantly Greek neighborhood of Fener, Istanbul, with the Greek School, built in the 1880s, in the distance. The row houses along the street follow the nineteenth-century typology in Fener and the adjacent Balat districts, where the Greek and Jewish populations lived. Photo by Mark Forte, 1998.

a Proustian reconstruction of Istanbul; and Latife Tekin, *Berji Kristin: Tales from the Garbage Hills* (1984)[29] about the castoffs of modern urban life; and the book of poems by Ilhan Berk, *Galata* (1985).[30]

Most of the earlier autobiographical works make references to the city's history and to the ethnically diverse population of Istanbul in the early twentieth century. Here, however, I would like to concentrate on *Kara Kitap* [The

Black Book] (1990; English translation 1994), a long and erudite detective novel by Orhan Pamuk.[31] Orhan Pamuk, who was born in 1952, is today one of Turkey's best-known authors. His work has been widely reviewed and translated, and has been compared with the works of Italo Calvino, Umberto Eco, Jorge Luis Borges, and Gabriel García Márquez. *The Black Book* is frequently cited as *the* contemporary novel about Istanbul. Not only is it full of architectural descriptions of buildings, street corners, and neighborhoods, but also it is permeated by the urban aura of the city, alternately a *flâneur's* paradise and hell. Pamuk said in an interview with *Publishers Weekly* (1994) that his aim was "to write a huge, richly textured narrative that would capture the schizophrenic angst of Istanbul, a city straddling two continents."[32]

The story is narrated in the third person from the point of view of Galip, a young lawyer whose wife, Rüya, has left him. Galip suspects that Rüya has left him for his older cousin Jelal, a popular journalist with a weekly newspaper column. In fact, every other chapter in *The Black Book* is one of Jelal's published columns of first-person essays relating reminiscences and ruminations about Istanbul. Galip studies these old columns with the fervor of a detective looking for clues of the crime, convinced that the columns contain the key to Jelal and Rüya's disappearance. What propels the plot and intensifies the tension in the protagonists' experiences is the dual pull of modernity and nostalgia. Modernity is identified with the eagerness to belong to the West, while nostalgia is reflected in the poignant childhood reminiscences embedded in the physical landscape of the city. This tension between modernity and nostalgia is not limited to the personal realm, but rather, becomes a reflection of the city's complex and enigmatic spatial physiognomy.

The Black Book is a labyrinthine novel, leading the reader down numerous paths that may or may not provide clues for the apparent mystery that holds the plot together. Yet the physical reference points in this four-hundred-page volume are all focused on Istanbul, and the European side of Istanbul at that. "By the time he was out on the street once again," Pamuk writes, "Galip had eliminated some of the clues and given prominence to others: They could not be outside of the city since Jelal could not live anywhere but in Istanbul. They couldn't be on the Anatolian side, across the Bosphorus, seeing how it wasn't 'historical' enough to suit him."[33] That there may be a broader country extending beyond the fashionable, historical Istanbul is not obvious here. Nor do we find any references to the earlier inhabitants, the rich multiethnic population that made Istanbul one of the most truly cosmopolitan cities in

FIG. 8.8. *The Alaca Imaret Mosque casts a shadow on the facing
  apartment buildings (author's neighborhood), Thessaloniki.
  Photo by Eleni Bastéa, 2000.*

the world in the early twentieth century. Fashionable in its postmodern stylistic sensibility, replete with references to Eastern and Western writings, *The
Black Book* is self-consciously directed to an international, bookish audience.
It is a rich cartography of space and literature, but not of history. It ignores
the fact that the built environment is also history's palimpsest.

I have selected to focus on *The Black Book* by Orhan Pamuk and on
the School of Thessaloniki because these works represent polarized view-
points on history and the built environment, and not because they are representative of national approaches. Clearly, the positions of the characters
do not necessarily reflect the authors' positions. Nevertheless, I consider the
protagonists' particular views on place and history to be representative of
at least one segment of the Greek and Turkish populations, a particular segment upon which each author decided to shine his literary light.

FIG. 8.9.
Akropoleos Street,
Upper Town,
Thessaloniki. Photo
by Mark Forte, 1982.

I began studying novels about cities on either side of the Aegean because I was looking for the voices of the departed. I wanted to see if the common histories of these lands, their Byzantine and Ottoman pasts, have left their traces in the modern countries' literatures and national consciousness. Although there are writers on both sides of the Aegean who explore history and the built environment in varying degrees, others ignore the echoes of past residents in their stories. Out of the complex matrix of overlapping historical and geographic lines, many writers carve out their own familiar space, their own mental or real neighborhood that they visit and revisit as a refuge from the ghosts of the departed. Perhaps it is a case of historical amnesia, a form of self-preservation.

A marked success of each state's nationalist project. I believe that the selective historical and spatial awareness depicted in the literature discussed here does not reflect only one author's view of a city. It allows us to understand also how some of the inhabitants may view that same city.

As an architectural historian I had long assumed that buildings, street corners, and cities communicate their history to us—visitors, scholars, inhabitants. However, as I reflect on this material and on my own early memories of architecture, I have come to realize that sensitivity to built form does not in and of itself presuppose a historical understanding of that form. Buildings do not reveal their past to us any more than families reveal their own past to strangers. Embedded in our built environment, the histories of those who came before us will remain locked in oblivion, until we become ready to decipher them with care and compassion.

ℭ

Notes

The epigraph is from Susan Griffin, *A Chorus of Stones* (New York: Doubleday, 1992), 8.

1. I presented earlier versions of this chapter at the fifty-fourth annual meeting of the Society of Architectural Historians, Toronto, Ontario (Apr. 2001), and at the Comparative Literature colloquium at Washington University in St. Louis (Oct. 1999). I am indebted to Engin Akarlı, Esra Akcan, Mark Forte, Hercules Millas, and Müfide Pekin for their comments and suggestions. I would also like to thank my former colleagues at Washington University, Randolph Pope and Robert Hegel, for offering me an interim academic home in comparative literature, as I undertook my forays into literature, memory, and place.

2. Pierre Nora, "From *Lieux de mémoire* to Realms of Memory," in *Realms of Memory: Rethinking the French Past,* vol. 1, under the direction of Pierre Nora, trans. Arthur Goldhammer, English-language edition ed. Lawrence D. Kritzman (New York: Columbia University Press, 1996), xxiii–xxiv; John Gillis, introduction to *Commemorations: The Politics of National Identity,* ed. John Gillis (Princeton, N.J.: Princeton University Press, 1994).

3. For the possible influence of the memory of place on two prominent modern architects from Greece and Turkey, respectively, see Eleni Bastéa, "Dimitris Pikionis and Sedad Eldem: Parallel Reflections of Vernacular and National Architecture," in *The Usable Past: Greek Metahistories,* eds. K. S. Brown and Yannis Hamilakis (Lanham, Md.: Lexington Books, division of Rowman & Littlefield, 2003), 147–69.

4. Vasilis Dimitriadis, *Topographia tis Thessalonikis kata tin epochi tis Tourkokratias, 1430–1912* [Topography of Thessaloniki during the Turkish Rule, 1430–1912] (Thessaloniki: Society for Macedonian Studies, 1983), 463–64.

5. Peter Mackridge and Eleni Yannakakis, introduction to *Ourselves and Others: The Development of a Greek Macedonian Cultural Identity Since 1912,* eds. Peter Mackridge and Eleni Yannakakis (Oxford: Berg, 1997), 13–14.

6. Eleni Bastéa, "Thessaloniki," in *Encyclopedia of Vernacular Architecture of the World,* vol. 2, ed. Paul Oliver (London: Cambridge University Press, 1997), 1491–92.

7. Alexandra Karademou Yerolympos, *I anoikodomisi tis Thessalonikis meta tin pirkagia tou 1917* [The Replanning of Thessaloniki after the Fire of 1917] (Thessaloniki: Municipality of Thessaloniki, 1985). See also Alexandra Karademou Yerolympos, *Metaxi Anatolis kai Dysis: Voreioelladikes poleis stin periodo ton othomanikon metarrythmiseon* [Between the East and the West: Northern Greek Cities during the Period of Ottoman Reforms] (Thessaloniki: Trochalia, 1997).

8. Richard Clogg, *A Concise History of Modern Greece* (Cambridge, UK: Cambridge University Press, 1992), 101.

9. Agis Anastasiadis and Panos Stathakopoulos, "The Physiognomy of Upper Town in History, City Planning, and Architectural Typology" [in Greek], in *I Thessaloniki meta to 1912* [Thessaloniki after 1912] (conference proceedings, Thessaloniki, Nov. 1–3, 1985) (Thessaloniki: Municipality of Thessaloniki, 1986), 525.

10. Peter Mackridge, "Cultivating New Lands: The Consolidation of Territorial Gains in Greek Macedonia through Literature, 1912–1940," in *Ourselves and Others: The Development of a Greek Macedonian Cultural Identity Since 1912,* eds. Peter Mackridge and Eleni Yannakakis (Oxford: Berg, 1997) 176.

11. Ibid., 178.

12. Ibid., 180.

13. Ibid., 182.

14. Ibid., 179–86; Nikos Karatzas, ed., *Oi pezographoi tis Thessalonikis, 1930–1980* [The Fiction Writers of Thessaloniki, 1930–1980] (Thessaloniki: Epilogi, 1982); Roderick Beaton, *An Introduction to Modern Greek Literature* (Oxford: Clarendon Press, 1994).

15. Hercules Millas, "The Exchange of Populations in Turkish Literature: The Undertone of Texts," in *Crossing the Aegean: An Appraisal of the 1923 Compulsory Population Exchange between Greece and Turkey,* vol. 12, ed. Renée Hirschon, Studies in Forced Migration (Oxford and New York: Berghan Books, 2003), 221–33. See also Iraklis Millas, *Eikones Ellinon kai Tourkon* [Representations of Greeks and Turks] (Athens: Alexandria, 2001).

16. Yorgos Ioannou, *I protevousa ton prosfygon* [Refugee Capital] (Athens: Kedros, 1984). English trans. by Fred A. Reed, *Refugee Capital* (Athens: Kedros, 1997).

17. Yorgos Ioannou, *To diko mas aima* [Our Own Blood] (Athens: Kedros, 1978), 183.

18. Paul Connerton, *How Societies Remember* (Cambridge, UK: Cambridge University Press, 1989) and Daniel L. Schacter, *Searching for Memory: The Brain, the Mind, and the Past* (New York: Basic Books, 1996).

19. Zeynep Çelik, *The Remaking of Istanbul: Portrait of an Ottoman City in the Nineteenth Century* (Seattle: University of Washington Press, 1986).

20. Bernard Lewis, *The Emergence of Modern Turkey* (Oxford: Oxford University Press, 1961).

21. Sibel Bozdoğan and Reşat Kasaba, eds., *Rethinking Modernity and National Identity in Turkey* (Seattle: University of Washington Press, 1997).

22. Çaglar Keyder, *State and Class in Turkey: A Study in Capitalist Development* (London: Verso Books, 1987), 79, cited in Ayhan Aktar, "Homogenising the Nation, Turkifying the Economy: The Turkish Experience of Population Exchange Reconsidered," in *Crossing the Aegean: An Appraisal of the 1923 Compulsory Population Exchange between Greece and Turkey,* vol. 12, ed. Renée Hirschon, Studies in Forced Migration (Oxford and New York: Berghan Books, 2003), 81.

23. Ziya Gökalp, *Turkish Nationalism and Western Civilization,* ed. and trans. Niyazi Berkes (New York: Columbia University Press, 1959), 137, cited in Aktar, "Homogenising the Nation, Turkifying the Economy," n. 23.

24. Halide Edib (Adivar), *The Turkish Ordeal: Being the Further Memoirs of Halidé Edib* (1928; Westport, Conn.: Hyperion, 1981).

25. Aziz Nesin, *Istanbul Boy,* trans. Joseph S. Jacobson. Multivolume (Austin, Tex.: Center for Middle Eastern Studies, 1977–1990).

26. Irfan Orga, *Portrait of a Turkish Family* (London: Eland, 1950).

27. Maria Iordanidou, *Loxandra* (Athens: Hestia, 1963). Turkish ed.: Maria Yordanidu, *Loksandra: İstanbul düşü,* trans. Osman Bleda (Istanbul: Marenostrum series of Belge Yayınları, 1995).

28. Ahmet Hamdi Tanpinar, *Huzur* (Istanbul: Renzi Kitabevi, 1949).

29. Latife Tekin, *Berji Kristin: Tales from the Garbage Hills,* trans. Ruth Christie and Saliha Paker (London: Marion Boyars, 1993; Turkish ed. 1984).

30. Ilhan Berk, *Galata* (Istanbul: Adam, 1985).

31. Orhan Pamuk, *Kara Kitap* (Istanbul: Can Yayinlavi Ltd., 1990). *The Black Book,* trans. Güneli Gün (London: Faber and Faber, 1994).

32. Interview with Orhan Pamuk, *Publishers Weekly* 241, no. 51 (Dec. 19, 1994): 36 (2).

33. Ibid., 193.

Part Three

Personal Cartographies

chapter nine

Beirut, Exile, and the Scars of Reconstruction

CATHERINE HAMEL

My era tells me bluntly:
you do not belong.
I answer bluntly:
I do not belong.

Here are some words. Some are mine, others are borrowed. Words not so much for you, but provoked by you, provoked by the particular space outlined by the forced migration of war. The war that unfolded in you stopped our meetings abruptly. Too young to understand or have the ability to rebel, I was stolen from you and you stolen from me. Furtively shipped out to foreign soil, I never had the opportunity to package you neatly before we were separated. Change is expected with the passage of time, but war has eroded that original version of you. I no longer know you, yet live and write to your memory and what it still evokes in me. Survival abducts one from tradition, friends, culture, all that is familiar. An origin is lost and in its place a rift settles. "For an exile, habits of life, expression or activity in the new environment inevitably occur against the memory of these things in another environment. Both the new and the old environments are vivid, actual, occurring";[1] a conflict between two spaces that never ceases. This displacement leaves scars that reassert themselves in spatial experience. The ruptured past assertively weaves itself into the present, shaping the space of

FIG. 9.1.
Weaving #1, 2001

exile with its memory. The civil war of our country has shuffled and reshuffled the lives of its people. It shuffled them in and out of their homes, in and out of each other's homes, in and out of other people's countries, in and out of their own bodies. There were hours of anguish in immigration booths, hours of hope in returning flights, patient hours cramped in resettlement homes, hours safely working in adopted lands. For sixteen years you provided the landscape of progressive deterioration of war. Since 1991, you offer the rare opportunity to see a city's erasure and reconstruction. You have become a case study of postwar reconstruction that has captured the attention of the world. Beirut is being reborn, the optimist says; the cynic sees the scars of reconstructive surgery.

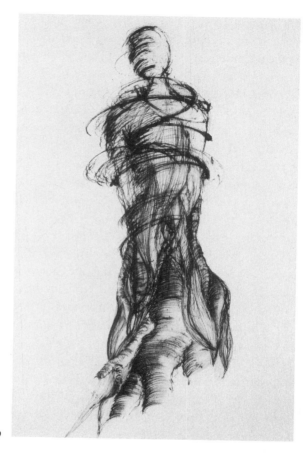

FIG. 9.2.
Grafting #1, 1999

I try to understand you.
Now I am a shadow
Lost in the forest
Of a skull[2]

"Do you go back often?" I am repeatedly asked. A faint smile lingers in my silent gaze. I never left. Migrants are those who move for interrelated personal, economic, political, or religious reasons. Definitions of migration appear quite simple and to the point: to be on the move; to pass periodically from one place to another; to leave one's country. The precipitating factors, experiences, implications, and meanings of migration are as varied and complex as the definitions are simple. Forced migration, where the movement or passage is not by choice but a flight for survival, is by and large prompted by persecution, massive human rights violations, and armed conflict. Millions flee their homes and country of origin and relocate in a foreign environment to avoid inhaling death daily. Severed, we are displaced in order to survive, grafted onto a new footing, seemingly preserved from the ravages of war by exile.[3] A graft is the insertion of something into an alien body so that it is accepted, as if belonging there. The process involves the act of cutting, insertion, and waiting to see the development of a new hybrid. The graft is also the shock. It is a process that structures the experience of the forced migrant. There is uncertainty in the experimental nature of a graft. Which two species will result in success, which will result in deformity, which will not survive? Always there is a scar. For the exile it becomes a delicate balance to dwell in conflicting identities, although there is nothing delicate about the circumstances, nothing delicate about tracing and retracing, like a faithful dog, this passage to oblivion.

The passage of time allows hope to be grafted onto despair. The exile can spend years perfecting the art of forgetfulness, but one encounter, one smell, one landscape and all mnemonic tricks dissolve, years of adaptation lost—suffocated memory that detects the trace of oxygen is revived with the strength of a last gasp, with striking clarity. It is an act of sheer determination that makes one move with agility under this weight that escapes most, who do not understand this need to retrace these scars collected. Who decides the necessity? A scar is the residue of healing as well as injured tissue.

> We no longer meet.
> Rejection and exile keep us apart.
> The promises are dead, space is dead,
> Death alone has become our meeting point[5]

One of the physical consequences of the war's urban geographies is your own division into two opposing spatial units. Your East and your West became separated by a line of confrontation that forged itself through your streets with

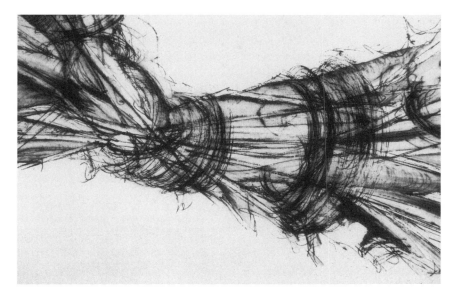

FIG. 9.3. *Departures #4, detail, 2002*

blood and destruction. According to some, this "green line," as it was known, was a term borrowed from military mapping vocabulary. A more populist view traces the name to the relentless vegetation that took over the asphalt and ruins. The growth of this wildlife that choked many of the streets and buildings was fueled by years of ruptured water pipes and overflowing drains. It was a dangerous urban forest planted with mines and unexploded shells hidden in the roots and foliage.[5] Although there were numerous demarcation lines that appeared and disappeared over the years, the green line had the most impact. You no longer existed undivided. The characteristics of the opposing areas and their inhabitants were embedded in people's mental geography with little room left for those who refused to belong to either camp.[6] Your two sectors were further divided by forced evictions that caused more segregation. Internally exiled, people were forcibly displaced within the borders of their own country. These mental geographies were continuously changing according to the surge of militia rules and the areas of fighting. People had to draw up continuously shifting maps of their world and had no instruments to assist them but their wits and their senses.[7] The boundaries and horizons within which they could circulate and interact continued to shrink over the years. A new generation of children and adolescents has grown up thinking that their social world cannot extend beyond the confines of the small communities where they have been compelled to live.[8] They endured through the years and witnessed their city and country being transformed until it became unrecognizable. With the official end of the war, barricades were pulled down and the country opened up to all its citizens. The dismantling of militia territories did not erase the demarcation lines still deeply embedded in the minds of the people. They soon began to venture into new territory and the exiled returned to lay their footprints in the rubble of war. A tradition has been born since, a ritualistic *Lebanese tour de force*. It is a yearly drive of will around Lebanon across visible and invisible boundaries to reassert this newfound freedom of movement, but the movement is across the whole country, not just the city. It is a reminder and an assertive act on this freedom that your inhabitants forget in their daily life, segregated still by habit.

A moment is born of a meeting between city and rejection
I got engaged to it, I offered it my ring
at every occasion that time suffocates me, I provoke it—
That moment lives with me now
at the height of its journey.[9]

Returning to a promised city that can never be delivered means the dismantling of the structure that holds up this longing. It means letting go of so much that is but a mere memory. A mere memory, is there such a thing under these circumstances? Memory establishes the meaning of the past. For the exile, it is the sense of loss that frames a past that has been frozen, and a future that has been stolen. My life was to unfold in you. Instead, you unfolded in me. So many versions of you have been unraveled so as to weave the veil through which I view all other space, all other cities. I tried touching my way through the world. Your space transformed itself into a scab on my finger, numbing, selectively stopping

FIG. 9.4.
Weaving #4, 2001

the sensation, always distorting, hiding, guarding the possibility of a full interaction. You have become my theater of pain. Yet you are my only hope. The pain of your loss has embedded itself inside me in such a way that I cannot experience space outside of your boundaries, the boundaries of disillusionment, of imagined perfection, of constructed futures, of distortions, of comparison, of constant disappointment.

ℭ

FIG. 9.5.
Beirut Landescapes #1,
detail, 1998

I said: That is the way to my home—he said: No,
you will not go through, and he lifted his gun . . .
OK. I have in each district
friends and all the houses of the world.[10]

With all the attempted returns over the years, the most shocking one was in
the summer when they declared the war was over. They claimed it was over.
They! They are the same ones who decided when it began. No one really won.
No one really could. There was no family left, no familiarity, merely strangers
in a landscape defaced by sixteen years of war. I had longed for that moment

for so many years that I had forgotten what I was going back to. We landed with the usual sweep the plane makes over the sea. That is when the war was shocked back into my existence. All memories were erased, all expectations forgotten. Where the airport once stood, the defiant guard of the country, slumped lethargic rubble, infested with rats and gunmen. We maneuvered our way in the dark among the debris, no signs telling us which dark hole led to which search patrol. Outside, where once there were memories of happiness now lingered the smell of death. Driving through the ruins, I felt like the late arrival at a murder scene. The body had been cleared away, yet the blood still flowed. Driving up to a checkpoint was a normal occurrence of this war. Your arteries, your veins, each possible path of circulation pinched to control the flow. What they were checking for had always been a mystery. Most of the guards were young boys, puppets to their hormones. I remembered seeing them standing by their gates. They were bored. Caught up in justifying their existence, the relevance of the moment was lost to them. Others were men, fully developed aggressors; efficient in their methods, they were searching for scapegoats on which to unleash their bigotry. A few rare gentler faces believed they were sustaining a semblance of order.

Upon coming to one of the control points that littered the roads of our city, we learned, with experience, to slow the car enough to assess the situation without raising suspicion. The seconds gained were used to determine the kind of predator ahead. However grave the outcome of the assessment, it was always too late to turn back. Sometimes a wager was made. Was the man in uniform the kind one looks in the eyes? While others our age were practicing the look of seduction, we practiced casting a direct look absent of defiance. A sharp glance waged a duel that was a guaranteed irritant to these men and their weapons. The arrogance betrayed a disrespect of the tool that their hand so casually rested on. It looked almost accidental, a consistent accident. The fingers never moved away from the trigger's reach, occasionally caressing it with a frightening sensuality. This casual stance in combat takes experience. The same experience that betrays the muscular twitch, the traces of perspiration on the smooth surfaces as the hand moves restlessly. Yes, it is almost casual for the untrained eye.

FIG. 9.6.
Beirut '91, 1997

*The killing has changed the city's shape—This
rock
is bone
This smoke people breathing.*[11]

This lifetime around, as we made our way through your streets, the silence
was unbearable. Each barricade we approached was empty. These are structures built to house aggressors and intimidate all who approach them. Yet
there they stood, defying all expectation. The car slowed down out of habit.
Inside the sandbags the imagination had etched a dead body. Weeds attempted to commemorate these graves. Even they succumbed and wearily rested
their foliage to dry. The moment is hard to define in words, yet it is so defined.

Veiled in silence you were resting after human violence had ceased. After the last mortar had exploded, the last gun shot, the last breath exhaled, another faceless victim laid dead. Danger lurked ready to pounce from the open wounds, ready to cripple from unexpected ammunition in the ground. Buildings had dissolved, the clean lines of their forms colliding. They sculpted views of the past, views of cruelty, of danger, of terror, of survival, of death. Ruins betrayed the stages of desolation. After the first few years, rummaging through war-torn areas, one saw abandoned buildings furtively clinging to themselves. Glass was shattered, metal bent, but traces remained of the lives they held before the destruction began. With the passage of time, even buildings lost their flesh. Repeatedly broken, glass returned to its origin and blended with the sand; wood was burned; metal sold. Only the defiant stone remained. One building was testing its structure, battling for balance and integrity. In the maze of its rubble, among the stench of inhumanity, a white shirt fluttered to dry. It made brisk movements to avoid the dirt that surrounded it, in its attempt to stay clean for its owner, for those few instances when it initially rested on his skin. It was not a desperate flag of surrender. It was the symbol of defiance, of survival, of one man and his family. This is the presumptuous reading that a stranger, looking for a sign of hope, assigns the situation. For the family, probably the remnant of a family, for that solitary survivor, the likely reality was that no alternative existed; there was nowhere else to go. The plight of the refugee reached him in his home. Metaphors can be conjured to describe the first footprints through ruins at the end of war. They remain feeble attempts. After the generic heading, it is in silence that the rude awakening from your nightmare exists. A momentary daze before the erasure of the brutal reality begins.

Whatever comes it will be old
So take with you anything other than this
madness—get ready
To stay a stranger . . .[12]

It was the familiarity of chaos that made one belong to you. The beauty of our country lay in the familiarity of its disorganization. Like a private room

FIG. 9.7.
Beirut Landscapes #1,
detail, 1998

that conceals itself, revealing a mess to uninitiated eyes. To the occupant, subtleties denoted each vicinity. When seeking out a person or a place, no direct and efficient route led to one's destination. Directions were given in reference to tree characteristics, potholes, and eccentric neighbors. You had belonged to your inhabitants not because they traded their body for labor and their money for land, not because they had a paper dispatched by the authorities telling them what parcel they can love and own, but because they appropriated moments and seeded themselves. Some passed these moments on for generations, others forged their own. My drive at the dawn of peace that claimed such a deep groove in my memory had captured a fleeting moment, the skeleton of what used to be. You soon succumbed to cleanup and restructuring, under siege again as machines ploughed through the heavily destroyed layer. The lacerations revealed that you had wrinkled from the inside out. A history of thousands of years was exposed. Discoveries unearthed during the urban excavations were displayed in an open-air museum—a juxtaposition of the accelerated ruins of modern warfare and the dormant ruins that struggled against time to reveal traces of the lives they contained. They were exposed for the survivors who flocked to the site to see the streets and shape of their ancestral city. The bloodstains fresh on their hands, history revealed them to be brothers, sisters, cousins. Each stared at this revelation of a forgotten past, a deep historic existence denied for war. The purpose of war! It still evades most of them. Most except those who had risen to rule their kingdoms. There is a breed of men that triumphs in the convulsive state of violence. For every one of them a group is bred to follow the empty promise of direction. In the upheaval of war, these decisive men forged a prescriptive path that the uncertain ones followed, as a way out of the chronic doubt that plagued them. With the ease of clear orientation, they robbed and pillaged to gain the riches of the dead, of the exiled, of the country.

ϭ

Darkness.
The earth's trees have become tears on
Heaven's cheeks.
An eclipse in this place.
Death snapped the city's branch and the
Friends departed.[13]

Standing among the ruins, I wondered what your new shape would be. That moment was one of the last tentacles I had to reach toward what is and what used to be. I thought I could finally mourn. You retain your name but the scope of the destruction does not allow mere reassembly. "Nothing remains of the old city except the scent of it that blows from old notebooks," wrote the late Nizzar Quabbani.[14] My Beirut had become events and spaces connected by experience, deformed by memory, erased by distance. Gone are the landmarks and favorite corners that embraced the sun at certain hours of the day. Gone was the particularity of your space, the

FIG. 9.8.
Weaving #2, 2001

alternating texture of old and new, now leveled by the ubiquitous marks of guns and shelling. You are being redrawn in the minds of designers who project perfection and avert their eyes from the life that flows in you—minds that impose order on the meandering of human life, replacing it by a grid of connections and superimposed systems, modeled on foreign modern cities, plagued by neglect and efficiency. Safe, sterile, the stench of antiseptic rises as your soul is traded for order. Should they succeed, you will become a place built, like so many others, upon a structure subordinated to rules. The interaction of the individual and the world, that space from which thought grows, will be erased. Eventually, your inhabitants will probably adopt a complacency of clarity, born of order and predictability, that directs one to plan an adventure before embarking on it. "War accelerates the evolutionary processes that are eminent to all architecture."[15] Ruins emerge with striking rapidity. All previous time frames of old and new are erased. Modern warfare does not differentiate between old buildings and new buildings, old women or young boys. They are all targets, leveled in their destruction. Your reconstruction has accelerated the slippage of the present into the past with a violent break. Memory has been torn in such a way as to pose the problem of its embodiment.[16]

As your erasure continues, and the reconstruction shapes a new city, the memory of the old will become more and more confined. The past will crystallize and secrete itself in the intimate space of the human psyche, the only repository of the memory of war. Year after year, the hope of the end of war was inhaled, shots fired, the hope exhaled. The war has ended, but the homecoming will never occur. In this new city, the perpetual irresolution between memories of the old city and the spaces inhabited in other cities becomes the exiles' monument of war. With time, the new Beirut will mold itself to the particular experiences of its inhabitants. Like all cities built on sectarian and religious lines, its survival will depend on memory or forgetfulness. At the moment, it is a slow dance with Mnemosyne that allows its inhabitants to live together again. "We choose not to scratch the surface," one woman reflected. "We do not forget, we just choose not to scratch the surface so as not to expose the wounds of our past."

✆

The flower that tempted the wind to carry its perfume
died yesterday[17]

Discussions of postwar reconstruction often revolve around rebuilding the past or creating a collective amnesia. There are mentalities of survival and mentalities of nostalgia. Whatever the outcome within the structures built, regardless of their style and their intention, even in environments created that attempt to erase the horrors of the past, memory persists. War appropriates space beyond physical destruction. Memories, muted to the privacy of their creators, are housed in the bodies that roam your streets. Mutilated bodies,

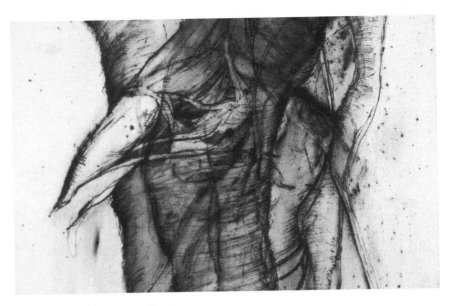

FIG. 9.9. *Grafting #2, detail, 2001*

with their scars visible, cast their own shadows on the redesigned maps of postwar landscapes. These tragic bodies stagger through your streets as live memorials. Your own physical repercussions endure. Disregarded concrete armors stand humbled as billboards, hard to avoid. A landfill has been created by the rubble of your destruction. The horror of your past used to create an environment for the future. It will be a silent memorial for a few generations, until people become too young to remember or care, or maybe simply prefer to forget. Until one day an acute historian, with the ability to capture subtleties on the outskirts of attention, discovers the slight change in your profile.

There is a style of buildings influenced by the military situation. With the destruction of the infrastructure, water cisterns began to emerge, rain water was collected, and wells were drilled for autonomous supply, which was then pumped when electricity became available. Electricity itself was creatively acquired from municipal cables. Buildings built in the era of war had a central generator or places for individual ones. These structures often included underground shelters or converted underground garages with storage areas built so that supplies could be stocked in protected areas. These new buildings were much sought after, as they had been the last guarantee of more-or-less normal living conditions.[18] Over-designed basements and thick concrete walls are strong reminders of the danger and violence that required this bunker mentality.

These new structures were built as extensions of the suburbs, intended to absorb the massive flux of displaced populations. As there were no municipal or civic authorities, the conditions that emerged constitute the most visible trace of the geographical upheavals caused by war.[19] Refugees arrived in large numbers and built structures in a hurry. Spaces were transformed. Exclusive beaches absorbed truckloads of refugees. The changing beach cabins, with their flowered shower curtains and small refrigerators for chilling beer and soda, became houses for whole families. But not all the displaced people were poor. Some of the new structures "reflected the relative wealth of the owners."[20] "Luxurious apartment blocks, in their ugliness, can mutilate a landscape just as much as, or even more than, the low lying temporary structures with their air of permanency."[21] The land had fallen victim to municipal neglect, causing the dehumanization of much of the living space. Hardly anything has been spared the commercial lust of war's predators. Homes were dwarfed by high-rise structures. Feeble, they sit in the midst of these giants that absorb their sun. Their inhabitants, veiled in constant shadows, have to rely on artificial light, when it exists, or candles, even on the brightest of Mediterranean days. Views were replaced by concrete and rooftops, the silence of the wind by toilets flushing, forests and gardens transformed into charred wastelands.

You asked me a question?
Embrace death first to ignite such a wound
Descend into my ashes and ask.
You ask which is my country?
My body is my country[22]

The physical reconstruction is expected to span thirty years, the human transition affecting at least two generations. Some people carry visible scars;

FIG. 9.10.
Deparrtures #1, 2002

others will live among those haunted by this vanished place, confined to origins stolen by the savagery of war. After seven years of rejuvenation, your past persisted. As you envelop me again, I discover that the designer's transformation only exists in pieces selectively imposed. Your Central District, the worst casualty, is being restored. Brand-new buildings reflect those not yet reclaimed in their lustrous glass, framed to heighten the contrast, framed to put the old to shame. High-rise apartments conceal their inhabitants in luxury, avoiding with violent cuts of roads and bridges that pierce through history and poverty blindfolded. How else would the consequences of war be erased? How else would the witnesses be effaced? The danger of such reconstruction, and what it decides not to see, lies in its potential to perpetuate the heart of an unstable and fragmented society, "an inaccessible ghetto of prosperity," in Michael Davies's words, building on the same political and social reactions that fueled the violence.[23]

The uninhabited, pristine new structures, waiting for the traces of life, seem oblivious to the life they await. So many of those hopeful apartments remain unfinished, naked concrete frames. Appropriated by squatters, they are transformed, subdivided by cardboard walls. These concrete skeletons stand as the hopeful ruins of reconstruction. Postwar reconstruction offers

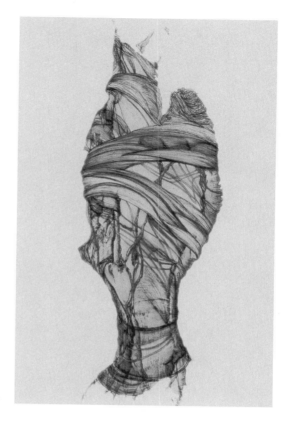

FIG. 9.11.
Adaptation #4, 2003

the opportunity to confront the social and political agendas in which architecture actively engages, while refraining from the seductive imagery of reconciliation.[24] Postwar reconstruction describes a condition of havoc, but also of anticipation. In the act of making and building, all those scripts that architects from around the world dream of, but seldom see performed, begin to materialize.

Space is charged. It cannot remain neutral to those who have seen politics and the degradation of humanity play itself out in it. When existence is shaped by the consequences of its loss, space cannot be reduced to formal manipulation. Time heals. Not my time. Twenty-four years and a single image can dissolve my heart in tears, twisting a narrow vein I thought had dried up. I have explored cities around the world in a futile effort to adopt them—adapt to them—a futile effort to love what I can only teach myself to

FIG. 9.12.
Adaptation #3, 2003

appreciate. After so many years it is your shadow that is being addressed. A shadow outlined for you even if it does not correspond to your shape. My mind wonders at the existence of this silent conversation. It is more of a soliloquy my brain performs for my hands. My hands perform for my pain. Within this cycle of submerged and emerging memories, lamenting memories, deceiving memories, it is hard to write as if the events are meeting these words for the first time. With each attempt, they remair rapped in that moment where silence reigns, before words finally merge into speech.

All drawings are by the author, Catherine Hamel, and represent a selection from the solo exhibit displace/graft/retrace. *All are ink and wash on watercolor paper.*

Notes

The selected verses are from the poem "The Desert," by Adonis, excerpted from the following two sources:

Eli Reed and Fouad Ajami. *Beirut: City of Regrets*. New York: W. W. Norton and Company, 1988.

Adonis. *Mémoire du vent: Poèmes, 1957–1990*. Preface and selection by André Velter, trans. Adonis and André Velter (Paris: Gallimard 1991). English trans. C. Hamel.

1. Edward Said, "Reflections on Exile," *Granta* 13 (1991): 172.
2. Eli Reed and Fouad Ajami, *Beirut: City of Regrets* (New York: W. W. Norton and Company, 1988).
3. Jean Said Makdisi, *Beirut Fragments: A War Memoir* (New York: Persea Books, 1990), 85.
4. Reed and Ajami, *Beirut*.
5. Gavin Angus and Maluf Ramez, *Beirut Reborn: The Restoration and Development of the Central District* (New York: John Wiley & Sons, 1996), 8.
6. Michael F. Davies, "A Post-War Urban Geography of Beirut," European Association for Middle Eastern Studies Conference, Warwick (July 1993): 1, at http://almashriq.hiof.no/lebanon/900/902/html/index.html.
7. Makdisi, *Beirut Fragments*, 73.
8. Samir Khalaf, "Urban Design and the Recovery of Beirut," in *Recovering Beirut: Urban Design and Post-War Reconstruction*, eds. Samir Khalaf and Philip Khoury (New York: E. J. Brill, 1993), 32.
9. Adonis, *Mémoire du vent: Poèmes 1957–1990*, preface and selection by André Velter, trans. Adonis and André Velter (Paris: Gallimard 1991). English trans. C. Hamel.
10. Ibid.
11. Reed and Ajami, *Beirut*.
12. Ibid.
13. Ibid.
14. Reed and Ajami, *Beirut*, 47.
15. O. Møystad, "Morphogenesis of the Beirut Green line," Beirut (1993): 4, at http://almashriq.hiof.no/lebanon/900/910/919/beirut/greenline/index.html.
16. Pierre Nora, "Between Memory and History: *Les lieux de mémoire*," *Representations* 26 (spring 1989): 7.
17. Reed and Ajami, *Beirut*.
18. Davies, "Post-War Urban Geography," 5.
19. Ibid., 6.
20. Makdisi, *Beirut Fragments*, 77.

21. Ibid., 90.
22. Adonis, *Mémoire du vent.*
23. Davies, "A Post-war Urban Geography of Beirut, " 6
24. Hashim Sarkis, "Territorial Claims," in *Recovering Beirut: Urban Design and Post-War Reconstruction,* eds. Samir Khalaf and Philip Khoury (New York: E. J. Brill, 1993), 102.

chapter ten

Diffused Spaces

A Sacred Study of West Belfast, North Ireland

CHRISTINE GORBY

*H*istorically, scholars have defined the sacred and profane as a binary set of opposites between the church (sacred) and city (profane), while neglecting the possibility of more complex or ambiguous readings. Analyzing the social constructions outside the church, in particular, can contribute to new definitions and valuations of sacred place in the public realm, the setting where the sacred exists amongst the profane. By stripping sacred space of "its politics and real history," our understanding of how sacred and profane spaces are organized or constructed never goes beyond "poetic metaphors."[1] This is critical for the primary "site of speculation"[2] in this study—the Catholic and Protestant neighborhoods of West Belfast, North Ireland—because political, social, economic, and religious identities have long interfaced there. Even though dramatically decreased church attendance and twenty years of banal urban redevelopment appear to have systematically eliminated the sacred in the religious geography, cultural changes continue to give rise to new forms of spiritual statement. Sacred memory is not disappearing, then, but is continually being redefined and renewed within the public streets. In this chapter, I will join together "myth" and "mapping" in order to create a mythology of "social collectiveness"[3] through the religious geography of Belfast.

How I Came to Study Belfast

In this chapter I explore how spirituality structures the built environment, a hidden history within cultural and social development. In my research, which I began in 1995, I have found that religious geographies are rarely explored and understood. What constitutes the sacred, then, seems to be left to the mind or body of each person to decipher alone. When anthropologists or religious scholars have explored the sacred, their cultural studies are either so defined or inaccessible as to make it difficult to pose general questions for other settings. I felt that the lessons I learned from the study of Belfast would have wider implications because there are many other cities, like Jerusalem or Rome, where sacred spaces have long found expression in the urban realm. I also found that there was a potent but unexplored link between memory and the sacred, hinted at in many texts but never fully explored beyond or outside the church. Given the global decrease in church attendance, but widening interest in spirituality throughout the world,[4] it seemed that the most active statement of sacred memory today would not be found in the church but outside, amongst the "profane" spaces of the city.

Unlike most outsiders who venture to Northern Ireland, family or religious ties did not lead me to Belfast. I was intrigued by the outright neglect of Belfast by researchers and the press since the height of sectarian violence there in the early 1970s. Before the most recent peace negotiations, when scholars and journalists did write about the city, they focused almost entirely on the religious conflict, with very little insight into reform or reconciliation efforts. The collective aspect of religious experience or shared sacred memory also led me to study Belfast. On the surface, the idea of anything collective in Belfast seems difficult or even impossible to imagine. The inconsistent nature of political authority on the physical geography makes the neighborhoods surrounding the city center appear isolated and fragmented. My hope was that a closer analysis of the city, then, would reveal elements of continuity and connection that are not (yet) apparent in the city's fabric.

If the church is no longer the primary mechanism through which shared sacred memory is constructed, through what vehicle does sacred memory find expression now? Though shared sacred memory might be found in the "silent witnesses" of the conflict,[5] I was not interested in "memorializing" memory by revealing people's private, individual grief. Memory might also be found in the large numbers of paperback thrillers that make false portrayals of the city by exploiting modern-day violence and fear. At this point I started to look more closely at sacred memory in the city through the modern myths of Belfast. These myths are not artificial or transient in nature but active, vital forms of memory, accepted by the culture as shared truths.

Current and Future State of the Project

The reflections on myth and memory and edited "field notes" that follow will together become the foundation for a future physical mapping of the city. To begin the physical mapping, I will layer and register a time-series analysis of historical maps dating from the 1500s to the present, in order to trace changes in the material fabric of the city over time. By studying how migration patterns and the rise of industrialization in West Belfast, for example, altered the marking of sacred memories over several centuries, I hope to discover how belief systems affected the form and structure of West Belfast neighborhoods. My plan is to integrate both the "myths" and "physical maps" of Belfast, so that they will become a framework for "a new mythology of the city."[6] In the long term, my hope is to make Belfast part of a larger study of cities focusing on the connections between memory and sacred space.

Purpose and Value of the Project

I undertook the mapping of West Belfast in order to record and remember important memories in the city history that are becoming lost. Studying and marking maps, walking and photographing neighborhoods with their abandoned high-rise Weetabix housing boxes, and other everyday inventories of places like schools, streets, and stores became my personal method for mapping visual memories and discerning sacred spaces.[7] Architectural historian Christine Boyer writes that "we are [all] . . . compelled to create new memory walks through the city, new maps that help us resist and subvert the all-too programmed and enveloping messages of our consumer culture."[8] In Belfast, though, what I am attempting to read is not a "consumer culture," but a religious cultural geography filled with indelible images of violence that are very difficult to overturn.

It is surprising that so little value has been placed on recording change in West Belfast. This is especially troublesome in a place where urban renewal programs of the past thirty years have fragmented smaller neighborhoods within religious communities[9] and where "religious/political lines have increased."[10] As Storr asks, "How does one represent a 'somewhere' that can never be fully comprehended, or whose specific parts cannot be made into a whole?"[11] In his 1941 novel, *Lost Fields,* Michael McLaverty considered the impossibility of mapping Belfast as he looked at the decay and destruction around him. Especially poignant are the lost streets McLaverty describes that are not lost in the sense of being able to be relinquished, but are destroyed, he says, beyond any possible reclaim.[12] Ironically, the "memory cannot be found in literature, the place where 'the passions are beside the facts.'"[13] Graham-Yooll, a journalist who traveled to Belfast in 1993, found it difficult to find anyone who "keeps a record of living comfortably in the front-line of fear."[14] How then, do you recover sacred memories in a city where so few artifacts or witnesses are willing to lay claim to their existence?

Reflections on Mythical Mapping and What Is Sacred

Throughout the history of Belfast many modern myths have evolved that have shaped the sacred expression of memory in the urban realm. A myth is a form of memory that originates as a single story from a ritual or sacred event.[15] The myth "narrate[s] human life and experience."[16] As it evolves over time, the myth becomes accepted by a culture or society as a reality or truth. "Myths are prose narratives which in the society where they are told are considered to be truthful accounts of what happened in the remote past. They are accepted on faith; they are taught to be believed; and they can be cited as authority in answer to ignorance, doubt, or disbelief. Myths are the embodiment of dogma; they are usually sacred and they are often associated with theology and ritual."[17] "But in the first instance the essential function of myth is to validate and justify, conserve and safeguard the fundamental realities and values, customs and beliefs on which depend the stability and continuance of a given way of life."[18] A mythology develops out of several narratives (or myths) that become complex, layered, and unified over time, so that the individual stories become part of a larger system of beliefs.[19] Mythologies are part of vital, living cultures, always evolving and active in the minds of their inhabitants. Modern mythologies, like memory, are "a current of continuous thought still moving in the present, still part of a group's active life, and these memories are multiple and dispersed, spectacular and ephemeral, not recollected and written down in one unified story."[20] Mythical mapping has been developed as a methodology that interweaves modern sacred myths with forms of mapmaking (both intellectual and experiential) to create a new mythology of Belfast.

Developing a spatial framework for what is "sacred" in the city is complex because it is never devoid of the political, economic, cultural, or social environment, making it a messy, often ambiguous proposition to sort out. Beyond the historic place that marks a narrative setting, the function of a sacred space goes further, by impelling one to recall something from the past that elicits a religious response.[21] A particular space to which a sacred narrative (or myth) is attached could invoke this religious response, as sacred places are the manifestation of sacred myths. Materials or the qualities of light or space could also contribute to the awareness of a sacred place, particularly when the sacred place is a psychological construction of the mind. When the sacred place is a physical or a mental construction, people often use the spatial classifications of mapmaking to locate themselves in relationship to the sacred. Centers, paths, and edges, for example, are geographic categories that help to locate and identify sacred places.

Mapping

Sacred places in Belfast are the manifestation of sacred myths from the city. By also exploring physical maps over time, I tried to imagine the city beyond the abstraction of their two-dimensional surface, where the coordinates, outlines of houses and lots, grids, scale, topographic lines, and other symbols are compressed. This is because no map is ever entirely neutral, making the process of mapping not only complex but also controversial. As instruments of knowledge and authority, maps can reveal how (sacred) territories are claimed and contested over time, how sacred spatial hierarchies are reinforced, or how access to (sacred) places is controlled historically. Maps make good witnesses. As visual texts they provide access to rituals, legends, and hidden or unknown narratives. By exploring the unique density of information in maps (the scientific or intellectual) with the kinetic aspects of perceptual experience (the experiential or mental), there is an opportunity to reveal the sacred territories of West Belfast.

Mapping involves a synthesis of both the intellectual (rational or scientific) and mental (psychological and perceptual) types of maps. The intellectual map refers to records fixed in time, or historical records. Authenticity is attached to intellectual mapping that draws on the need to rationalize and measure. Although the intellectual map is valued for its relationship to exact or real terrain, the complexity of ideas to be communicated often demands that this reality be limited or abstracted to be legible. Mapping reveals not only the material but also the mental (the psychological and perceptual) environment through the transforming aspects of journey and the evolving nature of time. Authenticity is attached to mental mapping because it more closely resembles actual experience. As my spiritual pilgrimage unfolded, I came to see that as a traveler, I could begin to understand West Belfast by creating a mental reconstruction of the city—a reconstruction that incorporated memory (time), narrative (tracing of motions, actions, gestures), and a record of my own direct experiences. Informal occurrences could be treated as spiritual landmarks with their own unique associative values.

What is compelling about the connection between myths and mapping is the moment when "myth and ritual combine to promote social collectiveness" through a mythical geography.[22] For example, E. O. James describes the "mythological topography" of native tribes of Australia, where people follow the same paths as their ancestors. They are guided by ceremonial sites (totemic centers) that protect those who walked along them.[23] Mythical maps, like the one just described, do not always have a formal expression; the collective understands them and there is no need to record or write them down. Scottish novelist Sara Maitland has also explored mythical geographies by studying pilgrimage routes that are marked on aged maps. Even though new maps are continually outdating the old ones, the old maps made by previous explorers serve a real purpose by encouraging others to reinvent new experiences and new maps along the same routes in order to "embody the sacred."[24]

Myth: The Sacred Body as a Present but Hidden Spatial Condition

The association of spatial direction with certain sacred values connects the body (movement) and boundary (geographical) within the mind and the imagination. It relates to the knowledge of something present but hidden, part of an initiation into the mysteries of the unknown. Historically, sacred frescoes in the crypts of medieval churches, for example, were known by their congregation but were made visible only once a year to a select group of the "initiated." Rilke refers to the example of the moon; even when hidden, it remains present within the mind.[25]

The relationship among religion, body, and geography first began with the idea of bearing witness—those who could testify to experiencing the resurrection of Christ. By the fourth century, the concept had evolved into the idea of martyrdom—those who were willing to be persecuted or sacrificed for Christ. The mythology of the religious culture has evolved to the idea of suffering with Christ, where the body has been made into a site for both sanctification and pain. The ritual becomes mythical by the continuous repetition of an event that connects a group or culture together.[26] Knee Cap Alley is a sacred place of power and suffering in West Belfast—known to insiders but unmarked and hidden to others. The terrorist rituals acted out there recall the rising, kneeling, and falling of a body during the positions of prayer. This association of pain and suffering with sanctification relates to the ambiguity and the multiple readings that sacred spaces often take on in the urban setting.

West Belfast is a confusing maze of "environmental walls, road enclosures, barriers and buffer zones,"[27] whose locations are understood to neighborhood dwellers and soldiers, but hidden to outsiders because they are never mapped. According to one visitor, the best guide to the city is the invisible map that "all locals carry around in their heads."[28] While centuries of religious conflict and violence have persisted in Belfast, the historical event that most clearly marks the renewal of "modern-day conflict" or "The Troubles" began on August 15, 1969. On this day, British troops were sent into the streets to take control of rioting in West Belfast, temporarily blocking off streets with a portable x-frame structure, or knife rest, strung with concertina wire. The first physical barriers made by soldiers were temporary structures. Later, soldiers built more permanent corrugated iron walls, with coiled barbed wire, in more sensitive areas,[29] forever altering the physical landscape of neighborhoods by reinforcing the boundaries of religious segregation. In the words of one resident, this was a time when "the voices and actions of the moderate [were] . . . much more difficult to find."[30]

Later the barriers became permanent "peace-line" walls—controlled places where sacred events and rituals continued to be recalled or played

FIG. 10.1. *(previous page) Map of West Belfast, North Ireland, before 1970, with drawing overlays from 1998. This map shows modern-day peace-line walls (in darkened lines), which are located between Protestant and Catholic neighborhoods in West Belfast. The peace-line walls are generally constructed of permanent materials, like steel and corrugated metal, and are fifteen to twenty feet in height. (See also figure 10.11.) New or rebuilt peace-line walls are also being made with more aesthetically pleasing materials, such as brick and stone. The "West Lag" highway, constructed in the early 1970s, is also drawn on this map to show how its construction affected settlement patterns in the West. It was built to connect the M1 and M2 Motorways, but it effectively acts as another wall cutting off the West from the Center City. (See also figure 10.2.) The peace-line walls were mapped on-site in 1998 and redrawn by Christine Gorby onto a map underlay from before 1970. The underlay was reproduced from an unidentified original in the collections of the Geography & Map Division, Library of Congress, Washington, D.C.* **Note map orientation: East is up.**

out. As defensive boundaries between Catholic and Protestant neighborhoods, the walls fit among each other like spaces between a maze path, physically marking differences that would otherwise not be legible in the urban fabric. Although some walls can be hundreds of feet long and several stories high, with effort one can eventually navigate around them to cross into "another" neighborhood, creating simultaneous conditions of porousness and impermeability in the city. Even though the peace-line walls disconnect what was once a continuous urban fabric, the memory of the former gridded street patterns of West Belfast remains suspended in the minds of the inhabitants (possibly to be later reclaimed).

Other boundaries physically mark shifts in religious territories that would not be apparent to the outsider. For example, religious territories are marked by street curbs and bollards that are annually repainted in the colors of each affiliation—the Irish tricolors of green, white, and gold used by Catholics and the red, white, and blue found in Protestant areas. The philosopher Maurice Halbwachs talks about memories that are linked to

FIGS. 10.3 *(left)*
AND 10.4. *(below)*
*Catholics and Protestants
paint bollards and curbs
annually in West Belfast to
mark boundaries between
their religious neighborhoods.
Photos by Christine Gorby, 1998.*

the time period in which they occurred.[31] Although repainting the streets is a ritual repeated annually, in the context of overall time it is rendered meaningless because the markings have had such an enduring presence on the landscape that their origin has been forgotten. Other conditions exist where no marks or tracings remain, except in maps, like the parish lines that once marked religious boundaries between neighborhoods. Watchtowers appear like multiples on the landscape but are never mapped. Similarly, concealed Royal Ulster Constabulary (R.U.C.) soldiers, Northern Ireland's police force (90 percent Protestant), who are posted along rooftops at entry points to religious neighborhoods, are not visible but known.

In the work of Northern Irish poet Seamus Heaney, marking and recording involves a need to escape from the presence of the city, removed and bounded from the disturbances of reality. Through a metaphorical structure of work, craft, and production, Heaney, an expatriate of Belfast, connects his mental conscious of Belfast with the tangible space of the rural Irish landscape through the voice of the "turf-cutter, ploughman, thatcher, water-diviner, salmon-fisher, or blacksmith."[32] In contrast to the destruction of Belfast city, the rural landscape is a sacred terrain to Heaney, a terrain where the boundary patterns of fields and hedgerows have remained unaltered for two centuries.[33] This venerated rural landscape recalls to him the memory of connectedness in the city, or what cultural historian J. B. Jackson calls the "collectiveness of society."[34]

Myth: The Cyclical Reenactment of Sacred Rituals in Spaces That Are Sought Out or Avoided

The cyclical reenactment of sacred rituals in spaces that are sought out or avoided evolves from a long history of foreign invaders who have controlled and shaped the city since its inception. The question of who should have authority over Northern Ireland—the United Kingdom, The Republic of Ireland, or most recently, Northern Ireland itself—continues to be at the center of the conflict between Protestant and Catholic communities today. Protestants (Ulster Unionists) on the whole believe that Northern Ireland should remain a part of the United Kingdom, where there is a Protestant majority. Catholics (Irish Nationalists) contend that Northern Ireland should become part of the Republic of Ireland, where there is a Catholic majority. Former English prime minister John Major first put the notion forth several years ago that the future of Northern Ireland should be determined by its own residents. This idea suggests that England will leave Northern Ireland when Catholics convince Protestants that this is an acceptable course of action.

The history of foreign invasion and control of Belfast and its surrounding region begins as early as the late twelfth century, when Anglo-Normans built a castellated fortification at the end of a *lough,* or long inlet, of the Lagan River.[35] Although there are no remains of this settlement, scholars generally agree that these first aggressors probably valued the site for its prime defensible position and because people and goods could be easily moved across the Lagan during low tide.[36] The translation of the first recorded name in this area from 1476, Belfast, or *Béal Feirste,* reflects its defense and transportation use, "the approach to the sand bank which led to the crossing place."[37]

As Belfast developed from garrison to market town between the twelfth and sixteenth centuries, control of the city and the surrounding Ulster region shifted between the local Irish, or Gaelic-speaking culture, and British Protestant colonists. For example, during the fourteenth century, Gaelic chieftains were able to take back much of their lands from the Normans in the Ulster region. By the late sixteenth century, though, Protestant English colonists began to exert force over the Irish after they recognized the development potential of their vast, open rural territories. Such interest prompted Queen Elizabeth I, near the end of her reign (1558–1603), to grant to her own colonists, such as the first Earl of Essex, Walter Devereaux (1541–1576), generous amounts of land. In the case of the first earl this included Belfast's Lagan River. Increasing tensions led Gaelic chiefs to challenge Protestant colonialists over control of the Ulster countryside. The nine-year-long battle ended in 1603, when forces of Queen Elizabeth I defeated the Irish chieftains, effectively ending their rule of the area.[38] Although chieftains were permitted to stay on their lands, not as Gaelic kings but as English nobles, the shift in authority to the British was not acceptable. British colonists took possession of lands of those who would not comply. By 1607 they had taken territory in six Ulster counties. This led five Irish chiefs to escape to the Continent in what became known as the "flight of the earls," prompting British Protestants to confiscate most of the remaining lands in the region.

With vast amounts of new territory available for colonial settlement, the British organized and promoted migration or "plantation" programs in

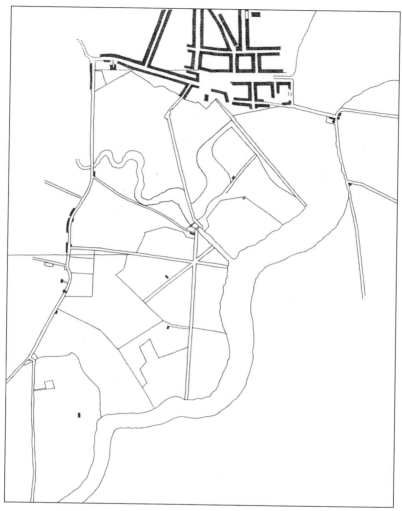

FIG. 10.5.

*Map of Belfast, 1783, showing the Belfast Lough (top right),
Long Bridge (below the lough), and Lagan River (below the bridge).
The Castle Gardens are located just below and in the middle of
the settlement area. The castle itself is shown by a small square
construction in the same area. Map redrawn by Christine Gorby and
reproduced from the original,* The Belfast Volunteer Review Ground
and Its Vicinity in the Year 1783, *in the collections of The Linen Hall
Library, Belfast, North Ireland.* **Note map orientation: North is up.**

both Belfast and the surrounding Ulster region.[39] Protestant immigrants from Scotland and England settled into several corporate boroughs throughout Ulster that were governed exclusively by British Protestant corporations.[40] With the granting of its charter in 1613 by James I of England (reign: 1603–1625), and the successor of Queen Elizabeth I, the new "Towne of Belfast" began its next phase of development into Ireland's most important colonial commercial trading center. British plantation probably reached its heights in the mid-seventeenth century, although passage continued well into the eighteenth.[41]

In Belfast the daily lives of new colonial immigrants and local Roman Catholics, who may have lived in the town as early as 1685, continued largely without incident.[42] In the early 1800s Catholics made up about one-sixth of the overall population, or twenty thousand people.[43]

As Belfast industrialized in the late eighteenth and early nineteenth centuries, however, tensions rose as massive "in-migration" to the city took place by Roman Catholics from the rural countryside. Although Roman Catholics remain a minority population in Belfast even today, migration had an enormous economic, political, and cultural impact on urban settlement patterns. One prime effect was the segregation of neighborhoods by religion. This occurred because jobs were almost always based on religious affiliation, with Catholics holding the lowest-status jobs.[44] New immigrants, whether Protestant colonials from England and Scotland seeking new opportunity, or Roman Catholics from the rural countryside fleeing famine and seeking work, often settled into areas near their jobs, thereby reinforcing settlement by religion. According to historian Fred Heatley, by 1850, Catholics, who made up one-third of the city's overall population of one hundred thousand, "were settled in religiously segregated quarters."[45] As time progressed, and tensions and violence increased, not only for jobs but also over the political question of "Home Rule" for Ireland, segregation rather than assimilation followed as people increasingly sought the protection of their own religious ethnic groups.[46]

As a manifestation of authority and control in the urban environment, religious segregation in Belfast is revealed through patterns of working, living, and worship.[47] According to Bill Morrison, "it is understood that territorial division along sectarian lines goes back to the founding of the city, and the 'holy wars' of Belfast over two centuries have altered nothing of the sectarian geography."[48] Boal and Douglas also support this claim, citing that segregation of

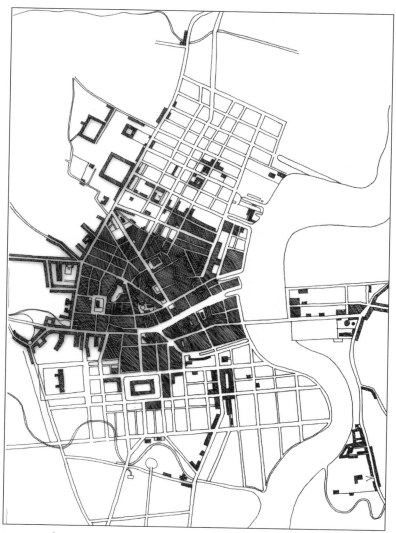

FIG. 10.6.

*Map of Belfast, 1814. The area to the west of the Lagan River is
known today as the Center City. What is now West Belfast is not
yet developed. Map redrawn by Christine Gorby and reproduced
from the original,* Plan of the Town of Belfast, *engraved for* Smith's
Belfast Almanack, *surveyor P. Mason, in the collections of the
Geography and Map Division, Library of Congress, Washington, D.C.*
Note map orientation: North is up.

FIG. 10.7.
Map of Belfast, 1897. This illustrates the vast increase in growth of Belfast as a result of massive in-migration, out-migration, and industrialization. Map redrawn by Christine Gorby from Marcus Ward's Shilling Map of the City of Belfast, *engraved and published by Marcus Ward & Co., Limited, Belfast, the Geography & Map Division, Library of Congress, Washington, D.C.*
Note map orientation: North is up.

Roman Catholics and Protestants was "characteristic of the city from its inception."[49] As forms of historical consciousness, peace-line walls could be seen as visible memories of actual physical confinement—social public expressions of prison internment and extreme suffering and deprivation. Alternatively, for those living on religious boundaries, peace-line walls are a form of protection, a defensible boundary between the private yard and house that many people

FIGS. 10.8 AND 10.9.
Contrasting wall mural images confront the passerby. A paramilitary mural shelters the side of a shop along Shankhill Road, a busy mercantile street in West Belfast. Another mural of Mother Mary and Child protects a retirement home on a nearby street. Photos by Christine Gorby, 1998.

do not want removed. While in some areas, discreet lockable doors are cut in the corrugated steel walls to ease navigation, making them permeable boundaries "open to passage,"[50] simultaneously other more permanent masonry and cast-iron walls are being extended and given permanent physical and, thereby, symbolic meaning. Transformational experiences can occur at the crossing point of these boundaries, as one shifts from one religious territory to another.[51] A Protestant man who was crossing through a Catholic neighborhood told me he made his presence as inconspicuous as possible when walking through religious neighborhoods not of his own affiliation.

Giant wall murals with highly charged militaristic images create forcible visual encounters before one enters the ordinary butcher shop, fruit vendor, or

FIG. 10.10. *View up the Shankhill Road, a major shopping corridor in West Belfast. Photo by Christine Gorby, 1998.*

dairy. As a mnemonic device, the enormity of these symbolic images, depicting bigger-than-life-size masked paramilitary gunmen or twenty-foot-high doves of peace, commands the constant attention of the outsider, while reminding the outsider to avoid entry into certain religious territories. The presence of these sacred shrines also indicates a loss of "communion" where the mural or object itself becomes the primary source for faith.[52] Mercantile streets, like the Shankhill Road, exist in a position parallel to twenty-foot-high ramparted avenues (or peace-line walls), built by military forces to disconnect Catholic and Protestant religious territories. One important mercantile street, the Shankhill Road, is located on block parallel to a very large-scale peace-line wall. Because of its massive height and length, this wall (composed of two twenty-foot walls with a zone between for military surveillance) continually commanded my attention as I walked along the Shankhill, cutting off every vista I attempted at the change of each block. Although the size and location of certain peace-line walls heightened the visual confrontation and disconnect between territories, other walls compel even the outsider to move forward. Painted murals on the ends of terrace buildings, for example, because of their imagery, appear to signify welcome sacred entry. In Catholic neighborhoods,

FIG. 10.11. *A peace-line wall was constructed one street parallel to the Shankhill. Photo by Christine Gorby, 1998.*

other immediate signals of entry are the street signs, using only the Gaelic language. The watchtowers, placed along peace-line walls, stand in contrast to the numerous Royal Ulster Constabulary (R.U.C.) police stations that are concealed or built inconspicuously within neighborhoods. Hidden labyrinthine street shapes in new housing developments promote confused movement, keeping the pace of nonresidents (and terrorists) at the perimeter, away from the collective sacred domestic settings.

Ritualized parading is a kinetic form of boundary making where select streets become sanctified spaces and religious territories become simultaneously encountered and avoided. Every July 12, to mark the victory of Protestant William III, known as "King Billy," over Catholic James II at the Battle of the Boyne, Protestant paraders symbolically march not only through their own religious territories but also those of enemies (spaces they would like to reclaim). The largest number of parades (over 75 percent) is organized by the Protestant community through the "Loyal Orders" (including the Orange Order, Apprentice Boys, and Royal Black Institution).[53] These fraternal organizations provide links to their countries of origin, and give religious legitimacy to a land that was historically taken by aggression.[54]

FIG. 10.12. *View to a dark throughway at the end of a West Belfast street. While access is preserved to row housing on the left, the unmarked R.U.C. station on the right creates a forbidding presence. Photo by Christine Gorby, 1998.*

Although church services regularly occur at various points along the parade routes, establishing "the renewal of faith that occurs at particular place[s] of pilgrimages,"[55] the parading has incited some of the worst religious violence during the conflict. In some ways parading becomes uniquely connected with the songs, readings of sacred text, and spiritual events that take place along the pilgrimage routes of Jerusalem.

People mark few religious memories directly outside their houses. A window covered with newspaper clippings describing a recent sectarian killing was the only memorialization I found, as I walked through the streets of the neighborhoods. Personal sacred relics, then, seem to be confined to the most private realm of the protected and defined boundaries of the home. Even though people may not mark their memories for public display, burials are ceremonies where the private grief is displaced into the public realm. Old black English-style cabs, ceremoniously drawn together into a sacred

FIG. 10.13.
*The protected view above
the passageway, shown
in fig. 10.12, is strewn
with debris. Photo by
Christine Gorby, 1998.*

circle, mark these rituals. Monuments do not appear to be for public enshrinement. Only two sacred memorials, the mythical sites of remembrance, were discovered during my walks through West Belfast. Each was physically connected with a place of worship in Catholic neighborhoods. One, located in an entry courtyard of a nunnery, was a statue of Mary, protected by high walls on four sides, with a gated entry and cast-iron spikes. Another statue, of Jesus, also stood fenced away from direct experience at the crossroad of two important streets.

Myth: Belfast as the Earthly Garden

The myth of Belfast as "the earthly garden" comes from panoramic-like murals of the same name painted on the walls of buildings in West Belfast. The images depict children running through paradisiacal places of abundant flowers and open green space. They promote the garden as a site for therapy in contrast to the many other images in the neighborhoods that

FIGS. 10.14. *Nature finds its expression in West Belfast through the mural* Garden of Belfast. *Photos by Christine Gorby, 1998.*

depict scenes of violence and control. By using natural images to show how God protects and nourishes humans, this kind of "figural nature" shows people how they, too, might experience the divine.[56]

The mythical origin of Belfast as the "earthly garden" comes from a veneration of the natural and rural landscape that can be traced back to the sacred earthwork constructions in Belfast by the earliest Mesolithic hunters and Neolithic farmers. The Giant's Ring and *raths,* or ancient ring forts, still mark some of the sacred territories of these ancient settlers. The memory of the rural landscape is also still evident in the nineteenth-century settlement patterns outside the city and throughout Northern Ireland, which changed dramatically as famine and poverty forced rural farmers to the city for employment.[57] Existing clustered farms were broken up and the landscape became dominated by small (mostly rectangular) fields bounded by hedgerows. This pattern has remained unchanged to the present day, making the rural virtually sacred terrain in contrast to the ever-changing Belfast city. Unlike Dublin, London, or Edinburgh, both rural and urban areas in North Ireland were unaffected by the eighteenth-century English "landscape gardening" movement.[58] As a consequence, large park systems were never integrated into the larger urban plan of Belfast. The memory of the "garden" remained in the rural landscape.

Continuously moving between the distant geographies of Belfast, the mountains toward the west, and the capitalistic city center to the east, is one example of the many paths between sacred demarcations in neighborhoods and the religious importance attached to certain geographical phenomena. A west-east movement historically dictates liturgical movement. Medieval maps and churches are also oriented to the east, toward the rising of the sun (the site of resurrection). The imposition of sacred spatial hierarchies, for example, on the Falls Road in Catholic West Belfast, is exemplified by a statue of Jesus at the high end of this long important road. The rising street also simultaneously provides a view toward the distant mountains. As the only visible spiritual landmark in the entire neighborhood, it is a literal but important hierarchical site of sacred memory. Jamie Scott and Paul Simpson-Housley also write about the literal or symbolic role of particular places, regions, or geographic phenomena in the development of religious self-understanding.[59]

The idea of garden as the site of therapy and positive spiritual participation has recently found formal expression in West Belfast after the awarding of over two and one-half million pounds sterling from Millennium Funds for open spaces. The multiple parks that are planned "aim to raise the pride and awareness of the beauty and value of open urban spaces, and to provide badly needed community facilities," while also addressing the needs of specific groups such as single mothers, the elderly, the disabled, and victims of Troubles.[60] One of several examples includes a small in-fill park on the peace-line between the Shankhill and Lower Falls areas, where an overgrown high wall will be removed and hard landscaping reduced. Another new park will preserve part of an existing rath (ancient fort) as part of the design.

Sacred centers are also illuminated by capturing select, framed views of intimate, spontaneous moments, the kinds of associative experiences that arise from drifting. For example, I once heard two women and a minister, blocks away on the Shankhill Road in Protestant West Belfast, singing sacred hymns, their voices greatly amplified by speakers and a narrow, rising street. On closer view, a churchlike manger gave them spiritual cover during their hymn-making. Thick landscaping on a metal fence bounded them from potentially dangerous outsiders.

Cemeteries in West Belfast are destinations and homes for the righteous dead, where persons viewed as religious martyrs or ethically correct members of religious groups are buried. Headstones in these sacred spaces are symbolically taken out into the social collective spaces of the city and re-created on walls of buildings as over-scaled epitaphs to each victim being sanctified. A Catholic wall painting of Bobby Sands, who died on a hunger

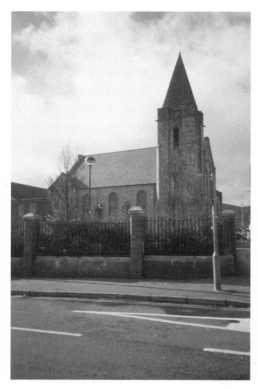

FIGS. 10.15 AND 10.16.
*Two women with a priest
in attendance sing religious
songs beside a church. A
gate and "manger" cover
protects them. Photos by
Christine Gorby, 1998.*

FIG. 10.17. *Stonehenge-like boulders line neighborhood streets in West Belfast where housing stock has been demolished, creating vast open areas. Although the stones are placed on empty sites like this to prevent joyriders, their placement also suggests a mystical presence. Photo by Christine Gorby, 1998.*

strike in 1981, is a good example. The symbol of the person merges with and becomes a new reality within the collective memory. Moving the righteous dead back into the main public thoroughfares to be encountered on a daily basis parallels an ancient Zen Buddhism funerary ritual. The "substitute body" is a practice in which the individual mortal body is transformed into the collective immortal body.

Earthly gardens in Belfast are sacred centers where people navigate but where there is often little evidence of collective gathering. Sacred centers can have conflicted or contradictory meanings as in the large, unplanned green spaces where terrace housing blocks were long ago demolished. Long paths of enormous boulders appear along the edges where housing once stood. Even though the boulders were placed there to prevent the onslaught of joyriders, they are symbolic of Stonehenge and other sacred gatherings still found in the urban and rural landscape of the British isles (such as the raths, or ancient forts).

Sacred centers have been formed out of neglected spaces. Ironically,

FIG. 10.18. *A public park in a West Belfast neighborhood, surrounded on three sides by housing. Photo by Christine Gorby, 1998.*

planned parks have been developed adjacent to the peace-line walls. Neglected, wasted space becomes reclaimed and remade again as a collective territory. Another example of a sacred center through which people move but where there is little sign of communal gathering is located in a Protestant neighborhood near a religious boundary. A community center with a militaristic mural on the garden-side wall was built at the base end of a large, triangular park. This pastoral rolling garden acts as a sacred center for the neighborhood, reinforced by continuous houses that bound it on all sides and three streets that also direct movement back to the park. The uninterrupted gaze between the park and the full-size paramilitary figures painted on the wall gives a strange human scale to this place. The garden shape creates tension because the heightened perspective of the funnel-like triangular form continuously directs one back to the mural on the community center. Memory becomes a form of both social practice and political engagement—a spiritual space for both communal gathering and political resistance.

FIG. 10.19. *The focal point of the park is this painted mural. Photo by Christine Gorby, 1998.*

Through a time-series analysis of historical maps and personal experience, mythical mapping is used as a methodology to explore how mental and physical boundaries mark public sacred territories between Catholic and Protestant communities in West Belfast, North Ireland. Although twenty years of anonymous redevelopment in West Belfast continues to eliminate systematically urban memory, cultural changes continue to give rise to new forms of sacred statement. Social conditions outside the formal confines of the ritualized sacred place, the church, contribute to new definitions and valuations of sacred space. By diffusing and relocating neighborhoods where political and social identities strongly interface with spirituality, a new consciousness of sacred memory can be revealed. Although it is sobering to consider that each group constructs memory from "the chaos of bloody happenings,"[61] the call by poet John Hewitt for "a new mythology of the city"[62] gives hope for the reclamation of sacred memory over a present history that seems to focus only on control and violence.

Notes

1. Roger Friedland and Richard D. Hecht, "The Politics of Sacred Place: Jerusalem's Temple Mount/al-haram al-sharif," in *Sacred Places and Profane Spaces: Essays in the Geographics of Judaism, Christianity and Islam,* eds. Jamie Scott and Paul Simpson-Housley (New York: Greenwood Press, 1991), 25, 24.

2. Robert Storr, *Mapping* (New York: The Museum of Modern Art, 1994), 14.

3. E. O. James, "The Nature and Function of Myth," in *Anthropology, Folklore, and Myth,* ed. Robert A. Segal, Theories of Myth Series (New York and London: Garland Publishing, Inc., 1996), 175.

4. Steve Bruce, *Religion in Modern Britain* (Oxford: Oxford University Press, 1998).

5. Jacques Derrida, untitled lecture, Pennsylvania State University, Department of Philosophy, April 1, 1998.

6. William Neill, "Re-Imaging Belfast," *The Planner* (Oct. 1992): 9.

7. Weetabix boxes refer to high-rise housing schemes built in West Belfast and other surrounding areas to rehouse residents after their low terraced housing blocks were demolished in the 1960s and afterward. The high-rise "boxes" that have not been demolished at present are mostly abandoned and are slowly being demolished.

8. M. Christine Boyer, *The City of Collective Memory: Its Historical Imagery and Architectural Entertainments* (Cambridge, Mass.: The MIT Press, 1996), 29.

9. Geraldine Boothman, "The Impact of Urban Renewal on Neighborhoods," *Ekistics* 44, no. 263 (Oct. 1977): 189.

10. Kate Kelly, "The Future: Views of the Women of Belfast," *Index on Censorship* 8–9 (Sept.–Oct. 1993): 22.

11. Storr, *Mapping,* 15.

12. Michael McLaverty, *Lost Fields* (New York and Toronto: Longmans, Green and Co., 1941).

13. Andrew Graham-Yooll, "Belfast," *The Antioch Review* (Oct. 20–23, 1993): 287.

14. Ibid.

15. Although I found in my research that there is no one universally recognized meaning of myth, there appears to be agreement on certain aspects of the term.

16. James Engell, "The Modern Revival of Myth: Its Eighteenth-Century Origins," in *Allegory, Myth, and Symbol,* ed. Morton W. Bloomfield (Cambridge, Mass.: Harvard University Press, 1981), 268.

17. William Bascom, "The Forms of Folklore: Prose Narratives," in *Theories of Myth: Anthropology, Folklore, and Myth,* ed. Robert Segal (New York and London: Garland Publishing, Inc., 1996), 2.

18. James, "Nature and Function of Myth," 180.

19. Engell, "Modern Revival of Myth," 264.

20. Boyer, *City of Collective Memory,* 67.

21. Ellen Ross, "Diversities of Divine Presence: Women's Geography in the Christian Tradition," in *Sacred Places and Profane Spaces: Essays in the Geographics of Judaism, Christianity and Islam,* eds. Jamie Scott and Paul Simpson-Housley (New York: Greenwood Press, 1991), 101.

22. James, "Nature and Function of Myth," 175.

23. Ibid.

24. Ross, "Diversities of Divine Presence," 109–10.

25. Roy Woods, "Against Mapping Invisible Worlds in Rilke's Duino Elegies," in *Mapping Invisible Worlds,* eds. Gavin Flood and Emily Lyle (Edinburgh: Edinburgh University Press, 1993), 141.

26. James, "Nature and Function of Myth," 175.

27. Kelly, "The Future," 22.

28. "Dividends of Death," *The Economist* 306 (March 26, 1988): 51.

29. Jonathan Bardon, *A History of Ulster* (Belfast: Blackstaff Press, 1992), 284.

30. Fred Heatley, "Community Relations and the Religious Geography," in *Belfast: The Making of the City, 1800–1914* (Belfast: Appletree Press, 1983), 142.

31. Boyer, *City of Collective Memory,* 26.

32. Terry Eagleton, "Review of Field Work," in *Seamus Heaney,* ed. Michael Allen, New Casebooks Series (New York: St. Martin's Press, 1997), 103. Eagleton is citing Frank Ormsby, *Poets from the North of Ireland* (Belfast: Blackstaff Press, 1979), 8.

33. Building Design Partnership, *Belfast Urban Area Plan,* vol. 1 (Belfast: Ministry of Development, 1969), 215.

34. John Brinckerhoff Jackson, *Landscape in Sight,* ed. Helen Lefkowitz (New Haven, Conn.: Yale University, 1997), 164.

35. J. C. Beckett, "Belfast to the End of the Eighteenth Century," in *Belfast: The Making of the City, 1800–1914* (Belfast: Appletree Press, 1983), 13.

36. F. H. A. Aalen, *Man and the Landscape in Ireland* (London and New York: Academic Press, 1978), 305.

37. W. A. Maguire, *Belfast,* Town and City Histories Series (Keel, Staffordshire: Keele University Press, Ryburn Publishing, 1993), 11. Maguire is citing Deirdre Flanagan, "Belfast and the Place-Names Therein," *Ulster Folklife,* trans. A. J. Hughes, 38 (1992): 79–97.

38. Maguire, *Belfast,* 12.

39. Philip Robinson, "Plantation and Colonization: The History and Background," in *Integration and Division—Geographical Perspectives on the Northern Ireland Problem,* eds. Frederick Boal and Neville Douglas (New York: Academic Press, 1982), 19.

40. Beckett, "Belfast to the End," 14. Ulster refers to the historic province of Ireland that was made up of nine counties. Northern Ireland refers to the area created in 1921 that is composed of six of the original nine counties of Ulster. Catholics typically use Ulster to describe their country; Protestants use Northern Ireland.

41. Robinson, "Plantation and Colonization," 19.

42. Frederick Boal, "Segregating and Mixing Space and Residence in Belfast," in *Integration and Division: Geographical Perspectives on the Northern Ireland Problem,* eds. Frederick Boal and Neville Douglas (New York: Academic Press, 1982), 251. Boal is citing Emrys Jones, *A Social Geography of Belfast* (London: Oxford University Press, 1960), 48.

43. Heatley, "Community Relations," 129, 133.

44. Ibid., 133, 138.

45. Ibid., 136, 137.

46. "Home Rule" concerns the question of whether Northern Ireland should be ruled by the United Kingdom, which has a majority Protestant populace, or by the Republic of Ireland, whose population is largely Catholic. Although the modern-day political radicalism, or "The Troubles," as they are known, began in 1969, recorded rebellion over the control and authority of the Ulster region and other territories goes back to the thirteenth century.

47. Boal, "Segregating and Mixing," 253. Belfast historian Frederick Boal has surveyed the available census information to trace segregation by religion groups in Belfast. In 1911, the year of the earliest available data, within Belfast County Borough, 41 percent of Catholics lived on Catholic streets and 62 percent of Protestants lived on Protestant streets. By 1969, according to the data within the same locality (but not including newly developed, less-segregated suburbs outside the city), the number of Catholics living on Catholic streets increased to 70 percent, while the number of Protestants living on Protestant streets increased to 78 percent. For more information, see Frederick Boal's article, "Segregating and Mixing."

48. Bill Morrison, "Making Belfast Work," *The Planner* 76, no. 49 (Dec. 14, 1990): 33.

49. Boal quantified the degree of ethnic segregation during the years for which data is available, including 1911, 1969, and 1972. He found not only a high degrees of ethnic separation at the beginning (41 percent of Catholics and 62 percent of Protestants) but also an increase in segregation later in 1969 (56 percent of Catholics and 69 percent of Protestants) and in 1972 (70 percent of Catholics and 78 percent of Protestants). See Boal, "Segregating and Mixing," 251, 253.

50. Leonard Thompson, "Mapping an Apocalyptic World," in *Sacred Places and Profane Spaces: Essays in the Geographics of Judaism, Christianity and Islam,* eds. Jamie Scott and Paul Simpson-Housley (New York: Greenwood Press, 1991), 117.
51. Ibid.
52. Surinder Bhardwaj and Gisbert Rinschede, "Pilgrimage in America: An Anachronism on a Beginning," in *Pilgrimage in the United States,* eds. Gisbert Rinschede and Surinder Bhardwaj (Berlin: Dietrich Reimer Verlag, 1990), 14.
53. The Orange Order was founded in 1795 and was composed of conservative Protestants from the Church of Ireland. The United Irishmen was founded in 1791 and was made up of a Catholic membership. At the founding of these two organizations, the Protestant Presbyterians, who were considered especially liberal, were generally more sympathetic with Catholics.
54. Bhardwaj and Rinschede, "Pilgrimage in America," 18, 23.
55. Northern Ireland Office; Bhardwaj, "Pilgrimage in America," 23.
56. Ross, "Diversities of Divine Presence," 107.
57. Aalen, *Man and the Landscape,* 142.
58. Building Design Partnership, *Belfast Urban Area Plan,* 215.
59. Jamie Scott and Paul Simpson-Housley, "Introduction: The Geographies of Religion," in *Sacred Places and Profane Spaces: Essays in the Geographics of Judaism, Christianity and Islam* (New York: Greenwood Press, 1991), xiii.
60. Quentin Fottrell, "Six Degrees of Separation," *Landscape Design Extra* (Mar. 1996): 5.
61. Chris Arthur, "An Image for Belfast," *The North American Review* 279, no. 6 (Nov./Dec. 1994): 14.
62. John Hewitt, cited in Neill, "Re-Imaging Belfast," 10.

℘

Bibliography

Aalen, F. H. A. *Man and the Landscape in Ireland.* London and New York: Academic Press, 1978.

Arthur, Chris. "An Image for Belfast." *The North American Review* 279, no. 6 (Nov./Dec. 1994): 13–15.

Bardon, Jonathan. *A History of Ulster.* Belfast: Blackstaff Press, 1992.

Bascom, William. "The Forms of Folklore: Prose Narratives." In *Theories of Myth: Anthropology, Folklore, and Myth,* ed. Robert Segal, pp. 1–18. New York and London: Garland Publishing, Inc., 1996.

Beckett, J. C. "Belfast to the End of the Eighteenth Century." In *Belfast: The Making of the City, 1800–1914*, pp. 13–26. Belfast: Appletree Press, 1983.

Bhardwaj, Surinder, and Gisbert Rinschede. "Pilgrimage in America: An Anachronism on a Beginning." In *Pilgrimage in the United States*, eds. Gisbert Rinschede and Surinder, pp. 9–14. Bhardwaj. Berlin: Dietrich Reimer Verlag, 1990.

Boal, Frederick. "Segregating and Mixing Space and Residence in Belfast." In *Integration and Division: Geographical Perspectives on the Northern Ireland Problem*, eds. Frederick Boal and Neville Douglas, pp. 249–80. New York: Academic Press.

Boothman, Geraldine. "The Impact of Urban Renewal on Neighborhoods." *Ekistics* 44, no. 263 (Oct. 1977): 188–95.

Boyer, M. Christine. *The City of Collective Memory: Its Historical Imagery and Architectural Entertainments*. Cambridge, Mass.: The MIT Press, 1996.

Bruce, Steve. *Religion in Modern Britain*. Oxford: Oxford University Press, 1998.

Building Design Partnership. *Belfast Urban Area Plan*, vol. 1. Belfast: Ministry of Development, 1969.

Collins, Brenda. "The Edwardian City." In *Belfast: The Making of the City, 1800–1914*, pp. 167–82. Belfast: Appletree Press, 1983.

Derrida, Jacques. Untitled lecture, Pennsylvania State University, Department of Philosophy, April 1, 1998.

"Dividends of Death." *The Economist* 306 (March 26, 1988): 49–56.

Eagleton, Terry. "Review of Field Work." In *Seamus Heaney*, ed. Michael Allen, pp. 102–6. New Casebooks Series. New York: St. Martin's Press, 1997.

Engell, James. "The Modern Revival of Myth: Its Eighteenth-Century Origins." In *Allegory, Myth, and Symbol*, ed. Morton W. Bloomfield, pp. 245–71. Cambridge, Mass.: Harvard University Press, 1981.

Fottrell, Quentin. "Six Degrees of Separation." *Landscape Design Extra* (Mar. 1996): 5.

Friedland, Roger, and Richard D. Hecht. "The Politics of Sacred Place: Jerusalem's Temple Mount/al-haram al-sharif." In *Sacred Places and Profane Spaces: Essays in the Geographics of Judaism, Christianity and Islam*, eds. Jamie Scott and Paul Simpson-Housley, pp. 21–57. New York: Greenwood Press, 1991.

Graham-Yooll, Andrew. "Belfast." *The Antioch Review* (Oct. 20–23, 1993): 286–96.

Heatley, Fred. "Community Relations and the Religious Geography." In *Belfast: The Making of the City, 1800–1914*, pp. 129–42. Belfast: Appletree Press, 1983.

Jackson, John Brinckerhoff. *Landscape in Sight,* ed. Helen Lefkowitz. New Haven, Conn.: Yale University Press, 1997.

James, E. O. "The Nature and Function of Myth." In *Anthropology, Folklore, and Myth,* ed. Robert A. Segal, pp. 172–80. Theories of Myth Series. New York and London: Garland Publishing, Inc., 1996 (originally published in *Folklore* 68 (1957): 474–82).

Kelly, Kate. "The Future: Views of the Women of Belfast." *Index on Censorship* 8–9 (Sept.–Oct. 1993): 18–22.

Maguire, W. A. *Belfast.* Town and City Histories Series. Keel, Staffordshire: Keele University Press, Ryburn Publishing, 1993.

McLaverty, Michael. *Lost Fields.* New York and Toronto: Longmans, Green and Co., 1941.

Morrison, Bill. "Making Belfast Work." *The Planner* 76, no. 49 (Dec. 14, 1990): 32–35.

Murray, Russell. "Political Violence in Northern Ireland, 1969–1977." In *Integration and Division—Geographical Perspectives on the Northern Ireland Problem,* eds. Frederick Boal and Neville Douglas, pp. 309–32. New York: Academic Press, 1982.

Neill, William. "Re-Imaging Belfast." *The Planner* (Oct. 1992): 8–10.

Northern Ireland Office. *Security, Crime and Policing in Northern Ireland: The Government Security Policy.* Belfast, May 1996, http://www.nio.gov.uk/pol_intro.htm#comdiv.

Poole, Michael. "Religious Residential Segregation in Urban Northern Ireland." In *Integration and Division—Geographical Perspectives on the Northern Ireland Problem,* eds. Frederick Boal and Neville Douglas, pp. 281–308. New York: Academic Press, 1982.

Robinson, Philip. "Plantation and Colonization: The History and Background." In *Integration and Division—Geographical Perspectives on the Northern Ireland Problem,* eds. Frederick Boal and Neville Douglas, pp. 19–48. New York: Academic Press, 1982.

Ross, Ellen. "Diversities of Divine Presence: Women's Geography in the Christian Tradition." In *Sacred Places and Profane Spaces: Essays in the Geographics of Judaism, Christianity and Islam,* eds. Jamie Scott and Paul Simpson-Housley, pp. 93–114. New York: Greenwood Press, 1991.

Scott, Jamie, and Paul Simpson-Housley, eds. "Introduction: The Geographies of Religion." In *Sacred Places and Profane Spaces: Essays in the Geographics of Judaism, Christianity and Islam,* pp. xi–xiv. New York: Greenwood Press, 1991.

Storr, Robert. *Mapping.* New York: The Museum of Modern Art, 1994.

Thompson, Leonard. "Mapping an Apocalyptic World." In *Sacred Places and Profane Spaces: Essays in the Geographics of Judaism, Christianity and Islam,* eds. Jamie Scott and Paul Simpson-Housley, pp. 115–27. New York: Greenwood Press, 1991.

Woods, Roy. "Against Mapping Invisible Worlds in Rilke's Duino Elegies." In *Mapping Invisible Worlds,* eds. Gavin Flood and Emily Lyle, pp. 139–49. Edinburgh: Edinburgh University Press, 1993.

chapter eleven

Profaning Sacred Space

Los Angeles in New Mexico

V. B. PRICE

"What we do anywhere matters, but especially here," Edith Warner wrote in her journals at Otowi Crossing, New Mexico, in 1933. The owner of a celebrated tea shop, traveler's inn, post office, and supper refuge for the scientists of the Manhattan Project, Edith Warner is the quintessential New Mexican. She loved the land and its people so deeply, she accepted responsibility to nurture and respect what she loved. She continued in her journal, "Mesas, mountains, rivers and trees, winds and rains are as sensitive to the actions and thoughts of humans as we are to their forces. They take into themselves what we give off, and give it out again. I wonder if it is my hatred and fear that turned the cedars brown and if the tumbleweeds ate my thoughts of some people."[1]

People who have identified with New Mexico tend to have thoughts like Edith Warner's, though rarely so eloquently put. Moving into an old railroad building on the Rio Grande in the late 1920s, living within walking distance of her friends in San Ildefonso Pueblo at the bottom of the "hill" in the Jemez Mountains that would eventually become the site of Los Alamos, Warner felt she had come home to New Mexico, even though her birthplace was in Pennsylvania. She endured many changes in her more than twenty-five years at Otowi, including the fantastic growth that took place around Los Alamos and in the Española Valley during World War II.

FIG. 11.1. *Albuquerque—canal, at the Nature Center, looking south. Photo by Mark Forte, 2004.*

She wrote in a Christmas letter in 1951, "How to endure the manmade devastating period in which we live and which seems almost as hopeless to control as drought; how to proceed when leadership seems utterly lacking, when individuals and nations seem stupid and arrogant; these no one human can answer."[2]

These are the same kinds of questions that have plagued many New Mexicans during their state's phenomenal growth since the end of the war. In the 1970s, New Mexicans used to call such growth "Californication." Now we call it sprawl, like everyone else. But disrespect by another name stings the same. And the pain is more than what those catchphrases can convey. When you live in a state of under one million people and watch it more than double in population in a little more than forty years, disrespectful growth comes to seem like an unstoppable disease. To this species of economic and stylistic colonialism that comes with rapid change, nothing matters but expansion.

FIG. 11.2. *Albuquerque, looking cross I-40, toward the volcanoes. Photo by Mark Forte, 2004.*

The landmarks and civil comforts of your home place turn over every three years or so in a dizzying future shock, especially if your downtown historic buildings have been demolished by urban renewal and replaced with a succession of fad and generic structures. Fundamentally, such disorientation comes about not only by erasing historic memory, but by taking suburbanism into what for many people is the holy land of the New Mexico high desert, and forcing the oases of New Mexico towns and cities to be desiccated by the asphalt, junk-building world of Californicated mall culture. Those who think of New Mexico as their homeland, and that includes, in my book, everyone who identifies with the spiritual and familial magnetism of the landscape, personally mourn the obliviating changes that come with that kind of growth. It offends our memory of what peace and majesty mean as defining qualities of New Mexican sacred space. Something precious to us has been profaned.

In its simplest sense, to profane a natural or human place of spiritual power is to deny its potency, treat it with disdain, and victimize it. In order to exploit, one must first devalue. Tyrants dehumanize opponents, callous land speculators denigrate the very landscape they want to sell and "improve."

People all over the world continually experience the helpless misery of witnessing beloved places, icons, and venerable ways of life degraded into mere objects of opinion or spaces of exploitation. As Edith Warner would say, exploiters do not think that New Mexico really matters to anyone.

New Mexico is starting to forget the meaning and value of places that cannot be commodified, like communal land grants and community water rights. But, obviously, it did not use to be that way. Pueblo and Hispano builders, through both materials and a pragmatic respect for light and natural resources of all kinds, made human structures that honored the dignity of the land itself. In much the same way, the Anasazi ancestors of the Pueblos gardened by using every available water supply, irrigation method, and mulch, and by establishing their gardens at the end of flood fields. Ancient builders and their Hispanic counterparts knew the value of land and light and built to connect with them wherever they could.

Until almost the middle of World War II, Albuquerque was a little city, a rail center for the region, and a crossroads connecting the famous Route 66, east and west, and U.S. 85, north and south. Its Hispanic Old Town was founded in 1706, and the villages and haciendas north and south along the Rio Grande formed a pattern of farming communities that lasted for well over three hundred years. The Rio Grande irrigated Albuquerque's rural valleys so they became a major agricultural powerhouse, with the Rio Grande being called by some "The American Nile." Fruits and vegetables were sent west by rail as far as California. Old Town, with its original Spanish mission church and Hispanic neighborhoods, was not incorporated into the rest of Albuquerque, with its railroad downtown, until 1949, nine years before I arrived. Downtown then was the small but vibrant hub of the city, with numerous eccentric architectural gems, including the mission-style Alvarado Hotel, the Taos Pueblo–like Franciscan Hotel, the Pueblo deco Kimo Theatre, which is the only one of those buildings still standing. Route 66 went right down the middle of downtown, where it was called Central Avenue, and U.S. 85, called Fourth Street, intersected it in the heart of the cityscape. That crossroads, incidentally, bore the passage of the first atom bomb, soon to be exploded at Trinity Site, as it rolled out of Los Alamos through Albuquerque and south to its final destination south of Carrizozo.

As I drove east from Flagstaff to Albuquerque for the first time, towns, pueblos, hamlets, and settlements all seemed like islands of humanity, tiny oases in the midst of a vastness as inhospitable as it was magnificent. Driving

FIG. 11.3. *Albuquerque, downtown Central Avenue (Route 66), north side. Photo by Mark Forte, 2004.*

over the top of Nine Mile Hill, I first looked down into the Albuquerque Basin, at about 3:00 in the afternoon, not unlike Bernal Diaz de Castillo's first sighting of the valley of Mexico in all its grandeur. But Albuquerque was not the gold and white metropolis of Tenochtitlán. It was a little urban oasis in the Middle Rio Grande Valley, backed by huge mountains, with a wide river and a gorgeous, vibrant, green *bosque* running through the heart of the urban core. It felt right that the biggest city in New Mexico should be tiny and contained, and radiating with the sense of refuge. When I drove up Central Avenue that day, past Old Town and through what I would come to see years later as an eight-block-long living museum of American architecture from 1880 on, and then up the sand hills to the University of New Mexico, I found a further, deeper refuge, an oasis within the city. That is what the central campus of the University of New Mexico felt like the first time I drove up Cornell. With its Pueblo-Spanish-style buildings that looked not unlike the mesas and bluffs that I had passed on Route 66, and its unmistakable sense of place, it made me feel instantly at home. All my memories and expectations of the built environment, ingrained in me from Los Angeles, were instantly replaced with my unformed and inarticulate love of New Mexico, all memories, that is, except for the sea, which I eventually came to equate with the desert.

The architecture downtown was a fabulous mix of 1950s brutalism, mission, Santa Fe style, and Puebloid hotels, a Pueblo deco theater, Italianate mansions, a tile replica of the Doge's Palace in Venice, an evocation of the Parthenon, and virtually every other kind of building style one could imagine coming west with the railroad. I suppose one might call that architectural colonialism too. But I prefer to think of downtown before the days of urban renewal as a reflection of New Mexico's character as the most culturally diverse and fascinating state in the union. And nowhere did it invade the desert and mountain landscapes.

In 1958, Albuquerque was still what it had been since the war—the commercial center of the state; an amalgam of ranching and farming lifestyles; a collage town; a military R&D headquarters; a meeting place for Anglo, Hispanic, and Native American cultures; the home of the largest "Indian School" in the West; and a city that was contained by mountains, mesas, and volcanos, with an almost-wild river running through it. Albuquerque was an oasis of civility and culture in the high desert.

It was not more than ten years, however, until the oasis had been invaded by Los Angeles–style asphalt deserts, in the form of interstates, strip malls, and massive shopping malls that drained downtown of its vitality. When I was nineteen, I got a job as a roustabout at the circus-like opening of one of the first big developments on the West Mesa, called Paradise Hills. The grand opening featured James Garner as Maverick, and offered food and drink to all and sundry. Little did I know that the Paradise Hills opening-day circus signaled a boomtown growth west into the high-desert landscape that forty years later would desecrate the sand hills and contribute to Albuquerque perilous water shortage.

It took me until I turned thirty-one and started reviewing growth and planning in the city to realize that the place I loved was already a lost place and was losing itself right before my eyes, sprawling into the desert, and welcoming Californicated desiccation into its inner precincts. That sense of waking up one day to future shock is part of the phenomenon of living in slow towns that become boomtowns.

Although downtown Albuquerque fell on hard times that lasted for more than forty years, the University neighborhood and its Nob Hill shopping area

FIG. 11.4.
Downtown
Albuquerque from
Pat Hurley Park.
Photo by
Mark Forte, 2004.

stayed virtually the same, and even became more prosperous with the federal Main Street Program of the late 1980s and the 1990s. The more I came to understand the city, the more internal oases appeared to me, until I could see Albuquerque as an archipelago of oases in the rural north and south valleys, and in the small villages in the mountains and upriver. In an increasingly generic city, with its sprawl and interior desertification, the spirit of New Mexico tenaciously held on, and does so to this day.

As an architectural critic in New Mexico, I have written about these intense feelings of grief and anger at disrespectful change for over thirty years. To make sense of my emotions I had to develop a theory early on. It goes like this. Everyone has an opinion about how places make them feel, even if it is never voiced or consciously recognized. So it is not unrealistic to infer that all places have meaning, however fragile and unexpressed. Land struggles occur not only over profit, but also over different value systems.

Such differences become glaringly apparent, for instance, when acequia associations in northern New Mexico view water and ditch systems as a sustaining and fundamental part of their life, while urban developers view water as a mere commodity. Our meaning of place is associated, inevitably, with our life experiences, both culturally and historically.

This understanding became clear to me when I started reviewing the built environment of Albuquerque for alternative newspapers, treating the cityscape in much the same way as one would respond to a work of art. As a journalist, I worked to give verbal form to what I knew were largely unconscious and visceral responses to where I was. For the most part, my responses came to me simply as forms of pleasure or pain. But I was fascinated, almost tormented, by my own reactions. Why did certain places make me feel miserable, while others ennobled me and filled me with ease and joy? I have spent over three decades trying to answer these apparently simpleminded questions. And as a writer and a teacher, I have tried to help others articulate the emotions of their own responses to place.

Basically, though, it is about love or the lack of it. As physician authors of *A General Theory of Love* have written, "Love is not just the focus of human experience but also the life force of the mind, determining our moods, stabilizing our bodily rhythms, and changing the structure of our brains. The body's physiology ensures that relationships determine and fix our identities. Love makes us who we are, and who we can become."[3] Although the authors are speaking of human relationships, I have always believed that the same holds true between people and places.

New Mexico is the fifth largest, most culturally isolated, among the least populated, and most "foreign" of the fifty states. New Mexico and parts of Arizona are the last bastions of fully intact Native American cultures and languages in North America, and the original, sustaining Hispanic heartland north of the Rio Grande.

Trying to make sense of my intense feelings about New Mexico has been a highly charged enterprise for me, as I quite literally fell in love with the cultures, landscape, and history of this place, in much the same way that Edith Warner did close to fifty years before I arrived. The pervasive emotions of my relationship with New Mexico are so integral to my personality by now that I have to be careful not to confuse clear-headedness with avid-heartedness. Putting aside obvious political and commercial design strategies that humiliate or entice a populace, the meanings of places are associated with our own emotional overlays from the past. Much like a behavior or word or situation that triggers off powerful reactions from the past to relatively mundane matters of the moment, all places incite within us patterns of memory associated with subtle sensual cues.

That being said, the meaning we give to places also reflects an infinite variety of cultural symbols and personal metaphors that refine our responses. Having a conversion experience with a place, however, changes your life forever. The experience can even replace the deep reference point of your childhood home, or can combine with it to give you an often untidy and unruly set of rooted expectations. I believe that is what happened to me in New Mexico.

I struggled as a critic with the Californication of New Mexico in the 1970s because I did not want my first hometown, Los Angeles, to obliterate my new home with urban forms appropriate to one of the largest and most congested cities in the world. I had memory conflicts between my early years in Los Angeles, which can be described as an orchard paradise and a vast beach resort that ran amuck, and the rest of my life in ever-changing Albuquerque, which could also be described as having run amuck from its early days as a crossroads and railroad town. Many of my critical stances against generic impositions on the New Mexican landscape come from my antipathy to Los Angeles, which has oddly dissipated as I have grown older, though I still find L.A. surrogates in the desert west to be absurd.

I came, eventually, to see these memory conflicts in terms of the metaphor of light—the light on the Pacific Ocean and the light of the New Mexico high desert. Early Spanish adventurers in the Southwest also referred to New Mexico as the land of clear light. Disrespectful change sucks the light right out of a place, usually with its byproduct, the choking brown haze of air pollution. It creates a deadness where light should be. And light is what defines beloved ideals wherever they are.

When I first drove across the Arizona-New Mexico border in 1958, at age eighteen, I had come from a landscape obscured and insulted by smog. I had to drive seven thousand feet up into the San Bernardino Mountains to leave the Los Angeles basin's visual and pulmonary purgatory. By the time I had reached the long red bluffs outside Gallup, New Mexico, even I, a hardened teenager normally oblivious to anything but girls, sports, and my own insecurities, even I could tell the land of clear light was the most beautiful place I had ever seen, even more transforming for me than the ocean had been. And I could see so much of the land from virtually any vantage point, a terrestrial version of the solace and dignity of the sea.

Many years later, my oldest friend, the late Michael Jenkinson, adventurer, river runner, author, wrote a book called the *Land of Clear Light*. With his lyrical prose, he described the architectural effects of shadow and luminosity on the landforms of New Mexico, so many of which seem like habitations of the gods. So the idea of "clear light" for me, now, has a personal sadness in its shadows, the loss of candor with a lost friend, and the gradual loss of the landscape I came to as a boy, watching it devoured by the cancerous built environment I had left behind. Light still fills the New Mexican land, though, with a metaphysical joy and a lucidity that feels both internal and transcendental, much as the memory of friendship does.

Recently, I read about the quality of light in ancient Greece, a light so clear, with lines of shade so precise, that fluted columns were designed to catch the pure fine lines of shadow.[4] Far from being intellectual abstractions in stone, Greek architecture embodied the contemplation of space that was as natural and grounded as light on leaves. As I read this, I found myself flooded by recollections of buildings, like mesas, carved in light; like the Lukachuchi cliffs turning blood red in twilight; like Pueblo Bonito in Chaco Canyon bathed in the clear, cold moonlight; like the Zimmerman Library at the University of New Mexico, shimmering at early twilight.

My sense of place in New Mexico comes from the realization that buildings belong to the land, and that humans and landscapes create each other in a field of clarity and pellucid calm—a calm not unlike that which early dawn winter light brings to Chaco Canyon, when you can see morning stars in much the same way perhaps as Anasazi star watchers could see them 2,500 years ago.

Such fantasies and memories have caused me to expect, perhaps, too much from New Mexico's present built environment, commodified and abstracted, as it is, from its natural setting. But high expectations or not, there is a particular horror, not unlike the slow realization of the loss of memory in dementia, that comes with watching the monuments of your past ripped from the present to accommodate "growth." When the human and natural landscapes have continuity, they reflect your healthy memory; they are your memory in the flesh.

What, then, is the "mental environment" of designers who must work within the conflicting "memory cultures" of a fast-changing city like

Albuquerque, set in a vast, slow-changing place like New Mexico? The basic conflict in New Mexico, I believe, is between those who have deep, loving memories of what has been called not inaccurately "The Land of Enchantment," and those who have no local memories at all but try, instead, to make New Mexico and its built environments conform to generic patterns or to memories of their own hometowns. It is this conflict, and the context of future shock in which it flourishes, that causes in some the disquiet of disorientation associated with losing one's memory.[5]

I have stopped reviewing architecture, and now find my columns more environmentally than architecturally oriented. At some point, I could no longer deal with my two conflicting and irreconcilable memory contexts, those of design and economics, and those of social and humanitarian issues. Although I have learned to appreciate the happy madness and consumptive energy of my old hometown, Los Angeles, as some sort of marvelously dangerous and fascinating mutation that cannot be stopped, I still hate to see Los Angeles blustering its way into the life and environment of Albuquerque. It seems to me that this bullying invasion is designed to humble and eradicate the irreplaceable personality of Albuquerque as a New Mexican city.

Part of the reason I stopped being a reviewer of my city is that it came to me that no one in *particular* was doing that bullying. It was, instead, the full force of American consumer culture spreading its manifest destiny into every nook and cranny in the nation. I am surprised that Albuquerque has survived so long with much of its soul still intact. And it may have held on long enough to see the emergence of a true limit to growth that is specific, but not unique, to our region—the amount and quality of water available to us. Albuquerque has allowed itself to be dominated by generic urban forms on the assumption that it had an unlimited amount of pure fossil water in its vast aquifer. U.S. Geographical Survey studies in the last decade have shown that to be grossly inaccurate. In fact, Albuquerque's aquifer is draining so fast, it could have as few as twenty-five years left, without an outside water supply coming in, through a maze of lawsuits and political gambits, from Colorado.

And that is the principal lesson of disrespectful growth—it treats specific places, with their distinctive cultures and natural limitations, as if they conformed to some uniform standard of excess and exploitation—in other words, as if they had no meaning, no history, no network of memories and natural patterns unique to themselves. The individuality of places does not matter to those who profit from disrespectful growth. And I believe such places eventually pay a heavy price. Not only do they lose themselves, but they also can come to lose their imported prosperity in the life-and-death competition among cities, large and small.

My memories of that first sensation as a teenager of being in a holy land of light have never left me. Such idealization of light is familiar and empowering to people whose minds have been transformed by the pure vastness of New Mexico and its refined sense of distance and perspective. Surely, for Albuquerque, a middle way that accommodates growth and preserves the city's New Mexican personality is both the only honorable and the pragmatic strategy to thwart the miseries of disrespect and environmental ruin. As Edith Warner said, "What we do anywhere matters, but especially here."

Notes

1. Patrick Burns, ed., *In The Shadow of Los Alamos: Selected Writings of Edith Warner* (Albuquerque: University of New Mexico Press, 2001), 165.
2. Ibid., 112.
3. Thomas Lewis, M.D., Fari Amini, M.D., and Richard Lannon, M.D., *A General Theory of Love* (New York: Random House, 2000), viii.
4. J. Donald Hughes, *Pan's Travail: Environmental Problems of the Ancient Greeks and Romans* (Baltimore: Johns Hopkins University Press, 1994), 12.
5. Anthony Anella and Mark C. Childs, *Never Say Goodbye: The Albuquerque Rephotographic Survey Project* (Albuquerque: The Albuquerque Museum, 2000), 25.

Part Four

Voices from the Studio

chapter twelve

What Memory?
Whose Memory?

THOMAS FISHER

*I*n my first day at architecture school, my studio professor said that he would teach us how to think like architects, which would demand that we forget all that we thought we knew about the subject. That one comment by that professor, as I later learned, turned out to be prophetic. Many in our profession have real ambivalence about memory of the past, an ambivalence that arises from the way we teach and think, and that reveals a lot about the strength and weakness of architectural education and the field in general.

The strength of our discipline lies in the peculiarly Socratic way in which architects learn and then apply those lessons to the world. At a time when many professionals present themselves as experts, coming to pre-defined problems with solutions, architects try, as did Socrates, to redefine clients' problems, to expand their considerations, to question their assumptions. Not until the completion of a project do many clients realize that they have received an education as well as a building. Also, at a time when higher education so often involves the absorbing of information in ever-larger classrooms, the one-on-one conversations in the architecture studio between students and professors, aimed at challenging beliefs and revealing what we don't know, continues a Socratic form of learning all but lost in universities. Few professors in other fields spend so much time with so few students with so little structure to such a great effect.

There is a weakness to this Socratic method, however, that the remark of my first-year professor exposed, had we known enough then to see it. In the Socratic urge to challenge, create, and resolve, many architects try to forget the past, especially their own past before becoming architects, or the past of their clients. It is as if with new buildings should come new people, without memory. Significantly enough, Socrates himself distrusted memory. In Plato's dialogue, "Theaetetus," Socrates argues that memory, which he likens to impressions in soft wax, is "indistinct . . . easily confused, and effaced,"[1] making it a primary source of error in our thought and action. We do not err, says Socrates, when dealing with visual images or abstract ideas. He demonstrates this by saying that he knows, in looking at his two companions, Theaetetus and Theordorus, that they are not the same person, or in thinking about an abstract idea, like the number twelve, that it is not the number eleven. "The only possibility of erroneous opinion," says Socrates, "is when . . . I try to assign the right impression of memory to the right visual impression."[2]

This distrust of memory has affected the architectural profession as much as Socrates's form of dialogue. All professionals, of course, share a distrust of memory to some extent, seeking to avoid the errors that come from not remembering something correctly. But architects have an especially difficult time with it since, unlike other professions such as medicine and law, we do not have well-documented procedures or cases to rely on for our decisions. In our more heuristic discipline, where trial-and-error and rules-of-thumb count for much more than in most, architects must depend upon their memory as a tool and so need to keep it clean, uncluttered, and free of old ideas. Even when dealing with the certain knowledge that Socrates saw in visual images and abstract ideas, architects tend to store that knowledge in their memory, for personal reference, rather than have a set of images or ideas that everyone in the field shares and agrees upon as true. And yet, because the profession depends upon memory to such an extent, it also seems to be more wary of it, more cognizant of its limitations. My first-year professor did not want us to forget everything, just those things that might undermine the new memories we were going to acquire.

If architects cannot escape memory in the process of designing, neither can the profession avoid it in the interaction with clients and communities. Human beings, organizations, environments—all come laden with memories and associations of various kinds. Although this often makes the design process more difficult, as architects occasionally trigger in clients a painful reminder or unpleasant association with something said or drawn, memory and architecture in most projects remain closely intertwined. As Gaston Bachelard writes, "Memories are motionless, and the more securely they are fixed in space, the sounder they are."3 But how, then, does the architect strike a balance between a wariness of memory and a need to embrace it?

I encountered that dilemma repeatedly during the years I worked as an editor of the magazine *Progressive Architecture (P/A)*. Many architects presented their work to us as acts of pure will and imagination, emphasizing the originality of what they did and downplaying any connection to the past, either theirs or their clients'. When I inquired about such a connection, I usually got a denial, as if resorting to memory represented a sign of weakness, a giving in to nostalgia. The shorthand for this was, "I am not a postmodernist," even from those who had made their name with that movement. And when architects did acknowledge influences from the past, they usually referred to architectural history, listing the landmarks that had influenced the project, a tactic that frequently backfired, since the new building rarely ranked anywhere near those mentioned as precursors.

I have also encountered this dilemma in a different form in the schools. Many faculty still emphasize the original and unprecedented in students' work and, indeed, in their own. As one faculty member said at the beginning of an awards program I participated in, "I won't recognize anything I've seen before." Meanwhile, other faculty have begun to emphasize and explore memory as a form of knowledge too-long neglected in architecture. Here, memory serves as a suppressed text in design and a potentially subversive activity that aligns well with the Socratic questioning that already goes on in the studios. The schools, however, need to ensure that this ambivalence about memory among the faculty does not itself become divisive. We need to value both forgetting and remembering, and hold them in a dynamic balance pedagogically as much as we do professionally.

There are, however, many forces in the profession at work to make us forget at least those parameters that lie outside our narrow professional realm. When editing *P/A*, for instance, I saw how much architectural photography reinforced the profession's ambivalence toward memory, typically excluding from the image people or the context in which a building stands—anything that might place it in time or connect it to what came before. When I talked to photographers about this, I often heard that they and the architects who hired them wanted to convey a timeless quality, which would be destroyed by too much context. That notion of timelessness, indeed, pervades both the profession and the discipline, as if it could make our work more lasting or more valuable, a kind of antidote to the increasingly flimsy materials with which we build. Even those who profess an interest in memory tend, oddly enough, to divorce it from time, echoing Bachelard's dismissal that "to localize a memory in time is merely a matter for the biographer and only corresponds to a sort of external history, for external use, to be communicated to others."[4]

Nor did we, as editors, agree among ourselves about the place of memory in architecture. Some of my colleagues saw our role as identifying the newest trend, covering the latest news, finding the most provocative building, with "memory" relegated to the occasional preservation issues that we published. Others, myself included, thought that we could not separate the present from the past, imagination from memory, and the final building from the process of its creation. In the final years of *P/A*, the latter view won out and we began talking about the process by which buildings came to be, the connection of a building to the architect's entire body of work, and the ways in which people inhabiting the buildings thought about them and used them. This brought warnings from some architects well served by the old *P/A* that we were ruining the magazine—all of which reinforced in my mind the division within our field about memory, and the fear that memory might somehow corrupt our imagination.

The real question is not whether memory matters to our imagination—that I think is hard to refute—but *whose* memory do we draw from when we design? The psychologist William James acknowledged that "memory requires more than mere dating of a fact in the past. It must be dated in *my* past. In other words, I must think that I directly experienced its occurrence."[5] This, however, creates another dilemma for architects. Becoming an architect involves the accumulation of memories—trips to architectural landmarks, visits to the cities of the world—essential to do this work. But in doing that, architects also potentially isolate themselves from the very people who commission them or who use their buildings, who may have no connection to the images that architects remember. How, then, does one think like an architect without forgetting how nonarchitects think? And how can architects' memories connect to the memories of those for whom they design and who inhabit their buildings?

This dilemma has, to a certain extent, become universal. The isolation of the architectural culture from the larger world reflects the efforts of other subcultures to do the same. The growing interest in memory, indeed, arises in part from the current fascination with cultural identity, in which people, cast adrift in the global wash of international capitalism and Western consumerism, seek bonds with other people through a common past. How much, though, should architects express their own identity culture, and how much should the profession set that aside and represent the identity of other cultures? And how can architects represent the memories of others, when many subcultures now coexist in the same geographical areas, sometimes as clients for the same project? Certainly one of the most important questions every architect must now face is not, What can I imagine from the material I have been given? but, Whose memories should I draw from in my imagining? The wrong answer to that question can dramatically reduce the chances of a design being accepted by a community, or constructed as designed, or cared for and used as intended once completed.

The architectural profession has been, perhaps, too quick to blame the clients or the public in such situations. In fact, drawing from the experiences and memories of the client and those who will use a building need not diminish the quality or imagination of a design. I know of two internationally known architects who have recently designed innovative, imaginative projects for the same public client. However, as I write this, one is under construction and the other has met with some resistance from the client group, largely I think because of the memories each draws from. The architect of the building being constructed has taken many of his design cues from the experiences and identity of the people who will use the building, having met with them on several occasions. The other architect, no less talented, has drawn, instead, mostly from his own experiences, from previous buildings he has designed, and from his extensive knowledge of architecture. His design is just as powerful as the other, but it has met with much less favor because, as a person representing the client said to me, that building is about him, not about us.

At *P/A*, we often received projects at one extreme or the other. On occasion, we would review projects that literally represented the culture of the client: a Native American school that looked like a sacred animal of that band or a Mexican American community center that used the bright color and abstract ornament of Mexican architecture. The less literal the building's representation, the more likely we would be to accept it for publication, although we did ask ourselves how much our lack of experience with such cultures affected our decision. At the other extreme, we often received material on buildings that represented the architectural culture, with direct references to particular buildings lodged in our discipline's collective memory. Although such architecture proved easier to judge and to write about, since we shared the memory referred to, I did wonder what meaning those visual "quotes" might have for anyone other than an architect. What value did these architectural references create? I think that the most challenging buildings sought to translate the memories of a people or place into architecture, without either mimicking or mocking them. Significantly, much of this work came from architects in regions that still had a strong cultural or geographical identity and that still seemed to value a collective memory: architects like Brian MacKay-Lyons, in Nova Scotia; David Salmela, in northern Minnesota; the late Sam Mockbee, in the deep South; Richard Fernau and Laura Hartman, in the Bay Area; and John and Patricia Patkau, in British Columbia.

Why do the architects in these places value memory in ways that others do not? I think most architects and most communities have come to think of memory as either passive or automatic, something that occurs without our having to work at it, certainly without having to enlist our imagination in it. One reason for this stems from our ignoring a distinction that the ancients made between "natural" and "artificial" memory. The former is what we now think of as memory: the remembering of things we perceive or experience. But the latter—"artificial" memory—consists of remembering factual information, a critically important skill in ancient times, when literacy was not widespread and books were rare. The skill of remembering factual information remains important among traditional communities even today, as they value the continuity of their oral histories and dissemination of their knowledge. Architecture long served as the basis of that artificial memory, evident in the anonymously written Roman treatise on rhetoric, *Ad Herennium*.[6] It gave ordinary people instruction in how to construct a "memory palace," an imaginary building whose elements could help us remember factual information. Every space and object in the memory palace was associated with particular data: a stair, for example, might help one recall important chronological dates in history, or an object on a shelf might help one remember aspects of a particular technology or cultural ritual.

The author of the *Ad Herennium* clearly had a Roman building in mind when advising about the design of a memory palace. The imagined structure should contain a series of intercolumnar spaces that are similar, but not identical, and that have a distinguishing mark at least every fifth space, as an aid to memory. The spaces should be deserted, so as not to distract us, and each intercolumnar space should be neither too large, lest it hold too many different things, nor too small, to prevent overcrowding. Within each space, one would then place objects or images associated with a particular memory, much as the Romans placed the booty of war or offerings to the gods within the intercolumnations of a public building or temple. Here, though, the *Ad Herennium* recommends not restraint and order but "similitudes as striking as possible," objects or images of "exceptional beauty or singular ugliness," that are "disfigure[d]" or "stained" or that have "comic effects." The more exaggerated the object, the more easily remembered.

Treatises such as the *Ad Herennium* remained in use throughout the Roman period and were revived in the late Medieval period. By the mid-1600s in Europe, however, the use of architecture as a memory device began to fade.[7] In our times, the tradition has remained alive in only a few relatively isolated populations, such as the Pueblo tribes of the American Southwest. As Native American writer Leslie Marmon Silko recounts, the Pueblo Indians record the history of their bands not chronologically or in writing, but through the telling of stories of events associated with and recalled by features in their landscapes.[8]

Donlyn Lyndon and the late Charles Moore recall this Roman tradition in their book, *Chambers for a Memory Palace*.[9] They argue that by creating certain archetypal spaces—axial spaces, columnar spaces, spaces that climb hills or sit under great roofs—architects can make a more memorable environment. Lyndon and Moore organized the book in the form of a memory palace, with each of its chapters or "chambers" associated with a particular theme. They also bolstered their argument with ethics: "Places that are memorable are necessary to the good conduct of our lives,"[10] they claim, recalling Saint Thomas Aquinas's belief that systems of memory "were a part of ethics . . . [and that] memory images in bodily form . . . [prevented] 'subtle and spiritual things' falling away from the soul."[11]

Lyndon and Moore's reference to memory palaces is not trivial. As we saw in the *Ad Herennium*, the more empty a space and the more unusual an object in a memory palace, the more likely it is that we will remember it along with the associated information or ideas. Lyndon and Moore take this to the next step and propose "that architecture must be considered this

290 | Thomas Fisher

way."[12] They suggest, in short, that architects should design physical space as they would a memory palace, conceiving of the built environment as a mnemonic, or memory, aid. Though few architects think of their buildings this way, the mnemonic tradition in architecture does remain. Architectural education, for example, has kept alive a version of the memory palace method, teaching students to image three-dimensional spaces, to judge the appropriate placement of objects within them, and to associate both spaces and objects with meaning. The magazines also echo that tradition by publishing photographs that often present the most idiosyncratic buildings in the most dramatic and memorable ways.

Lyndon and Moore's book, however, raises a question about the time-frame in which memory occurs. The authors acknowledge that the memorable spaces they have in mind stem from their own experience, gained from traveling around the globe. But even though they found these spatial qualities "present in architecture throughout the world,"[13] can a specific set of spaces or forms be universally memorable, as Lyndon and Moore claim? Or is memory something that every individual brings to a place, making it memorable regardless of its physical features? The writer John Brinckerhoff Jackson makes the latter argument. "It is my own belief that a sense of place is something that we ourselves create in the course of time. It is the result of habit or custom . . . [and not] an unusual composition of spaces and forms."[14]

Time is the critical issue here. Lyndon and Moore's argument appears true for those who have no long-term relationship with a place, such as tourists looking for the photo opportunity or architects on the grand tour. But as J. B. Jackson observes, involvement with places over time can make even the most mundane space a part of our memory because of the events that have transpired there. Although the making of memorable spaces by architects will continue to matter, especially to those who seek to attract attention or visitors, we should not forget the imaginative ability of ordinary people to make the most unremarkable space memorable over time. Our duty, as architects, lies in our accommodating the memory and imagination of others, in making space that is not so personal or so inflexible that it leaves out the possibility of others appropriating it for themselves.

During the last years of *P/A,* we planned to send architectural writers to randomly selected places on the map to write about the ordinary places, people, and events they found there. We ended up doing relatively little of this, but I still think such an exercise would begin to address some of the issues J. B. Jackson raises about seeing architecture in time and the memory of architecture in relation to the events occurring there. Until we understand how places contribute to the memories of ordinary people and how our own prearchitectural memories play a role in this, we will remain, I believe, an isolated and misunderstood profession. Architecture deals with time as well as space, with memory as well as form, and the more expansive we are with the former, the better the latter will become.

Notes

1. Plato, "Theaetetus," in *Dialogues of Plato,* Great Books of the Western World (Chicago : Encyclopedia Britannica, 1952), 7:540.
2. Ibid.
3. Gaston Bachelard, *The Poetics of Space,* trans. Maria Jolas (Boston: Beacon Press, 1969), 9.
4. Ibid.
5. William James, *The Principles of Psychology,* Great Books of the Western World (Chicago: Encyclopedia Britannica, 1952), 53:425.
6. Frances A. Yates, *The Art of Memory* (Chicago: University of Chicago Press, 1966), 5–21.
7. Jonathan Spence, *The Memory Palace of Matteo Ricci* (London: Faber & Faber, 1988).
8. Leslie Marmon Silko, "Landscape, History and the Pueblo Imagination," *Antaeus* (autumn 1986).
9. Donlyn Lyndon and Charles W. Moore, *Chambers for a Memory Palace* (Cambridge, Mass.: The MIT Press, 1996).
10. Ibid., xii.
11. Spence, *The Memory Palace,* 13.
12. Lyndon and Moore, *Chambers,* xiii.
13. Ibid.
14. John Brinckerhoff Jackson, *A Sense of Place, A Sense of Time* (New Haven, Conn.: Yale University Press, 1994), 151.

chapter thirteen

(Re)Placing, Remembering, Revealing

Understanding through Memory and Making

RACHEL HURST and
JANE LAWRENCE

> *On whatever theoretical horizon we examine it,*
> *the house image would appear to have become the*
> *typography of our intimate being. . . . Not only are our*
> *memories, but the things we have forgotten are "housed."*
> *Our soul is an abode. And by remembering "houses"*
> *and "rooms," we learn to abide within ourselves. Now*
> *everything becomes clear, the house images move in both*
> *directions: they are in us as much as we are in them.*
> —Gaston Bachelard,
> *The Poetics of Space*, xxxvii

There are few certainties in the makeup of the beginning design student, but two that can be relied upon are the well-recalled experiences of place and a bundle of related memories.

This work describes a philosophy and methodology for the collaborative teaching of first-year architecture and interior-design students at the

University of South Australia, based on the pre-eminence of memory and experience in the perception of place.[1] An additional strategy to be outlined uses an alliance with the tangible and familiar realms of hands-on making and food to subvert conventional and potentially alienating languages of discourse. It examines the notion of origin through a consideration of memory, identity, and the diverse student condition. And it proposes that critical foundations for understanding of place include the recognition of the inherent sensuality of making and perceiving space, the acquisition of an architectural language, and the importance of the everyday.

A fundamental goal is to make learning an experience to remember. One way of achieving this is to attach a design exercise to a place or places beyond the campus. This enables students to discover and, in time, fondly recall the experience of the place and the particular lessons learned there. They are also able to make comparisons between different places—for example, between the city and the bush, between here and there, mapping spatial and qualitative distinctions between them. Such experiences become markers of progress on which to hang pedagogical insights.

Concepts of Learning

In the not-so-distant past, design education often began with a purge. Students were encouraged to expunge any preconceived ideas they had about design or the built environment, relinquish their judgments about taste or what constituted that elusive quality *beauty,* and generally consider themselves as tabulae rasae, ready to be enlightened about the nature of the designed world. Perceptual and technical skills were valued above individual experience and identity. Now with some radical shifts in the way we think about education and knowledge, it is recognized that each of us has a unique view of the world, and that learning is a continuous process from the cradle to the grave. In this model, the student is not so much a blank slate as an inscribed but mute one. We value the body of knowledge and experiences that students bring with them into the course, and set projects that reveal and reinforce their perceptions of place and space.

The approach of our first year embraces this understanding; our aim is to use students' existing perceptions of place as a basis for design education. Given that students are entering an unfamiliar environment and are

effectively amongst strangers, it is important that these memories are drawn
out in a simple and sensitive way, rather like the modest manner Australian
writer David Malouf uses to express the connection between formative
memories of place and identity:

> And it is this whole house I want to go back to and explore, redis-
> covering, room by room, what it was that I first learned there
> about how high, how wide the world is, how one space opens
> into another, and from the objects those rooms contained, and the
> habits and uses they were caught up in (including the forbidden
> ones), what kind of reality I had been born into, that body of
> myths, beliefs, loyalties, anxieties, affections that shape a life, and
> whose outline we enter and outgrow.[2]

Remembering Places

However, for students studying away from home, there may be a genuine
sense of placelessness, which requires them to establish a "home away from
home"[3] in order to sustain their identities at a critical stage in their lives—
like a homestead on the frontier. Clare Cooper Marcus, in her pioneering
studies of psychological attachments to home, elaborates: "Such place making activities are almost universal in childhood, regardless of culture social
context or gender. . . . For some people that place of initial separation and
autonomy, that secret home away from home, lingers in adult life as a powerful and nostalgic memory."[4]

For many of us, the most precious and poignant memories are of childhood places where we felt secure, safe and nurtured—our first dwelling or
dreaming places.[5] If one asks beginning design students to recall a memorable
place, the majority will describe, without prompting, in intricate and articulate detail their childhood home. The importance of these highly place-specific
memories in establishing identity and notions of self has been discussed by
writers in a range of disciplines, from philosophy and psychoanalysis to art
theory and education.[6]

To put this into practice we ask students to write a memory of a place,
articulating their sensory and emotive recollections of it. This is written on

FIG. 13.1. *"I remember, I remember: a personal postcard,"*
        by Lucy Weekes, 1999.

the back of a collaged postcard, which they produce in one of their first studio sessions, identifying them and their metaphorical or symbolic association with place by assembling carefully chosen images and/or text. These postcards bring to the surface the inextricable links between memory identity and place, meeting one of the central themes of our teaching philosophy, to attune students to their specific context—where they are from and where they are now—physically, socially, culturally, and temporally. What also becomes apparent is the resonance of memory when it is associated with some rite of passage, newfound freedom, or skill. Serendipitously, for most students the experience of university is ripe with the potential for just such pivotal events, rites of passage, sexual exploration, mobility, and increased independence. The marriage of learning with such experiential freedoms can kindle a memory and understanding that last.

Synchronicities

In conventional educational settings, students may recall parts of a lecture, elements of a studio, and the tension of a critique, but the potent memories are those that synchronize with these liberations of thought, sensuality, and rebelliousness. For us, these synergies are easier to elicit away from the restraints of the campus, particularly because of the quality of the environment surrounding the city of Adelaide.

Like most Australian cities, Adelaide is isolated by great distances and, while aspiring to global sophistication, it has a sometimes parochial quality in design and cultural attitudes.[7] There is a sense that although Adelaide is a very comfortable place to live, it is also a very good place to leave. Sadly, some of the best designers often aspire to practice elsewhere, rather than using their talents to improve the quality of local architecture.

The University of South Australia's faculty of Art, Architecture and Design is housed in a new purpose-built campus located in the heart of the city. The campus design is repetitious, and like many corporate and institutional buildings, it is the product of economic rationalism, a climate that is not always conducive to design teaching. However, Adelaide is favored in its siting. It is lineal, bordered by the sandy beaches of the southern ocean on one boundary, and rolling, vegetated hills on the other. Both of these areas are within a ten-kilometer radius of the campus. Arid deserts and wetlands are less than two hours' drive away. These conditions are seductive for off-campus teaching and provide the canvas for intense learning experiences.

Revealing Places and Familiar Things

The practice of teaching design off-campus is no novelty, and its value has been recognized and exploited by many leading architectural educators. Often, the principal intention is for students to experience firsthand the dynamic perception of space and form by visiting architectural icons and to learn from the solutions of others. With a few exceptions, Australia does not have a resource of built landmarks and "meccas"—the infrastructural "conceived spaces" described by philosopher Henri Lefebvre in *The Production of Space*.[8] But our reasons for off-campus teaching are not an apology or substitution for that. The objective is to let the unadulterated and sometimes humble places, the

FIG. 13.2.
At the beach: Memories
of play underwrite
the initial projects.
By Enzo Caroscio's
student group, 1993.

"perceived spaces,"[9] reveal solutions and prime the students for lessons that become ingrained not just metaphorically, but literally.

This idea has been powerfully expressed in recent political debate about Aboriginal reconciliation, when a tribe of elders, in a bid to establish a common language with politicians, asked them to meet on Uluru territory. They said, "Let the land get into them. You sit in the dirt and it will affect you."[10]

Two of the initial exercises that make clear this connection between the students and the land involve a visit to the beach and into Tjukalu forest, where they explore the themes of landscape and materiality, passive assembly techniques, layering and massing, connection and structure, and composition. The projects examine the relationships between material and form, between designing and making, between design and place, and between design and memory.

FIG. 13.3.
*In the Bush: Within
Tjukalu forest students
hide gentle and
evocative spatial
interventions.
By Alistair
Cornell, 1999.*

A number of recurrent themes emerge for both Australian and overseas students and have place-specific characteristics. At the beach, memories of liberation, release, and introspection are common, often allied to the Australian holiday season with festivities of Christmas, New Year, and the ritualistic shedding of clothes and cares. These memories are often employed spatially to produce broad-scale compositions characterized by open vistas, loose and irregular geometries, and textural meanderings. In the forest setting, different patterns prevail, tending toward evocations of finely crafted secret cubbies and hiding places, intricately woven into the fabric of the bush and setting up internalized microcosms that invite occupation. In Bachelard's words, the *intimate immensity*[11] of the forest is revealed.

Working with onsite materials on a one-to-one basis and acquiring skill by making rather than abstracting are in some ways a reiteration of the

Bauhaus ideal of design mastery through material and technique—but here our students become proficient with bucket, sand, and shovels.

In "feeling the immediacy of the material and the place,"[12] the novice design student, who otherwise does not know the parts of the design equation, is given an intrinsic starting point that is not in any way simulated. Designing space is, after all, the central and critical activity to be mastered, but it is "an abstract undertaking for beginning design students."[13] Methods that allow *hands-on* engagement with the actual *stuff* of architecture and design are more persuasive and tangible to initiates than ones that require mental visualization, drawing skills, or scaled representations. Visual and tactile immediacy alleviates the barriers of language and encourages communication and social interaction between students and staff. Where protocol between these groups has been more formal in other cultures, the process of making and doing becomes a congenial and responsive medium of translation.

By using familiar materials, sites, and equipment, students are able to embark on what might otherwise be dauntingly abstracted explorations. Although overseas students may not have the same cognizance of these sites, similar qualities of nature, recreation, and retreat accord with comparable places in their homelands. Like the evocations of play inherent in the design activities they undertake there, the places visited are reminiscent of childhood adventures and provide an introduction to the Australian environment. They set up a recollection of past excursions against which students may see their multiple and continually shifting concepts of self and place. And in these initiatory games they are, in the language of the philosopher Michel de Certeau, beginning to practice space, "to repeat the joyful silent experience of childhood; . . . in a place, *to be other and to move toward the other.*"[14]

Memory Places

In a project inspired by Charles Moore and Donlyn Lyndon's *Chambers for a Memory Palace,* and its underlying tenet that "ideas are made memorable by locating them in space,"[15] the emphasis is on designing a place that offers occupants a memorable experience. Students were first required to design a series of sitting places using no more than two materials. Various conceptual approaches were explored, from refinements of conventional seats, to examining ideas of the body and form, through to abstracted representations.

FIG. 13.4.
A Memory Place:
Students condense a
series of memories
to produce their first
building design rich
in text and texture. By
Diana Atanasov, 1998.

Then, students were asked to map a site close to the campus, revisiting it a number of times to establish both the physical qualities of the place and a body of personal memories associated with their visits. Many of the mappings conveyed nuanced sensory readings of the site, presented in highly charged and evocative ways. The next stage was to design a compact sitting or resting place that would instill strong positive memories of the place itself, the journey there, and the experience of resting—a contemporary dwelling or dreaming place.

Like the recollections of beach and bush, the memories that develop here have similar themes. As the students become adept at reflecting on idiosyncratic perceptions, they begin to blur the short-term memories of site visits with longer-term recollections and more codified cultural understandings of place and dwelling. For example, one student who mapped the physical and historical reality of a particular tree recalled his experiences of a childhood treehouse for the philosophical and theoretical basis; in the spatial and material design of the dwelling place, he deliberately evoked images of Australian vernacular and indigenous shelters. These exercises demonstrate that although memory operates as a complex and interconnected resource for design inspiration, the way it is employed by individual students is not necessarily linear or predictable, even when common themes habitually recur.

Tents, Tempts, and Tense

Later in the first year, we conduct a major project that investigates the way in which interior design and architecture respond to and integrate within the urban or rural context, and the relationship of a design to its location with respect to climate, materials, and topography. In social terms, we address the issues of community, habitation, and consumption. Part of this project is conducted on a camp. Projects have included conceptual designs for coastal villages and universities and the fabrication of tents on a limited budget.

Although these camps have not been without incident—excessive behavior and overindulgence seem inevitable—the students regard them as a major exercise during which they enjoy the relationship between work and play. This project, which affords them newfound freedoms and experiences, also underscores the value of establishing a studio culture in first year, one that ultimately forms the basis for an ongoing cohesive and supportive network.

The concept of unique, site-related projects is a useful one for architectural teaching, and is used throughout the architecture and interior-design courses at our university. In subsequent years, and in a variety of subjects from design to construction, projects are based in the Outback, such as the Miners Memorial on the Line of Lode at Broken Hill, the Wheal Hughs Mine Visitors Centre, Moonta, and the Warburton Project for local Aboriginal communities.[16]

A Memory Bank

If the aim of the architect and interior designer is to contribute to the making of memorable places, then the design educator needs to have a store of memorable places as a reference. By taking students off campus, we establish a shared body of experiences that are rich in textural, temporal, and scalar qualities of space and can be used for future teaching practices. Staff and students can later refer to and recall these experiences from memory, rather than relying on the more conventional teaching aids.

Students have often visited places like the beach and bush previously, and our prompting to appraise from a perspective influenced by personal recollections validates what they bring with them, and encourages them to find their own voices for design. But most important, off-campus teaching gives the students a real affection for and understanding of the Australian place. This is in accord with contemporary professional and political directions in supporting the development of a truly Australian architecture, in place of the traditionally Eurocentric models, and the growing momentum for national independence, as Australia moves toward republicanism.

Reproducing the Material World

The twin strategies of memory and off-campus teaching are further applied to typological studies of built environments. The discourse of typology is a means to understanding context at a variety of scales and "offers a known framework in which creative change can take place."[17] Often, the patterns or forms studied in the context of architectural education are architectural paradigms, most of them physically remote from Australian students, yet part of their collective cultural memories. However, these may not be as revelatory of persistent human patterns of dwelling as humbler, unadulterated, ordinary places. The locations we choose for our studies reflect incremental, day-to-day habitational patterns, as opposed to those produced by a rational tectonically conceived and linear process.

In a pivotal project, students are introduced to the "implicit and largely invisible" ways of typing and its capacity "to reproduce the material world and to give meaning to our place in it."[18] The project has three components. The first part examines the fabric of varying urban and country landscapes, streetscapes, buildings, and materials; in the second part, students produce a portable food container informed by the essential characteristics of their chosen place. Finally, they design an in-fill building that addresses context, material, and function from a typologically and place-specific perspective.

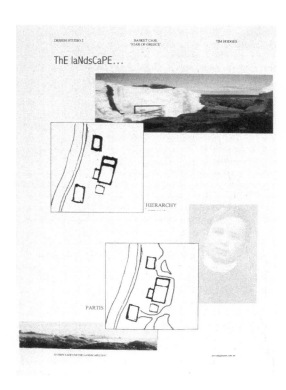

FIG. 13.5.
The Material World:
Typological mappings
recall physical and
personal information.
By Tim Hodges, 1999.

The purpose of this program is to enable students to acquire a design vocabulary and cultivate their existing "dialects" of architectural elements. In recognition of the difficulty of developing a design process, educators have sought ways of bridging the territory between the known and the unfamiliar. A recurrent tactic has been through analogy or metaphorical association with other spheres of cultural expression, such as literature, text, art, and, to a lesser degree, music. These have become accepted canons for design analysis and inspiration. However, for some students, these analogies are foreign in nature and content and can confound rather than clarify.

Remembrance of Things Past

A more tangible and familiar sphere of cultural reference can be found in gastronomy, and our methodology exploits this territory as well. Food and architecture are "an immensely versatile mythic prototype, an art form, a medium for commercial exchange and social interaction, the source for an intricate panoply of distinguishing marks of class and nationhood."[19] Beyond the power food exerts over individual recollection is its fundamental status as a manifestation of collective beliefs and cultural significance. Its universality and accessibility in these respects makes it an effective agent in teaching, an aide-mémoire on both a personal and communal level.

As practiced, gastronomy is a universal activity but one that "cannot be isolated from the full cultural social and physical experience."[20] While it crosses over multidisciplinary barriers of human and natural sciences, it retains intimate regional and personal significance. It is therefore a revealing and reflexive medium for cross-cultural teaching, especially when coupled with the operation of memory. For, as the Proustian reminiscences prompted by the taking of tea and madeleines[21] illustrates, "a taste acquired is rarely lost; and taste and smells which we have known in the past recall for us, as nothing else can, the memories associated with them."[22] Not only does food possess the status of a language, a means of discourse, instruction, and control—"gastronomic utterance, because the desire that it mobilises is apparently simple, demonstrates in all its ambiguity, the power of language"[23]—but also the "hidden entailments"[24] inherent within privilege we regard as central aspects of architecture and its use. Its intrinsic qualities as an essential everyday activity, the substance of which is often shared and produced communally and subject to time and place, make it a rich field of association. In addition, our memories and associations with food are inseparably linked to place. One can't read about the discovery of foreign places without connection to food, and in the academic realm, contemporary interdisciplinary research crosses boundaries of geography, gastronomy, and cultural studies.

Recipes and Rituals

Comparisons and connections can readily be made between food/place and architecture/place. For example, the elements and ingredients of regional cuisines and vernacular architectures invariably originate in a pragmatic use of local raw materials. Yet this simple determinist view neglects more subtle and complex connections between place and these realms, where physical and built characteristics of light, texture, color, and economy correlate not only with gastronomic qualities such as taste, pungency, plenty, and balance, but also with profound beliefs related to cosmological and agricultural readings and husbanding of the land.

In addition, parallels can be drawn between the typological study of architecture and the manner in which we inherit our tastes, recipes, and rituals of eating—both are continuums of knowledge. "Feasts, by means of structure and ritual, use the powerful connotations of food to recall origins and earlier times. They also attempt to be events in themselves unforgettable, in order to furnish recollections for the future. Recipes and the lore are to be handed on by us to be used in ritual celebrations."[27]

Basket Cases

The heterogeneous nature of the student body is put to advantage by encouraging students to explore and disclose their specific sociocultural heritages, not only of place and place making but also through considering the essential element of food. After examining and recording typological analyses of their places of origins, students design and fabricate basket cases from genius-loci materials. They employ spatial configurations and assembly techniques informed by their observations. These vessels contain a portable feast of foods associated with the selected area that each student concocts and assembles individually.

For example, interior compartmentalization conveyed patterns of spatial hierarchy; symmetrical or asymmetrical dispositions conveyed relationships between repetitive spaces and unique components; the envelope of containers projected responses to expression of structure, materiality, and form; the selection and arrangement of food and beverages made reference to social and agricultural customs and the functional criteria of edibility, portability, and waste. The project culminates in a communal picnic.

Problematically, heterogeneity in teaching has often been undermined by an underlying belief in eventual assimilation. However, what seems to be apparent is that certain groups resist this process (albeit passively). Now, when debate about the multicultural has legitimized the idea of separateness and difference, this assumption can be challenged openly with strategies that were once considered divisive. In responding to this, and eager to

FIGS. 13.6 AND 13.7.
Basket Case: Recollections of cultural origins become potent design references. By Reiko Kobayashi, 1999.

continue the momentum of cross-cultural understandings of self, place, and memory emerging from other projects, we separated a group of students from places outside the normative condition (i.e., urban Australia). The range of countries and regions was far reaching: from Norway to El Salvador, Mildura to Manchester, and from the Pilbara to Bali and beyond.

The response from this group was one of immediate engagement with the project, both intellectually and verbally. Overseas schemes showed a clearer understanding and perpetuation of type on macro and micro scales. Local schemes, on the other hand, tended to emphasize expressionist and eclectic attitudes to design. It could be postulated that distance enabled a willing acceptance of—perhaps a nostalgic yearning for—archetypal and stereotypical building forms and context. In communicating their schemes, it appeared that international students possessed an innate awareness of cultural continuity, and in the act of translating, refined their own (design) language[26]. In Visser's words, they "are eating cultural history as well as family memories."[27]

The potentially intimidating conventional studio and critique processes were disarmed by the exotic and unorthodox nature of the project and its products, and students appeared to gather confidence to enter into design discourse on this and subsequent related programs. The physical sharing of the outcomes at the picnic was a tangible manifestation of cross-cultural curiosity, and enabled students to discuss the origins of their work convivially.

On reflection, however, we observed that students, working in locations selected for their clear and archetypal expressions of food, place, and architecture relationships, inevitably regurgitated to some degree the status quo, rather than expressing their own values and memories. It needs to be acknowledged that the cultures of food and architecture are being similarly affected by globalization and consumerism, and the way students identify themselves through food and place is likely to be different from traditional patterns that have informed the theoretical discourse of both architecture and gastronomy.

Forgotten Generations

We are now at a phase of evaluating and refining the project, given that it proved successful in a number of ways. If one uses the Brillat-Savarin aphorism, "Tell me what you eat and I will tell you what you are"[28] as a tool to

FIG. 13.8. *Nut Case: The ordinary container becomes the extraordinary object. By Amber Lewis, 1999.*

investigate the student condition, this project reveals a group of students who have "gone from custard to olive oil in one generation,"[29] and where "food as a commodity is consumed not simply for its nourishing or energy giving properties, or to alleviate hunger pangs but because of the cultural values that surround it."[30] This new generation is eating product identity, advertising, and packaging as much as the food itself.

In response, and with the intention that our programme has currency, accessibility, and meaning for students, a series of small projects has been designed to embrace a quality often forgotten in conventional academic environs—the presence of contemporary youth culture. Devices such as common objects and materials in uncommon conjunctions, contemporary symbols, and street argot, are used to further deinstitutionalize the project and suggest lateral approaches to the task of design. The first project—*nut case*—requires students to reconfigure, in one studio session, a disposable food or beverage container to create a holder for a handful of nuts. Here we explore ideas of containment, materiality, adaptation, connection, the body, semiotics, and tectonic form. In the second exercise, named *Generation xxxx* after an Australian beer, students produce a series of images and text that encapsulate

FIG. 13.9.
Generation xxxx: *The project
illustrates contemporary
attitudes to food and place.
By David Lazic, 1999.*

their personal, cultural, and collective identities of food and place. This project "celebrates the potential for inventiveness within the ordinary and is thereby genuinely 'of its moment.' It may be influenced by market trends, but resists being defined or consumed by them."[31]

Informed by both typology and popular culture, and continuing the themes of memory, place, and making, they proceed to the design of the basket case described previously, and then to the design of an eating place, e.g., noodle bar, bush tucker grill, and Internet café.

Invisible Pleasures

The relationship of these small, metaphorical yet practical projects to the eventual task of designing space and buildings is of more consequence than may at first appear obvious. The oft-quoted aphorism of Mies, "God is in the details," seems peculiarly grandiose and inappropriate here to explain the relationship between the part and the whole. A more empathetic voice belongs to Witold Gombrowicz, who states: "I have had, you see, to resort more and more to very small, almost invisible pleasures, little extras. . . . You've no idea how great one becomes with these little details, it's incredible how one grows."[32]

The metonymic nature of these projects as a foundation for design thinking attempts to instill attitudes that challenge the orthodoxy of existing architectural practice. They endeavor to respond to the dynamic situation of work patterns, the contested influence of home and parental responsibilities on societal structures, and the impact of technology in refiguring physical and organizational aspects of work places. In their incremental accumulation of experiences, they mimic the operation of memory and the manner in which we acquire our deeper understandings through apparently innocuous discrete events.

In his *Critique of Everyday Life*, Henri Lefebvre theorizes: "What is the goal? It is the transformation of life in its smallest most everyday detail. . . . Why wouldn't the concept of everydayness reveal the extraordinary in the ordinary?"[33] The prompting to appraise the design characteristics and aesthetic qualities inherent in familiar places (beach and bush, street and shed) and activities (eating and making) implant a respect for the quotidian, the routines of daily life, and sets up a continuum between students' previous observations and their new roles as "designers." Just as Christopher Alexander's seminal works[34] reveal the worth of empirically observed patterns in architecture, and remain accessible texts for beginning design students, so in revisiting these common places and rituals we emphasize that designing is enriched by collaborative practice and the everyday.

Reductionist models of teaching have supported the heroic myth of the individual designer making a distinctive statement in a pure space. The practices we employ are by comparison group based, the places we visit are not sacrosanct, and design is taught as a shared endeavor that counters rational egocentric attitudes to design. In rethinking architectural practice and education, we need to take account of the everyday, and acknowledge domestic life, for "there is poetry and consolation in the repetition of familiar things."³⁵ "Architecture may take on collective and symbolic meaning, but it is not necessarily monumental."³⁶ Bachelard's metaphor of the evening lamp on the family table as the center of a world has particular resonance in light of the strategies we use, where "the familiar world assumes the new relief of a dazzling cosmic miniature."³⁷ Rather than commence design as an exercise in "otherness," our practice reconsiders the everyday as a basis for architecture through two means, the highly tangible and the imagined, drawing in each case upon individual memories of self and place.

Invisible Realms

The non-negotiable aspect of our approach is the genuine experience of space in lieu of the virtual. Beginning design students, if they are to resist what has been described as the "reductive non participatory threat constantly present in the electronic media and all forms of simulation,"³⁸ need to feel directly and keenly the total sensory stimulation involved in perceiving a place, and recognize themselves that their previous spatial experiences are part of that sensing. Architectural theorists Alberto Perez-Gomez and Louise Pelletier highlight the paradox that "while our culture seems to be in the process of questioning the 17th century notion of a division between mind and body, cyberspace embodies precisely that division. . . . A major problem with the discourse on cyberspace as a medium for architecture seems to be a pervasive and radical gnosticism that forgets 'prior' experience."³⁹ The intelligent use of the computer in architecture education requires mediation by "language and a poetical and ethical articulation."⁴⁰ How appropriate then is the balancing stratagem of memory, off-campus teaching, and gastronomy, where experience is ultimately participatory and unreplicable, stimulated through the other senses but remaining intensely personal? It is not, after all, the agreed significance or merit of places visited, and things made and consumed, or even their embodying some humbler but shared human values about our built world. It is more that the journeying to, and the otherness of place, sets up the invisible central realm of architecture, the place where we engage with one another.

In summary, our studio method recognizes the intense and inextricable link between place, experience, and memory as a universal characteristic and fundamental starting point. This becomes the deep harmonizing rhythm against which idiosyncratic personal melodies of memory are set in counterpoint. Students are set design tasks that foil stereotyping by drawing specifically on their cultural perspectives, while establishing a body of equally place-specific memories to reflect upon. A cyclic and cumulative process, it deliberately chooses languages of discourse with origins in sharing and communality, against which differences can be writ large and, in their everydayness, subvert the conventional ones of academia.

Notes

1. In this chapter we use the term *place* in the sense employed by Christian Norberg-Schulz (*Meaning in Architecture,* ed. Charles Jencks [London: Cresset Press, 1969], 226), that is, "places that give form and structure to our experiences of the world." See also Edward Relph, *Place and Placelessness* (London: Pion Ltd., 1980).
2. David Malouf, *David Malouf: Johnno, Short Stories, Poems, Essays and Interviews,* ed. James Tulip (St. Lucia: University of Queensland Press, 1990), 207.
3. Clare Cooper Marcus, *House as a Mirror of Self* (California: Conari Press, 1997), 25.
4. Ibid., 21.
5. Gaston Bachelard, *The Poetics of Space,* trans. Maria Jolas (Boston: Beacon Press, 1994), 6.
6. The range of disciplines is extensive, and pivotal theorists in the field of literature, philosophy, psychoanalysis, educational theory, art theory, etc. have dealt with the notion. See, for example, Carl Jung, *Memories, Dreams, Reflections* (London: Fontana Library, 1969); Martin Heidegger, *Poetry, Language, Thought* (New York: Teachers' College Press, 1991).
7. The peculiar qualities have been remarked upon by Salman Rushdie, speaking at Adelaide Festival of Arts Writer's Week. He expressed the view that Adelaide had an eerie quality, a perfect town for serial killers.
8. Henri Lefebvre, *The Production of Space,* trans. Donald Nicholson-Smith (Oxford: Blackwell Publishers, 1991), 38–40.
9. Ibid.
10. Quoted from Paul Pholeros, "Learning from the Great Unmade Places of Australia" (lecture, University of New South Wales, Sydney, 1997), 29.

11. Bachelard, *Poetics of Space,* chap. 8.

12. Pholeros, "Learning," 29.

13. Pierre von Meiss, "Design in a World of Permissiveness and Speed," in *Educating Architects,* eds. Martin Pearce and Maggie Toy (London: Academy Editions, 1995), 111.

14. Michel de Certeau, *The Practice of Everyday Life,* trans. Steven Rendall (California: University of California Press, 1988), 110.

15. Donlyn Lyndon and Charles W. Moore, *Chambers for a Memory Palace* (Cambridge, Mass.: The MIT Press, 1996), xi.

16. These projects were initiated by the university in association with local government and community groups to give students the opportunity to design and construct buildings in rural and isolated areas.

17. Doug Kelbaugh, "Typology: An Architecture of Limits," *Architectural Theory Review* 1, no. 2 (Nov. 1996): 47.

18. Karen Franck and Lynda Schneekloth, *Ordering Space: Types in Architecture and Design* (New York: Van Nostrand Reinhold, 1994), 9.

19. Margaret Visser, *The Rituals of Dinner* (New York: Penguin, 1991), 2.

20. Michael Symons, "The Post Modern Plate: Why Cuisines Come in Threes," in *Australian Cultural History: Food, Diet, Pleasure,* ed. David Walker (Geelong: Faculty of Arts, Deakin University, 1996), 69.

21. Marcel Proust, *Remembrance of Things Past,* trans. C. K. Scott Moncrieff (London: Chatto & Windus, 1981).

22. Visser, *The Rituals of Dinner,* 29.

23. Ideas about food, language (and desire) are discussed in Marion Halligan, "From Barthes to Barmecide: The Tasting of Words," *Australian Cultural History: Food, Diet, Pleasure,* ed. David Walker (Geelong: Faculty of Arts, Deakin University, 1996), 29.

24. Richard Coyne, Adrian Snodgrass, and David Martin, "Metaphors in the Design Studio," *Journal of Architectural Education* (1994): 114.

25. Visser, *The Rituals of Dinner,* 29.

26. Anthony C. Antoniades, "The Exotic and Multi Cultural," in *Poetics of Architecture: Theory of Design* (New York: Van Nostrand Reinhold, 1992), 140.

27. Visser, *The Rituals of Dinner,* 30.

28. Jean Anthelme Brillat-Savarin, *The Physiology of Taste, or Meditations on Transcendental Gastronomy,* trans. Mary Frances Kennedy Fisher (Washington, D.C.: Counterpoint Press, 1999), 3.

29. Elspeth Probyn, "Alimentary Assemblages," in *Cuisines: Regional, National, Global Symposium Proceedings* (Adelaide: 1999), 6.

30. Deborah Lupton, *Food, the Body and the Self* (London: Sage Publications Ltd., 1996), 23.

31. Deborah Berke, "Thoughts on the Everyday," in *Architecture of the Everyday*, eds. Steven Harris and Deborah Berke (New York: Princeton Architectural Press, 1997), 223.

32. De Certeau, *The Practice of Everyday Life*, xxiv.

33. Henri Lefebvre, introduction to *Critique of Everyday Life*, vol. 1, trans. John Moore (New York: Verso, 1991), xxviii.

34. Christopher Alexander et al., *The Oregon Experiment* (New York: Oxford University Press, 1975); Christopher Alexander, Sara Ishikawa, Murray Silverstein et al., *The Pattern Language: Towns, Buildings, Construction* (New York: Oxford University Press, 1977); Christopher Alexander, *The Timeless Way of Building* (New York: Oxford University Press, 1979).

35. Berke, "Thoughts on the Everyday," 224.

36. Ibid.

37. Bachelard, *Poetics of Space*, 170.

38. Alberto Perez-Gomez and Louise Pelletier, *Architectural Representation and the Perspective Hinge* (Cambridge, Mass.: The MIT Press, 1997), 378.

40. Ibid., 380.

41. Ibid., 379.

chapter fourteen

Places Within and Without

Memory, the Literary Imagination, and the Project in the Design Studio

SHEONA THOMSON

This chapter inquires into the relationship between two inhabitable realms—one material, the other immaterial. These realms are the physically constructed spaces of architecture and those spaces that are conjured up in words—the imaginary and psychically charged spaces of literature. In particular, this chapter seeks to underline the potency of the relationship between the spaces constructed by architecture and the spaces constructed by words, and to consider how memory and imagination may be crucially engaged in this partnership at the level of design conceptualization. In doing this I will present some commentary on my own experience of thinking through the relationship of the real, the remembered, and the imagined and some of the sources that have influenced and tempered my thinking. I will then outline a project developed for first-year students at the Queensland University of Technology in Brisbane, Australia, that aims to harness and take advantage of this relationship at a number of different levels. The project developed out of this inquiry is called "Memory Palace."

Historically, the use of architecture in literature and, reciprocally, the serving of architecture by literature are enduring. For example, writers have long used architecture as literary allegory, for character definition, to symbolize, and to contextualize. As demonstration of the consistency and richness possible in the crafting of imaginary worlds out of the residues of memory, one has only to consider Italo Calvino's *Invisible Cities,*[1] manipulating, as it does, the knowledge and experience of the real and extraordinary place of Venice. The villas described by Pliny in his letters have preoccupied architects for centuries as an exercise in architectural reconstruction from a literary text.[2] Conversely, architects and theorists since antiquity have exploited the power of literature for speculating upon the possible origins and meanings of architecture. On a more prosaic level, architectural description is impossible without language and text as a medium of communication between professional and layperson. Client-architect dialogue relies on a series of iterations between image and word, between verbal image and pictorial image to confirm understanding.[3] This transaction is explicitly drawn into the "Memory Palace" project.

I began to seriously examine the connections between architecture and literature when preparing my undergraduate dissertation, which took as one of its subjects the idea of the house as container of memory and intimacy. This particular interest had bloomed from a seed planted much earlier, when as a beginning architecture student I was led into Gaston Bachelard's discussion of the poetic imagery of dwelling[4] through a project called "Abstractions of the House." Ostensibly, the project was designed to introduce us to concepts of metaphor in architecture, but it also opened up the possibility of designing prompted by poetic images of archetypes of spatial intimacy in texts. This was one of the threads I drew into my fledgling research.

In exploring these ideas about dwelling, I began with language, and specifically with words describing intimate space. I sought to shadow what was "kept" in language and, more important, how this meaning, particularly about place, is maintained. Language conditions things and places. It outlines, defines, and secures the essential aspects of things. For instance, the etymology of the word *house* in the English language reveals a more latent meaning of *to hide.*[5] This etymological footing secretly secures a very essential conception of the house as refuge, as separation. This example highlights the idea that language, while categorical, is also inherently evocative.

This wondering about the latency of meaning in language further developed through to a preoccupation with the inevitable and complex connections that language has with memory and imagination. Our use of language, crafted into poetic, literary description plays on, reveals, and extends the nuances of apparent and hidden meaning in the worlds of words. If language conditions things and places, then this revelation of meaning in the world of words could be enlisted in thinking about the shaping of space in architecture.

Bachelard's exegesis on the powerful images crafted in literature provides us with a way of thinking about designing more intentionally with these images in mind. Through his writing Bachelard introduces us to the pleasures of reverie possible through contemplating powerful poetic images. His emphasis on the intimate reflects on the resonance of these images, which he seeks to categorize as archetypes of intimacy and interiority—of nest, shell, hut, etc. His proposition is that we experience the recognition of powerful poetic images as a palpable "interior" reverberation. In furthering Bachelard's treatise, Edward Casey suggests that this reverberation is perhaps the echo of bodily experience felt in imagination—of memory kindled into something "new."[6]

In furthering my explorations I was led to reconsider the conviction that the imperative of architecture was to do with the learning and application of proper architectural knowledge through studying precedent and practice. Why couldn't we be drawn more often into learning about architecture by studying how it has been painted by Giotto, or described by Virginia Woolf, or for that matter, by being asked to reflect on our own recollections of place? I speculated that thinking about these imaginary sites of architecture contained some great potential.

Taking the "Grand Tour" of Europe gave me the opportunity to extend my mental library of architectural recollections. Grazing on these memories I began to reconsider Calvino's complex constructions in *Invisible Cities* and the value added to them by my own experience of Venice. Calvino's text had first shaped my youthful imaginings of the exotic city and later enlarged my own memories. I became fascinated with the idea that perhaps architecture has a notably compelling presence in literary description. For me, this seemed very much to be where a significant power of architecture lay, and I wondered if the true test of the memorability and imaginative endurance of a built reality is how it is latently retold and experienced through other media. In my design work I began to explore a formula for seeding yet-to-be-realized space with memories of place, wondering all the while about the idea of architecture as "reconstruction" of resonant experience, both imagined and remembered. It seemed to me that a fundamental aspect of designing was to invest the imagined with an anticipation of pleasure, of joys that we know are possible because our memories hold these things fast.

Another important influence in thinking through the relationship between place and the literary imagination has been the work of William Blake. Shortly after graduation, I attended a lecture by the eminent British poet and scholar Kathleen Raine[7], which further reinforced this profound alliance between the literary, the remembered, and the real. The lecture was entitled "The Spiritual Fourfold London" and explored William Blake's rapt connection with his "Albion," the city of London. Raine's objective in her lecture was to open for us Blake's compelling message that the world of memory and imagination must be reflected in every time and place we inhabit. She disclosed her seductive meditation on the lessons of Blake, which was that experience will, if we are attentive, present us with the unexpectedly familiar amongst the hidden, the secret in the known. Blake reminds us that what we may know as palpable and physical may be transformed into the ineffable in the alchemy of poetic description, and, in this transformation, the real will become more meaningful. Blake is also a great mentor in that his work binds word, image, and material fact so enthrallingly. The infinite iterations possible between the real, the remembered, the imagined, and the idealized are set in motion in his work.

How might we characterize these iterations not only from the point of view of literature and writing, but also from the point of view of architecture and designing?

In looking at the relationship from the literary view, the forms in which architecture and architectural images may be captured by the literary imagination are manifold. In literature, be it poetry, or legend, or story, the spaces of architecture may be invoked by a writer or poet to cultivate an atmosphere, define a temperament, set up a scene or express an idea. Spaces of intimacy, grandeur, terror, or felicity inhere in memory and can be effortlessly employed as literary images to reveal the principal preoccupations of the work in which they appear. In conjuring up such space in imagination, the writer or poet is apparently able to delve much farther than the architect into space's poetical, mystical, and mythical substance. In imagination the unconscious residues of experience and the metaphorical potential of architecture are sounded. The writer thus transforms the physical experience of architecture into an imaginary, even fantastic one. A physical reality becomes an imaginative, literary idea. The poet (and writer) "creates imaginary figments which, in a way, are more real than the physical reality itself."[8]

Our physical experience of architecture is apparently finite—bound by such constraints as time, place, and mobility. But literature offers us the opportunity to inhabit many different architectures in many different times and through this serves to strengthen our understanding of the chief poetic resonance of architecture—its latency, its capacity for shadowing forth the invisible and the illusory. This idea of latency is really the key in framing the portal between literature and architecture. Our individual interpretation of space and place is endlessly dynamic and subjectively charged with our own perceptions. A writer can offer us another experience of space—another point of view, no less subjective, but outside our own, and charged with a different perception.

We can see that from the literary point of view a writer or poet is able to take architecture very far—far beyond its physical reality—through the idealization that is possible in the virtual world of literary description. What is the import of this for the architect or architecture student? And what would be the point of structuring a project that explored this exchange between the remembered, the imagined, and the real?

The writer sounds the depths of the metaphorical potential of architecture, so the nature of the relationship between architecture and the literary imagination has obvious usefulness for appreciating and exploring the device of metaphor as the crossing-over of internal and external aspects, of the layering of the real and the known with the imagined. If the poetic transforms the real, what does the real need to be to facilitate this imaginative extension? How do we define architecture as an armature to which resonance will readily and inevitably cling?

If an architectural experience is resonant in some way, beyond the temporal confines of its immediate experience, then it can be secured in consciousness, in memory, to be shared through other devices (language, image) with other people. Through reading and writing we can share certain experience, and perhaps in so doing, also share an agreement about what is and is not resonant and memorable in spatial experience. Memory shapes itself as the harbor for the recollection of space. Imagination facilitates the blending of the experiences occupying this harbor to assist us in inhabiting the virtual worlds of literary architecture, constructed from the description of resonant space.

Language that describes experience can both capture and temper our quality of experience. This is what I try to secure in the student's understanding. If language can be so richly crafted in its striving to capture and share experience of place, then the framing of place and experience is not something to be glib about. Nor is it wise to be indifferent about one's own experience, memory, and imagination. The relationship between physical experience, memory, and imagination is potent. It is important that students are made conscious of the links between physical space, the space of recollection, and the imaginary. This consciousness is exercised in the Memory Palace project.

As I prepared the Memory Palace project I researched other projects that used literary texts as generators for design and reviewed the stated objectives and outcomes of these. Some studios were based on interpreting spaces described in novels, sometimes literally, sometimes symbolically. I became more interested in other studios that sought to use an "immaterial" medium (literature) to reveal the latent potential of architecture, supporting the premise that architecture and the understanding of it can be derived from things immaterial, rather than its practical, physical reality or its operation within a symbolic register. My preference, and the one I noted in these other studios, was to work with directing an "architectural" shaping of the space and spatial quality wrought in literary description.

The project that I developed to explore and engage the relationship between text and architecture is offered in studio at first-year level. Through the Memory Palace studio I intend to develop the beginning student's comprehension of fundamental spatial and formal values and to enhance their sensibilities concerning architectural qualities and how to deploy those qualities. Through the use of descriptive textual prompts as the basis for designing I aim to develop the student in his or her technique of working explicitly between word and image, between word and material construction, and back again through various iterations. I invite the students to formulate creative connections through the intertwined conduits of memory and imagination between words and their physical and archetypal counterparts.

The subjects of the text "brief" are presented as the recollections, ideals, and imaginings of a central protagonist or inhabitant. Recalled in the descriptions are places inhabited by the protagonist at one time or another. As is the case with all memories or daydreams, some of the descriptions are quite explicit and others ambiguous. Students eventually give form to these spatial ghosts of the protagonist's mind and in the process explore the ways in which these experiences, defined in the textual prompts, can be provoked, revealed, and recalled by architecture. Some visual material is presented in support of the text, and other fundamental agendas of relevance to beginning students

FIG. 14.1.
Collage of the
thematic of secrets
and shadows, by
Ingrid Anderson, 1997.

are addressed, namely, issues of history, character, scale, proportion, and aesthetic ideals in building and landscape.

Before dealing with the requirements of the protagonist, we examined the students' own conceptions of the key ideas in the program. Through a personal daydreaming exercise of remembering and imagining, the students were asked to consider their earliest or most potent recollection of space and determine how their surroundings had aided, if at all, in the construction of these recollections. Then, anticipating old age when one would be very much with one's memories, what did they imagine they would like to look back on? Would place play an important role? Would it be interesting and worthwhile to work these memories back into the place in which they would reminisce?

Also, to avoid a beginning that was too text based, and thus alleviate the anxiety that some students have about reading, we worked up some

FIG. 14.2. *Collage on the thematic of darkness and light,*
by Ashley Paine, 1997.

thematic collage images that would later have relevance for the protagonist's requirements. Each thematic was strong in its description and allowed the students to explore some possible relations between word and image and refine them into useful visual references that they could bring to the project and that could temper and be tempered by the protagonist's desires for space.

In consideration of the implications that literature has for revealing the poetic resonance of architecture, I ordered the descriptions of space that were given to the students very carefully. The descriptive brief texts are structured in layers, outward from a skeleton of geometry, form, and order. Some assumptions about the memorability of certain types of spaces are inferred in these descriptions—assumptions that, in concurrence with Bachelard's thesis, set the archetypal at the core of memorability. The descriptions seek to articulate some archetypical memorable "dimensions" of space, for example its roundness, its darkness, its depth, and scale.

In these descriptions I tried to order the language much as architecture is ordered, from a firm foundation through to the most temporal of elements.

The foundation of each description is an armature—a component of the descriptive text that serves as the ground, as the element, to which the moods and desires of the protagonist will inevitably cling. By layering this literary armature with ambiguous, shadowy, and occasionally slippery description, I aim to lead the students "beyond the fragile geometry of space,"[9] into an understanding of the mutability of form and material in imagination.

The kinds of places imaginatively constructed in the text are outside of the experience of most students, in that they may describe, for example, somewhere far away in place and time, or an unusual conjunction of material and space. The places described in the text are recognized through a working up of "archetypal" images and figures of architecture and through very sensual and sense-charged recollections and imaginings of place. So while the project appears, via the descriptive text program, to take beginning students out of the realm of the known, it also encourages the students to enlist their memories and imagination in the service of defining the unknown. In giving architectonic body to the literary phantoms of description, the students are working in the fertile realm between memory and imagination.

I have staged the project several times, with a different protagonist and varied programmatic description on each occasion.[10] The most successful incarnation of the project has been the Memory Palace of Hadrian. The success may be because I was able to draw out the character using a combination of forceful literary and architectural references. A composite character, Hadrian was mostly sourced from Marguerite Yourcenar's *Memoirs of Hadrian*,[11] but also from Pliny and Sir John Soane, with bridging by myself. Hadrian's Memory Palace was, in its general disposition, ordered according to the description of Pliny's Tuscan villa, which gave it a context, a site, and an orientation. The students were directed to design parts of the complex in detail, leaving the rest to exist as ground for the more significant figures of four companion rooms and gardens. These four pairings were: the Room of Golden Light and the Garden of the Sun, the Room of Water and the Garden of Reflection, the Room of Shadows and the Garden of Hidden Secrets, and the Room of Darkness and the Garden of Moonlight Blue.

Each of the rooms and gardens was defined not according to function, but through a poetic elaboration on the part of the protagonist as to how they would be experienced. This poetic elaboration consisted of a range of varying "modes" of description to underline for the students some of the ways in which space can be described and thus interpreted. To describe these spaces in different modes reminded them how architecture can be apparently factual, explicit, and unambiguous, but at the same time a refuge for many moods and characters, accommodating rich imaginative play. For example, in articulating the space and experience of the Room of Golden Light, I referred directly to the guidebook for Sir John Soane's house in Lincoln's Inn Fields in London. The Room of Golden Light was then secretly the twin of the Breakfast Parlour in Soane's own house. The students, for the most part, had no idea of this relationship. The accuracy of the guidebook description of the geometrical, spatial, and material characteristics of the real room ensured that the Rooms of Golden Light that sprang from the students' imaginations certainly shared some genes with Soane's delightful space. Interestingly, the slippery complexities of the real space, more difficult to capture in the language of the guidebook alone, were variously and ingeniously interpreted.

Hadrian's telling of space ranged over what he desired to see, to do, how his friends would react, how he wished to sit or lie, and especially how he felt and what he was reminded of.[12] As the agenda for the project stretched between introducing students to the poetic aspects of architecture to dealing with fundamentals of space, form, and order, the descriptions intentionally brought formal order and material mutability into coalition.[13]

Placed alongside the textual descriptions, as an appendix to each paired brief, were excerpts from other writings (not fictional) that further reinforced the poetic resonance of particular buildings and gardens for students to source and examine to extend their mental library for creating Hadrian's palace anew.[14]

In summary, the project is set up from the viewpoint that the capabilities of beginning students are often underestimated. By placing students into a world that is, or may be, quite different from those worlds that they know or experience every day, the literary descriptions of places developed out of Hadrian's "memories" provide a bridge between the students' imaginations and their architectural responses.

The project in its structure aims to cover a lot of territory. In providing beginning students with literary descriptions of places it invites them to explore thoroughly the creation of an architectonic structure to partner an imagined or remembered quality or experience. It provides them with the foundations of an idea about a place. It also invites them, on another level, to engage with architectural terminology (What is a spandrel? A segmented arch?

An axis?). More fundamentally, it aims to get students enthusiastic about the great pleasures of architecture and to reveal that these pleasures may be sought and enjoyed in the worlds of literature. Through this it engenders an awareness of the unquestionably poetic nature of architecture.

Understanding the engagement of memory by imagination helps students to reflect directly on, and develop, the potential of space. It also, quite particularly, seeks to draw the students toward a heightened valuation of their own memories of places and to find ways to access the unconscious recordings of memorable experience. Significantly, students can come to a realization about the value of their own experiences in design conceptualization, whether this is enlarging an image given to them in text or developing their own. For example, student Ingrid Anderson created a pair of spaces: the Room of Shadows and the Garden of Hidden Secrets. Anderson sought to temper Hadrian's forested description with her own recollections of the memorable worlds at the base of banyan trees. These trees have an elaborate structure of roots that exist above ground to naturally shape intimate, room-like spaces. Imaginative interpretations of the metaphors in Hadrian's language like this are encouraged in the Memory Palace project.

But perhaps its most important accomplishment is to make explicit the need for them to become critically conscious of experience and its many renderings. It provides each student with the foundations of an idea about resonant experience and its inception as harbored in memory, enriched by imagination, and constructed by architecture.

Notes

1. Italo Calvino, *Invisible Cities* (London: Pan Books, 1979).
2. See Pierre de la Ruffiniere du Prey, *The Villas of Pliny from Antiquity to Posterity* (Chicago: University of Chicago Press, 1994).
3. This has been neatly discussed in Dana Cuff and Elizabeth Robertson, "Words and Images: The Alchemy of Communication," *The Journal of Architectural Education* 36 (1982): 8–15.
4. Gaston Bachelard, *The Poetics of Space* (New York: Orion Press, 1964).

5. The word *house* in the English language has with some probability been referred to the verbal root *hud,* of *hydan,* meaning "to hide," as noted by Dr. E. Klein in *A Comprehensive Etymological Dictionary of the English Language* (London: Elseiver, 1966), 746.
6. For example, see the chapter on Bachelard in Edward Casey, *The Fate of Place* (Berkeley: University of California Press, 1997).
7. This was a lecture given in August 1991 to the Prince of Wales's Summer School in Civil Architecture at Magdalen College, Oxford.
8. Giambattista Vico, *On the Study Methods of Our Time,* trans. Elio Gianturco (Ithaca: Cornell University Press, 1990), 43.
9. This phrase was noted as the title of a book lying casually on the sofa next to Julie Christie in Nicholas Roeg's film, *Don't Look Now* (1973). It has stuck fast in my memory, but I know nothing more about its heritage.
10. The first staging of the project in 1996 was as an apartment of rooms occupied by a slippery character referred to as the Trickster. The next year, the protagonist was Hadrian (as discussed in the body of the text). Subsequent to this, I worked with the character of Orlando, drawn from Virginia Woolf's novel of the same name. I am currently working up a scenario that places the character of William Blake at the center of the exploration.
11. Marguerite Yourcenar, *Memoirs of Hadrian* (London: Penguin, 1959).
12. An excerpt from the brief for the Room of Shadows and the Garden of Hidden Secrets illustrates this layering of desires:

> I am reminded of so much in this room; the time I visited Bithynia and its sea of trees, the forests of cork-oak and pine; restful afternoons spent in the hunting lodge with its delicately latticed trellises. Of the shade house of my friend A, where exotic species grew beneath a filigree of layers of fine timber battens, carved here and there with botanical ornament. I long to feel in this room the splendour of high noon, the luminous glow of siesta time, when everything within the space bathes in a golden shade.
>
> Just as the boundaries of this room of shadows are layered with elements that make the play of light and shade within the room as varied and surprising as I could imagine, the edges of the garden are also layered, with trellises and narrow hedges. In these edges may be discovered little places, niches and the like, that hold statues and figurines collected in my travels from all over the world. In the time between day and night, when the world becomes indistinct, these figures appear to me as ghosts, reminders of time, peering out from their dark caves or shrouded veils, a whisper of their forms visible to me as they are caught in the last rays of the sun.

13. This can be seen in the description of the Garden of Moonlight Blue:

> Outside, the garden of moonlight blue is a space of scent and mystery. The inverse of the interior, its plan is one of circle in square. The circle circumscribes a sunken space into which I descend to sit against walls that are still warm from the day. These walls are just high enough to frame only a view of the firmament above—the great dome of the heavens. These walls glow blue in the light of moon and stars. Beyond the curved walls grow borders or arbours of scented flowers, thanks to which the night smells sweet. The floor of the sunken space is covered with a surface so polished that it captures in reflection the infinity above. I sit between these two heavenly discs and contemplate large thoughts. The rest of the garden, the square that contains the circle, is serenity itself. Four still pools lie quiet under the night sky. Between them paths lead to two opposing niches and a belvedere at the end of the garden. The niches contain two figures—one of Nut, the Egyptian sky goddess, the other, Orpheus, Greek God of the underworld. At the end of the garden the belvedere marks a point of prospect that complements the containment of the sunken space.

14. For example, material for these appendices was sourced from such texts as Henry Plummer, *The Poetics of Light* (Tokyo: a+u Publishing Co., 1987); Junichiro Tanizaki, *In Praise of Shadows* (London: Jonathon Cape, 1991); and Donlyn Lyndon and Charles W. Moore, *Chambers for a Memory Palace* (Cambridge, Mass.: The MIT Press, 1994).

Index